JUDITH GIENCKE KIMBALL, PhD, OTR/L, FAOTA

DIAL IT DOWN

A Wellness Approach for Addressing Post-Traumatic Stress in Veterans, First Responders, Healthcare Workers, and Others in This Uncertain World

Edited by Deborah Murphy
Portland, Maine
www.linkedin.com/in/DeborahMurphyWriterEditor

DEDICATION

To my family members who served in the armed forces:

My father: Lt. Col. Edgar J. Giencke, USAF Retired

My brother: Capt. Robert E. Giencke, USAF veteran, Biomedical Sciences Corps

My Son-in-Law: W. Lane Carpenter, US Army veteran, Expeditionary Force 1999-2000

To my two very special teachers and dear friends:

A. Jean Ayres, who did the pioneering work on Sensory Integration and inspired and challenged me to learn more about and do research on sensory integration issues.

Patricia Wilbarger, who did the pioneering work on sensory defensiveness and inspired and informed my clinical practice.

And to Charlie and our three daughters, Amy, Heather, and Emily, who lived with an Occupational Therapy Sensory Integration Clinic in our house and spent many hours helping me learn.

Dial It Down

A Wellness Approach for Addressing Post-Traumatic Stress in Veterans, First Responders, Healthcare Workers, and Others in This Uncertain World

©2021 Judith Giencke Kimball

print ISBN: 978-1-09837-466-2
ebook ISBN: 978-1-09837-467-9

Contents

FOREWORD

I first had the opportunity to work with Dr. Judith Kimball in the 1990s when I was a medical student and she was the director (and founder) of the award-winning occupational therapy curriculum and clinic at the University of New England. My previous background as a trauma survivor, and as a professional dancer who experienced significant physical injury, had given me what was to become a lifelong passion for understanding and working to heal the incredibly complex intersections of the physical and emotional components of trauma and post-traumatic stress. Dr. Kimball was among the most skilled, knowledgeable, and compassionate practitioners I encountered in this field during my education, and she has remained so during my thirty years as a physician affiliated with Maine's leading hospital systems and its osteopathic medical school, and in my private practice.

Over the years, I have had the privilege of treating patients with Dr. Kimball, including veterans with diagnosed PTSD and people suffering from chronic pain, and I was struck from the first by her unique ability to balance her rigorous research-based grasp of the neurophysiology and psychology of post-traumatic stress with a direct and deeply empathic connection to each patient. Judy's combined knowledge and warmth stand out on every page of this extraordinary book. *Dial It Down* is a much-needed resource on the effects of post-traumatic stress for both patients and medical providers. It combines a focus on practical daily strategies for healing with an open and accessible tone for general readers, as well as a solid research foundation with additional resources for those who may wish to explore this topic in more depth.

Dial It Down offers excellent self-assessment tools and guidance for individuals and families who've experienced trauma and its complex aftermath, along with an assurance grounded in the stories told by patient histories that healing and wellness *are* possible. As an occupational therapist, Judy has always been intensely focused on meeting her colleagues and patients *where they are* in their individual journeys toward healing, and her book similarly offers not a one-size-fits-all "prescription" but rather a broad range of possibilities for exploring, experiencing, and talking about post-traumatic stress. For clinicians like myself who treat those suffering from post-traumatic stress, *Dial It Down* offers a kind reminder of the questions we often don't think to ask our patients about the often-subtle after-effects of trauma, when we need to be mindful of its small and large daily impacts on individual sensory experiences, intimacy, and family life.

This book is truly a gift for those who've endured trauma, and a testament to Judy's singular understanding of the value of *connections*: the physical, mental, and emotional connections that each individual must navigate in their own unique way on their path toward better health; the importance of repairing the connections to support networks of family and close friends that are all-too-often damaged by misunderstandings in the aftermath of trauma; and finally, the crucial connections to society as a whole that often suffer due to a lack of understanding of trauma among the general public and even the medical establishment. Dr. Kimball provides us ways to explore, share, and talk about these matters.

As I write this in February 2021, all of us have recently experienced unprecedented levels of traumatic stress in our daily lives: the loss of routines and personal connections resulting from the COVID-19 pandemic; the economic uncertainties generated by this health crisis; and the political upheaval and crisis of the 2020 election cycle. The target audience of this book—first responders, military personnel, and frontline medical workers—have suffered greatly from these and other traumatic experiences and will benefit from the wisdom in these pages. But I also highly recommend this book as a path toward post-traumatic growth and healing for anyone who is struggling to repair personal, familial, and social connections in these difficult times.

Stephen Goldbas, DO
Whole Health Osteopathic Medicine
Portland, Maine
February 7th, 2021

PREFACE

The COVID-19 pandemic leapt to the forefront of the news and of all our lives across the United States just as I was completing my final draft of this book, which was originally intended to support veterans and first responders (police, firefighters, and EMTs) in finding ways to manage the trauma resulting from their prolonged exposure to life-and-death situations, a trauma that often disrupts not only their perceptions of personal security but also their most intimate connections with family and close friends.

The new national and global realities of COVID-19 tragically and exponentially increased the number of individuals experiencing trauma: frontline healthcare workers (doctors, nurses, medical technicians and assistants, and respiratory, physical, and occupational therapists); "essential" workers operating daily in unsafe or uncertain environments (postal and delivery service workers, grocery store and warehouse employees); and, in different ways, all of us, from COVID-19 patients and their families, to senior citizens and individuals with underlying health conditions, to unexpectedly unemployed workers, to school-aged children and toddlers (and their parents) who crave but suddenly faced the loss of in-person connections to extended family and peers. We have all, in different ways, been on the "front lines" of a war that has taken us far away from our former lives. We will all, even after the widespread distribution of effective vaccines and treatments, still carry some of the emotional, psychological, and physical impacts of this time.

The research- and treatment-based techniques for recovering from trauma described in this book can be applied across all ages (many of these were in fact first developed to aid children diagnosed with sensory issues) and professions. As the pandemic has demonstrated on a devastating scale, we all share the same biology and inherent vulnerabilities. But we also all share the same potential strengths that can help us, in both large and small ways, to regain a sense of security and connectedness.

I have expanded the language of this book to include COVID-19 frontline healthcare workers as well as the originally intended veterans and first responders. The traumas faced by these active-duty and medical personnel—living under threat for extended periods, whether the threat of gunfire or of potentially fatal infection, and being directly responsible for the lives of others—are comparable, and frontline medical workers deserve and can benefit from the same supports and treatments that are available to military personnel and first responders.

It is my desire that this book can offer hope to all these brave people and their families. It is my wish, as well, that it may be a resource for others—essential workers, parents, teachers, COVID-19 survivors and their families—looking for guidance in reclaiming a sense of safety, community, and self in the midst of our collective trauma.

INTRODUCTION:
Coming Home

Chris came back from his 2018 deployment in Afghanistan excited to be home, wanting to finally spend time beyond the limits of Skype and phone calls with his 10-year-old son, his 5-year-old daughter, and his wife, Emily. But things didn't go as he expected them to. His family threw him a big welcome home party. He enjoyed the barbecue and beer, but after 45 minutes, the music on the stereo speakers sounded too loud and the happy crowd of friends and relatives felt "too big" for his comfort level. There was too much movement, too much color in the decorations and bright spring clothes, and everyone wanted to touch him and ask him questions. It all felt like "too much," and he was glad when the celebration finally ended because he was anxious about "losing it." Emily wanted to know why he'd seemed so angry during the party. But he couldn't find the words to explain.

Jane, a nurse at a long-term care facility that experienced an outbreak of COVID-19 in the spring of 2020, described feeling "stressed" and "unsafe" even when at home with her family. She contracted COVID-19 from a patient, and after her recovery, she was able to return to work, but she continued to feel "very alert" in ways that included being strongly startled by noises at home that had never bothered her before, such as beeping household appliances.

Roy was a detective in a large urban police department. He'd been called to numerous active shooting situations, including one involving mass casualties. His wife was a retired police officer who experienced physical limitations due to an on-the-job injury. The couple decided to move out of the city to a horse farm in the country so that they could have a calm, low-stress home to return to each day. But Roy found that even in this quiet setting, he was still "on edge" and often not able to relax.

Dawn, returning home after working as a respiratory therapist in an overcrowded COVID-19 ICU apart from her family for two months, found herself responding in unexpected ways to her children. She'd been looking forward to relaxing evenings with them, but instead she often found herself agitated by their movement and noise and yelling at them to be quiet, when all they were doing was happily chasing each other around the house and laughing.

Steve, a Vietnam-era veteran, attended a Fourth of July picnic with his grandson and was embarrassed when he "hit the ground" as the first fireworks went off.

Marcus's family decided to go out to dinner several months after he'd returned from military deployment to a combat zone, but when they got to the restaurant, there were no tables where he could sit with his back to the wall to scan for every possible threat and escape route, so he insisted on leaving. He couldn't find the right words to tell his disappointed parents and sisters why.

These stories are all based on experiences described to me in the context of my work as an occupational therapist (OT) with veterans, first responders, and medical personnel. Your behavior at home may be very different than it was before your military service or frontline work. Is this simply due to increased anxiety from having been "under fire"? You probably don't think so because you were able to function very well *while on duty* in highly stressful situations. Why are you having problems adjusting to life at home where there's much less serious stress? What's different?

The answer is that *you* are. The trauma of active duty and frontline work—of experiences faced as a soldier, first responder, or medical professional—can actually change *how your brain processes* everyday sensations from the world around you. Your reactions to common sensations may have been fundamentally altered in ways that are just now being researched. Ways that respond to a physical solution, not just a psychological one—ways that are the subject of this book.

During active duty or frontline work, you needed to be vigilant to stay alive and effective, and the military or other training programs you completed (such as first-responder physical training and live drills, and medical residency with its stresses and repeated protocols) did an excellent job of preparing you to use your vigilance skills. You found that you were able to control your anxiety, stay focused, and get the job done even in difficult circumstances. How and why? In part because you knew that your military, first responder, or medical peers "had your back" and you had theirs. Additionally, members of the military and first responders must all meet physical fitness requirements. These often-daily physical workouts keep your body in top shape; but even more importantly, you may be surprised to learn that this *physical* training also *keeps your brain focused for optimal decision-making,* which can have a major effect on your behavior.

How do you see yourself now that you've returned from active duty or frontline work and aren't under the same training regime, facing the same demands and threats? Rather than reacting only to certain real danger situations, you may find yourself *over*-reacting in daily life. The responses that trouble you may often be related to the strange feeling that there's "too much" going on to keep track of—too much noise, too many smells, too much light touch, too much clutter (things out of place), and/or too much activity (too many things moving). What do these experiences have in common? They're all reactions to common sensations from the environment. But why is your nervous system reacting to them more intensely than it did before?

When you returned from active duty or rotated off your shift, you may have been told to control and reduce your vigilance responses (to "just calm down"), but most likely you weren't told *how* to do this. And you weren't told exactly *what* was going on in your body and brain as you tried, because science is only just starting to map how our brains change when exposed to the stress and trauma of war and sustained physical threats like those experienced by first responders and medical personnel. The military has taken the lead in describing some reactions to look for when its soldiers return from deployment, and it is working on ways to help soldiers cope (see BATTLEMIND, the Comprehensive Soldier and Family Fitness Program, and the Performance Triad P3 Program, discussed in Chapter 3). Programs throughout the country have been developed to help veterans reintegrate (see Chapter 13), and many police and fire departments and hospital systems have also started programs to help their members cope with the stress and dangers of their jobs.

But this book is about *a crucial missing piece of the puzzle*, offering hope and proven ways for *you to help yourself* respond more calmly and consistently to the issues of daily life after active duty, first responder work, or frontline medical work.

There's a Name for That Missing Piece of the Puzzle

It's called *sensory modulation challenges* (SMC), and you may have developed it due to the stress and trauma of your job. It's the reason you might find yourself overloaded by common sensory input from the environment that doesn't seem to bother other people, leading to hypervigilance and anxiety. It's why you may feel calm one minute but then "very anxious" or "very angry" the next. And why you may react to many things that "didn't bother you" before active duty or frontline work.

What Are Sensory Modulation Challenges?

Sensory modulation challenges are an *over-reaction to **common** sensory input,* and this over-reaction *can negatively affect daily functioning.* The prime directive of our brains is to keep us alive. This is accomplished by what I call the "staying alive reflex," the fight-or-flight response. It appears that trauma can *change* the way in which our brains respond to sensations, resulting in *over-alerting us to danger too often and keeping us alerted for too long.*

We're constantly bombarded in daily life by sensory input from all aspects of our environments—sight, sound, touch, smell, the shifting movements of our own bodies through space, and internal bodily sensations. For those with an "even" or "less reactive" nervous system, these sensory experiences enter our conscious awareness and alert us to danger only if they're out of the ordinary. For those of us with *sensory modulation challenges,* many sensory inputs result in more intense reactions, and these can have a profound effect on our lives and functioning.

Sensory modulation challenges have been well-documented in scientific studies and are now widely known as they relate to people (estimated at 10% of the population) who are *born with* these challenges. But little research has been conducted on people who acquire these specific neurological challenges through trauma *as adults*—those who suddenly find themselves at odds with places and people, even in their own homes and with close family members, where and with whom they've always felt comfortable and safe before. For the people like those mentioned above—Chris, Jane, Roy, Dawn, Steve, and Marcus—life after active duty or frontline work can feel as isolating and unsettling as suddenly being stranded on Mars.

People *without* sensory modulation challenges, those who have more "even" nervous systems, generally assume that everybody reacts as they do to the sensory experiences around them. Until sensory issues are described to them, they have no idea of the alternate ways in which someone with sensory modulation challenges may experience daily life events, and therefore might misunderstand your changed responses to sensory information. A person with sensory modulation challenges may overreact to any variety of "normal" sensory inputs—for example, to an unexpected light touch from a spouse, a sloppy kiss on the cheek from a child, cooking odors, noisy children, clutter, bright lights, restaurants, or even music.

While the brain generally interprets sensations on a spectrum ranging from "just right" (no threat here) to the need for self-preservation reactions of "fight-or-flight," it's much more difficult for people with sensory modulation challenges to keep themselves in that "just right place" of "even" responsiveness. This can be especially hard for someone who's had to be highly vigilant in order to survive dangerous situations such as military deployment, active police duty, or numerous COVID-19 emergency room shifts. Also, sometimes, returning soldiers, first responders, and medical workers can show what seems to be the opposite response—when maintaining that amped-up state of vigilance becomes simply too much for the brain, they may find themselves unable to take in more sensory input and "shut down" to any additional stimuli, thus appearing to be in an under-aroused or "freeze" state.

Why This Book

The purpose of this book is to help those with sensory modulation challenges (SMC) and those who live, love, and/or work with them to understand and *alter* the effects that SMC can have on all parts of their lives. A great deal about SMC is known—first and foremost, that this is **not** *primarily a mental health issue, but a neurophysiological difference in how the nervous system functions.* We know that people are born with a full range of sensitivity to sensory input—some are unusually sensitive, some are not sensitive at all, and others vary in their responses depending on the amount of sensory input they get. Excellent research and books have been written on this topic since the groundbreaking work of Dr. A. Jean Ayres in the 1970s (Ayres, 1972a, 1972b, 1979). Dr. Ayres' work helped families and people born with these issues to cope and live fulfilling lives. This book, written by a mentee and friend of Dr. Ayres, aims to bring this knowledge and understanding to people whose sensory processing ability has *changed.* We know that *trauma of any type can cause increased sensory sensitivity, and that with understanding and the use of self-initiated wellness techniques, a person can "dial down" that heightened sensitivity.*

If you are having difficulty with your reactions to life, you may have tried several approaches to getting relief from the emotional disconnect, anxiety, and physical symptoms you're experiencing. You may have sought medical help in the form of medications or psychological/behavioral strategies; you may have found a group of veterans or peers to share high-intensity physical experiences with; or you might have tried your own methods that may have included self-medication with alcohol or drugs.

This book describes a new strategy called "Dial It Down"—a wellness program based on your individual responses to sensory experiences in your environment. Dial It Down consists of techniques that you can implement *for yourself* in most situations. This book will explain how your nervous system works, how your nervous system interprets sensory input, and how to keep it functioning well so that you can participate more fully in your life. When you understand your own nervous system's responses, you can choose to "dial down" your reactions with sensory techniques, including basic physical activities you're already familiar with. As your nervous system is "dialed down," you'll find that many issues will become easier to deal with, and that if you're participating in medically prescribed treatments for trauma like psychological counseling, those important treatments will work more effectively (as will be discussed in later chapters, SMC is a key *part* of post-traumatic stress that's only beginning to be recognized).

The main concept of "Dial It Down" is to change the "set point" of your nervous system, to move it to a more modulated or centered place. If you start out from a centered or modulated point rather than a hyper-aroused or under-aroused state, you'll have a better chance of reacting more typically—with a greater feeling of choice and control—to incoming sensory input in your life.

This book will help you develop an easy individual wellness approach using sensory, mostly physical, methods to influence your nervous system every day—methods you may already be familiar with from military, first responder, or athletic training, but used in a way that fits in at home. Changes in how you handle sensory input can greatly improve your relationships with your partner, your children, and others. And once you understand which of your behaviors have a sensory basis, you'll find yourself in a better position to explain to family, friends, and colleagues of your choice what you're doing to keep your senses in that "just right place," and to let family members in particular know how they might help.

The book offers 15 participatory "Check-Ins" designed to involve you in the process of understanding sensory modulation challenges, deciding whether and how sensory modulation challenges are affecting you, and discovering and achieving your own personal ways to Dial It Down.

CHAPTER 1:

What are Sensory Modulation Challenges, and How Do They Connect to Trauma?

As noted in the Introduction, sensory modulation challenges are mainly an *over-alerting to common environmental input* affecting the body's sensory systems. We all have eight sensory systems "on call" at all times: the five best-known senses are hearing, vision, touch, smell, and taste/texture in the mouth; in addition, three lesser-known but crucial senses are movement and balance perception (the vestibular sense), joint and muscle sensations telling us where our bodies are in space (the proprioceptive sense), and our ability to feel what's going on inside of our bodies (the interoceptive sense, which includes hunger and fullness). Sensory input from these eight sensory systems is *constantly* being evaluated by our brains, 24/7/365. Your brain alerts you to the sensations coming into your body and makes you react when sensations reach a danger level.

These reactions are *not under conscious control*. After an initial alerting reaction to potential danger (your automatic fight-or-flight response), you decide what to do about it ("Is it really dangerous or not?"). In service members, first responders, and frontline medical workers, the most likely senses to cause "danger" reactions are hearing, vision, touch, and smell, with the four other senses—textures in the mouth, the perception of your body's movements, the perception of where your body is in space, and feelings from inside your body—being much less likely fight-or-flight causes.

Most people don't realize just *how strongly alerting* these sensory experiences can be to the nervous systems of people experiencing sensory modulation challenges (SMC), and how markedly these heightened sensory experiences can then *change their behavior* from their "normal" ways of interacting before developing SMC.

Jason, for example, after his tour of duty in Afghanistan, could no longer tolerate being kissed on the cheek by his teenaged daughter as her light touch now set off a fight-or-flight reaction and led him to flinch away. His unconscious *sensory* response greatly upset her, as a quick kiss had always been their goodbye ritual when she left for school.

Samantha, a first responder, found that she could only grocery shop late at night due to the sensory-alerting noise and crowds in the store during the day. This changed routine led to family arguments about the household responsibilities she'd always easily shared before with her husband and teenaged son.

What Causes Sensory Modulation Challenges?
What Causes Some People to Overreact to Common Sensations?

Some people are born with sensory modulation challenges—for instance, some individuals born prematurely or who've been injured during birth, individuals with autism spectrum disorders, and some individuals with ADHD. For others, the difference in reactions from the usual level occurs later and results from trauma: Experiencing physical or emotional trauma can cause the parts of the brain that protect us from danger *to stay on over-alert "just in case it happens again."* This is a very important function of the automatic parts of the brain that are responsible for keeping us alive—it's just that here, they become *too* active, and the brain has trouble reducing that over-alerting when we want to go back to doing things in places that aren't dangerous. Many usually harmless sensory inputs are interpreted by an over-alert brain as very dangerous, causing us to take evasive action by initiating a *fight-or-flight response*. In other words, *increased sensitivity to sensory input can be the result of a change in the **autonomic** (involuntary) nervous system's responses after a person is exposed to trauma.* Underreaction, an unwanted protective "shutting down" of the system due to too much input, can also occur.

How Is Behavior Affected? What Do We Know?

We know that *these reactions have both positive and negative features.* The choice is to use the sensory processing continuum to your advantage. For example, it's important to know when you are hypervigilant (over-alert) or hypovigilant (under-alert) and to recognize when staying this way is interfering with something that you want to accomplish (whether that "something" involves larger life goals or the basic act of dining out or spending quiet time with your family). The course of action described in this book is to use simple, nonmedical sensory wellness techniques to gain more control over your nervous system.

We know that sensory modulation challenges *affect the development and sustaining of relationships and intimacy.* Our levels of sensory modulation affect every interaction in our lives. If your level of sensitivity to sensory input is similar to your child's, partner's, or friend's, then you understand each other. For example, your military unit members or your police, fire department, EMT, or frontline medical colleagues understand what you've gone through and may experience similar levels of sensory modulation challenges themselves. But if your level of sensitivity to sensory input is different from others' levels, then sensory mismatches can occur, leading to misunderstandings that may be interpreted as emotional or psychological issues. If the level of a person's sensitivity to sensory input reaches a point that's out of sync with society's norms, *sometimes a mental health diagnosis may be given*, both to account for the person's actions and to get medical assistance for them. This can happen because many people do not understand that *sensory processing issues are a difference in how the brain interprets sensory input, not primarily an emotional problem.* If sensory modulation challenges are addressed, then important treatments for other issues, including the psychological and emotional components of trauma, are usually more effective.

We know that *the relationships that suffer the most when someone has sensory modulation challenges are the most intimate ones*, for example, the parent–child bond and the partner bond (including sexual functioning—more about that in Chapter 6). People with over-reactive sensory processing may respond differently from how they did before they experienced trauma to touch, among many other sensations, and the people in relationship with them need a road map for understanding what those different responses mean.

A very difficult issue for adults whose sensitivity to sensory input has changed through trauma is that *they know how they used to function.* They and those they're in relationships with know how they *used to* respond to sensory input, and have difficulty understanding the *changes* in their responses, which can be profound. For example, because her husband's nervous system was hyper-aroused to smell, Mary reported that he couldn't tolerate the scent of her shampoo when he came back from deployment (so after trying several different brands without success, she made the uncomfortable accommodation of washing her hair only once a week). Alec found that the household clutter he'd always accepted as normal before his deployment became so jarring to him afterwards that he'd sometimes yell at his spouse and kids to clean up or to "be more careful!" Though he always later regretted his outbursts and apologized, his initial response was an unconscious *fight-or-flight reaction* (because his hyper-alert sensory system reacted in the same way it had to the "war zone" possibility that something dangerous might be hiding in the clutter).

We know that *some people with sensory modulation challenges may be diagnosed with PTSD (post-traumatic stress disorder).* No one wants to hear a diagnosis of PTSD, especially in the military or as a first responder, and so many people never tell anyone about the difficulties they're experiencing. They just live with the pain of trying to cope with the changes that come from participation in war and from daily stress and trauma as a first responder or frontline medical worker. The wars our country has fought in recent years have resulted in many soldiers being diagnosed with PTSD, and PTSD is also increasingly being recognized in first responders (and now, anticipated in healthcare workers who have cared for record numbers of patients daily while facing the threat of COVID-19 infection). Those with PTSD have heightened (or sometimes depressed, "shut down") sensory arousal that affects their daily functioning. Recent research has demonstrated that much of what we know about variations in sensory processing can be applied to many veterans, service members, first responders, and frontline healthcare workers, both those diagnosed with PTSD and those not diagnosed with it. This is why I have chosen throughout this book to include the broader term "post-traumatic stress" (PTS) in addition to the specific *DSM-5* medical term "PTSD" (*DSM-5* is the fifth edition of the *Diagnostic and Statistical Manual of Mental Disorders* published by the American Psychiatric Association). *The SMC (sensory modulation challenges) seen in veterans, first responders and medical personnel suffering from post-traumatic stress and PTSD is separate and distinct from the emotional and mental health issues surrounding their trauma.* SMC is *just sensory,* reflecting significant changes in their responses to common sensory input from the environment. But *SMC frequently occurs with and is a key **part** of the symptoms of post-traumatic stress and the PTSD diagnosis that has, to date, gone undifferentiated and unrecognized* (Kimball, 2021, 2021a). If sensory processing problems are addressed, then medically recommended treatments for the emotional and mental health aspects of trauma (discussed in detail in Chapter 13) can be significantly more effective.

In other words, we know that anyone with diagnosed PTSD *likely* has some degree of SMC that *should be addressed* as part of their treatment—particularly through wellness strategies like those outlined in this book. The same is true of people experiencing post-traumatic stress. Please note that post-traumatic stress and PTSD should *never* be self-diagnosed but *should always be assessed by an experienced medical professional* to ensure that no key part of your diagnosis and road to wellness is missed.

We know that *some changes in reactions to sensory input are trained intentionally,* like the training to become hyper-alert to suspicious behavior that is needed by members of the military, police, and airport security officers. But *to use these skills is a choice.* When you find yourself living with a constant level of heightened arousal or under-arousal that interferes with your daily life, then sensory modulation challenges may be present.

What Keeps Our Sensory Systems Functioning Well?

The nervous system will function at its best if it's given particular types of input. These inputs are body movement in a rhythmic way (head through space, as in running or jumping), heavy work with the joints and muscles, and deep touch pressure to the skin. The strategic use of these actions is called a "*sensory diet*" because we need a certain level of sensory input for our nervous systems to react in healthy ways just as we need a certain level of food, and we need it spread throughout each day like food. If you're a veteran, then you have unknowingly used this principle in the active-duty military (particularly the Army and Marines) with the required daily physical training. *You know that daily physical training kept you physically strong, but it also kept you mentally sharp, maintaining your nervous system in that "just right range" to respond to all situations in the best way possible to keep you and your unit alive and to complete your mission.* Understanding your present level of sensitivity to sensory input is important. And *changing* your level through the actions described in this book can be a powerful life choice.

Background Information: Our Own Personal Sensory Perspectives

We all live in multiple environments: large physical outdoor spaces like parks or the neighborhoods around our houses and apartments; large indoor spaces like malls or stadiums; smaller personal living spaces; and many up-close surroundings that daily touch us like our clothes, scents, or a bath. We are aware of and can discuss most of our other differences (such as gender, race, religion, or politics), but we usually don't think that other people might experience *sensations* differently from us. We all have our own "personal sensory perspectives" or "sensory frames of reference." Those of us with an "even" nervous system have little awareness of the need to understand anything beyond our own reactions to sensation—mainly, that we only react strongly to sensation if there is "actual danger" involved *as we perceive it.* We assume that all people react as we do, that is, in a non-defensive way, to most sensory inputs from the environment. If we like a particular sensation, then we generally think that others will like it, too. As a result, we may judge others negatively or be surprised when they don't like the touches, sights, smells, movements, sounds, and sometimes textures in the mouth that are perfectly acceptable or pleasurable to us. And we're often deeply offended if others react negatively to sensations that originate with us, such as touching them or playing our type of music.

For example, after his deployment, Tom got upset with his daughter because he couldn't stand hearing the same "annoying" (as he called them) Disney tunes played multiple times on the way to school; she in turn was upset with him because he'd always previously "gone with" her music choices as a father–daughter bonding experience.

Learning how sensory reactions to the environment operate along a *continuum* can allow us to make adaptive life choices to *modulate* these reactions, mainly to calm our reactions when we're hypervigilant in everyday contexts like interacting with family members (and/or to discuss our "different" reactions with them). Modulating your sensory responsiveness levels is a life choice that has the potential to make a profound difference in your functioning.

A Little About the Science of Stress

To understand sensory modulation challenges and what you can do about them, it helps to start with a brief look at nervous system science, especially at how our nervous systems handle stress (arousal) and how this impacts our ability to function.

Figure 1:

Classic Arousal Curve

(Kimball, 1999, p. 130)

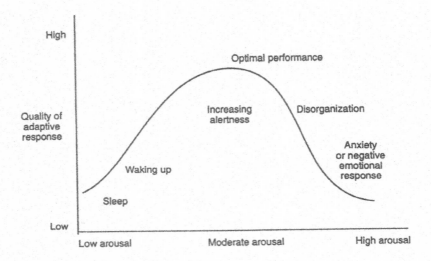

Figure 1 shows a classic stress–arousal curve associated with the part of the central nervous system that controls our levels of reactivity (Kimball, 1993, p. 98; 1999, p. 130). The "prime directive" of the nervous system is to keep us alive, so when the brain senses any danger, it reacts immediately with the classic fight-or-flight response. This is initiated by the parts of the brain *below conscious control*, mainly the amygdala (an almond-shaped area within the temporal lobe). The initial "danger" input–response loop doesn't involve the higher-level, thinking parts of the brain because these are too "slow" to immediately arm our bodies for most survival situations (like fleeing a tiger in the wild or veering from an IED in the road). So your body reacts before you're consciously aware of any need for a reaction, initiating a series of physical changes that make it easier to either fight or flee.

Your heart rate, blood pressure, and respiration increase in order to circulate more blood to the muscles of the extremities (your "fighting/fleeing" arms and legs) and to the brain. Hormones including adrenaline and gluta-mate that support fighting and fleeing are also released, so the body has all that's needed to react quickly and with strength and speed (see Appendix I for more information). At the same time, blood is shunted *away* from bodily functions that are "unimportant" during a survival reaction, for example, digestion. (Have you ever had "butterflies in your stomach" when anxious, nausea or diarrhea when very scared, or experienced digestive problems or constipation after chronic stress?)

What does your body *feel* like when it's ready to fight or flee? You are highly alert to sensations from your environment, for example, you look around, listen, smell, and *feel* more intensely. Your muscles are on alert for immediate bursts of action: in fact, feats of extreme strength (like parents lifting cars to save their trapped children) have been reported. You're not thinking about anything but the stimulus that alerted you to the need for a "staying alive" response. We all have and need these responses, but when our bodies react in a fight-or-flight mode to *everyday things* that are not in themselves perceived as threatening by most people, then we're said to have sensory modulation challenges.

Figure 1 shows what happens as the unconscious arousal level increases in our bodies from "normal" to a level that requires action. Note that "Quality of Adaptive Responses" (how well you do things) is on the vertical axis and "Arousal Level" (how much stress you experience) is on the horizontal axis. *Moderate* arousal results in optimal performance—for example, to have a "good day" or a "good meeting," you need to be alert but not overly anxious. When arousal increases beyond the moderate level, "disorganized" behav-ior can result. Think of the disorganization you feel if the stress of running late in the morning is suddenly elevated by your being unable to find the car keys that you were *sure* you remembered putting on the counter last night. If your arousal (stress) level goes still higher—if, for instance, after five minutes of frantic searching you still haven't found your keys—the behavioral impact will be "anxiety" or "negative emotional responses" (you might "lose it" and yell at someone close at hand [your partner or kids], or just bang around angrily expounding about the "$$##!! KEYS!"). If you stay stressed even *after* you find the keys, you may experience an even greater disorganized/negative response like driving too aggressively and risking a ticket or accident on your way to work.

People with even-keeled nervous systems can quickly recognize when they're over-aroused, and do something about it. They can easily (and often unconsciously) "self-modulate" if the situation calls for it. Those with sensory modulation challenges often cannot de-escalate as easily. This difficulty is compounded by the fact that it's harder for people with sensory modulation challenges to stay in the "optimal performance" range to begin with: people with SMC may move quickly from over-aroused to under-aroused, and vice-versa. It takes "less" to set them off, and once set off, they *stay* "off" for longer.

Figure 2:

Sensory Modulation and Arousal

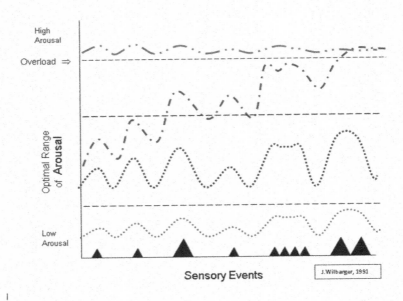

Figure 2 (Wilbarger & Wilbarger, 2001, p. 25) shows this dual SMC difficulty of going "off" more easily and staying "off" for longer periods. This chart results from turning Figure 1 on its side, with anxiety (high arousal/stress) on the top vertical axis and sleep (low arousal) on the bottom. Note that the

optimum range of arousal spans the middle of the chart. The varying-sized black triangles on the bottom of the chart represent any type of sensory event over the course of a day (like noise, a touch, movement, a smell, etc.). The *small* black triangles represent sensory events with low sensory intensity, such as a TV on low volume or soft music; the *large* black triangles represent sensory events with greater intensity, such as a glass dropping or a shout.

The second line from the bottom on the chart (square dots) represents the reactions of a person with a *modulated* nervous system. That person starts out well within the "Optimal Range of Arousal." Note that the line moves up as each sensory event moves the nervous system up to a higher stress/arousal level, but each time, the person's nervous system *is able to move back down* into a low/normal range of arousal after the initial reaction. Also note that while several large sensory events (at the end of the line) can put the person in "overload" (above the central range) *momentarily*, their nervous system can always get back down. A person with a modulated nervous system can get back to an even keel relatively easily even after *strong* sensory events.

The line above the modulated one (third from the bottom, dashes and dots) represents *the nervous system responses of a person with sensory modulation challenges of the over-arousal (defensiveness) type.* Note that *this person's responses are not returning to modulated baseline levels between sensory events, but are steadily climbing up over time, only coming down a little after each stimulus.* After a period of time, when they come down, they're only barely in the modulated range so that *it only takes a **small** sensory event to put them over the top to the point of "losing it," moving into overload.* The important thing to remember here is that **it was not the one specific small sensory event directly preceding their outburst that pushed the person over the edge, but the accumulation of sensory events.** The person may have outwardly appeared modulated (in control), but actually, their nervous system was at a place barely in the normal range and very near "overload."

Some psychologists might advise such a person to "eliminate the antecedent event." In other words, don't let the event that occurred just before you "lost it" happen again. But, in reality, the "antecedent event" itself had very little to do with causing the person to "lose it," rather, it was the *buildup* of arousing events in a nervous system that never fully came back down to modulation. This is why Dawn, for instance, the respiratory therapist who was mentioned in the Introduction, found herself at the end of the day yelling at her children for simply running around the house laughing; her nervous system was by that point at such an elevated level that even this "ordinary" boisterous movement and noise was enough to push her into overload.

Summary: Why We "Lose It"

So why does this happen—why do we "lose it" and blow up? As noted previously, the underlying mechanism of fight-or-flight is an *extremely* important response as it's *the central nervous system's primary survival action*, the "staying alive response." When we're threatened, we move into this heightened nervous system response—the intensity of which is directly related to the *perceived seriousness of the survival threat*. Keep in mind that *it is the individual's nervous system's* **perceived** *survival threat, not other people's perceptions of the situation.* Things that look like no threat at all to a modulated nervous system can look like a very serious threat to a person with sensory modulation challenges (Kimball, 1993, 1999a, 1999b).

Sensory modulation challenges of the hypoarousal type (low arousal) can also occur (see the bottom line on Figure 2). In this instance, the nervous system is under-aroused and does not respond readily to sensory input, or very rarely it's so over-aroused that it has to "shut down" to any more sensory input, and so it acts under-aroused (see Appendix I for further explanations of the science behind these issues).

All individuals with sensory modulation challenges can *improve* their reactiveness and their daily lives and relationships through the Dial It Down program described in the chapters that follow.

CHAPTER 2:

A Closer Look at Specific Sensory Modulation Challenges Post-Deployment or After First Responder or Frontline Medical Work

As mentioned in the previous chapter, being hypervigilant while in a war zone or as a first responder or frontline medical worker is essential to staying alive and performing your mission or job, but *remaining* hypervigilant afterward is not always beneficial to daily functioning. We know that the brain changes with the stress of war or sustained physical or psychological threat, and that returning it to the pre-threat level has historically been difficult, as has been shown by extensive Army studies as well as the personal narratives of soldiers experiencing difficulty post-deployment. Using a sensory-based wellness approach has the potential to help veterans, service members, first responders, and frontline medical workers to "Dial It Down" when experiencing issues around hypervigilance.

Hypervigilance reveals itself in several types of responses involving overreaction in all sensory systems, *particularly* in those sensory systems that are the *most important for staying alive in a war zone or other sustained-threat situations*. These are *tactile (touch), olfaction (smell), audition (hearing),* and *vision. Levels of hypervigilance in each sensory system vary by person.* The following sections contain examples of sensory modulation challenges that have been reported to this author by veterans, service members, first responders, and medical personnel who've found that they have become averse to certain common sensations. Understanding their reactions can help you better understand your own reactions—a crucial first step toward change.

The Visual System

Veterans and first responders, in particular, have commented on several visual sensory changes when they return from duty. Many have reported that in public spaces like restaurants or auditoriums, and even their own homes, they feel the need to sit with their backs to a wall and certainly not to a window. Jackson, an Iraq War veteran, told me that he asked his wife if he could shift their couch away from the spot in front of the living room window where she'd moved it while he was away, as he couldn't stand the "exposed" feeling of sitting on it there. Veterans and service members often attribute this type of unease to having always had someone "watching my back" while in the military, and not having that sense of unit security once they return home. While there's a definite truth to this, it's important to note that this type of heightened sensory response is also often seen in persons who are *born with* sensory modulation challenges: They frequently feel the need to sit with their backs to a wall in restaurants in order to keep an eye on the movement of people near them and to be sure that no one surprises them by approaching from behind. Many veterans and first responders additionally feel the need to be able to see and plan an escape route to keep themselves and their families safe.

Another issue that can over-alert the visual system of someone with sensory modulation challenges is seeing something lying in the road and not knowing what it is. In fact, anything that is *out of place visually* can cause an alert. The difference between someone with sensory modulation challenges and someone without is that someone without can quickly figure out what the visual irregularly is and stay calm, whereas the person with sensory modulation challenges may become highly alerted (as the out-of-place item could pose a threat) and may then have trouble calming down even *after* the item is found to be safe and just out-of-place.

In some cases, even the simplest visual clutter can be unsettling—as was true for Alec, a service member, mentioned in Chapter 1, who found that "normal" household clutter became so disturbing to him after his deployment that he'd sometimes yell at his spouse and children about it, outbursts he deeply regretted.

Visual clutter may be unsettling for frontline medical workers suffering from post-traumatic stress as well, given that high-stakes ERs and ICUs are organized according to strict, specific safety protocols, and anything "out of place" at work (gloves, masks, equipment) could signal a breach that risks both patient and provider infection. Hypervigilance in a hospital setting is positive and necessary, but if it continues *outside* of work and affects daily functioning, sensory modulation challenges might lead to fight-or-flight moments like Alec's of discomfort or "losing it" with family members.

Olfaction (Smell)

Smells are very alerting for most people. As will be discussed further in Chapter 5, smell is the only sensation that doesn't go through the thalamus—the "major traffic cop" of the brain—but instead goes directly to the limbic system—the "seat of emotions." The limbic system plays a key role in modulating the fear response and storing memories related to fear. Police and military veterans have told me that they always react to the smell of gunpowder and explosives such as fireworks—which is exactly what we'd expect them to react to. But when sensory modulation challenges and *over-reactivity* become an issue, these individuals may experience intensely negative responses even to common smells. This is why Mary, the wife of a service member, reported that her husband reacted negatively to the smell of her hair products, which he'd never noticed before his deployment. Another spouse revealed that her husband now couldn't stand the smell of the perfume he'd given her as a gift before his deployment. Similarly, while we would expect medical personnel to be alerted by certain smells associated with hospital settings (disinfectant, alcohol swabs, etc.), when *over-reactivity* becomes an issue, other strong scents may alert them and cause discomfort.

Audition/Hearing

We all know that sounds have the power to alert us strongly. This is why sirens are so effective: they're loud and pitched to get our attention. Another sound that nature has designed to be powerfully alerting is the cry of a small baby: it's developed to make us do something to check on the child's welfare.

The types of sounds we alert to are not just loud ones but can also often be very small ones that may be persistent or different from usual. Sounds like ticking clocks and dripping water are persistent, whereas unexpected noises like a soft *thump* in your house at night are "different." These sounds can have many meanings and cause many different responses. If a service member is in a war zone or a first responder is searching for a suspect, small noises can mean extreme danger, while if they're at home, a small noise may just be the cat brushing its tail across the door frame. One soldier revealed to me that he almost shot his wife one night when he'd been sleeping and she came home late: rather than taking his advice that she should be sure to make lots of noise when she came in, she'd decided "not to wake him up" and entered the dark bedroom quietly. He said he had his finger on the trigger to shoot, but something made him stop just in time.

Frontline medical workers may find themselves reacting with uncomfortable hyper-alertness to many "normal" beeping noises even outside of the hospital setting, for example, to alarm clocks, vehicle back-up alarms, car alarms, and national weather warnings on TV.

Another example of sound sensitivity is the difficulty in sleeping experienced by numerous veterans, first responders, and frontline healthcare workers. Many have stated that they have trouble sleeping as they're always "on alert." Sleep difficulties can include being alerted by any noise so that you can't get to sleep or stay asleep, or needing to get so exhausted that you "sleep like the dead" and are very hard to wake up. These are the two extremes of sensory responses: over-arousal/defensiveness, and "apparent" under-arousal. Remember that what looks like under-arousal may in fact be an example of severe over-arousal that causes the nervous system to "shut down" because it can't take any more stimulation (see Appendix I).

Tactile System (Touch)

By far the most complex and far-reaching problem for those with sensory modulation challenges, including first responders, returning veterans, and frontline medical workers, is touch. Touch is the strongest sensation involved in developing intimacy. And touch is the sensation that's *most often affected* in people with sensory modulation challenges. The tactile system has two distinct divisions in the brain. One division processes touch in an "evaluative" way to almost instantaneously assess the need to act or not with the fight-or-flight response. And the other touch system processes discriminative touch: pressure, pain, and temperature. If a person has sensory modulation challenges, a fight-or-flight response is more likely to occur, especially in reaction to a *light* touch. All of us respond with greater sensitivity to light than heavy touch—for example, if something touches you lightly, like a bug or a spider's web, you're more likely to take a swipe at the spot where it landed on your body to "protect yourself" compared with if something bumps into you firmly. People with sensory modulation challenges react *more often* and *more intensely* to light touch, and then have a harder time returning to a modulated state.

Touch is the main way in which we as humans are intimate with each other: It's a key part of how we show love to our children and connect with our spouses or partners, and this often involves light touch. For the person with sensory modulation challenges, light touch in intimate situations can become problematic by causing "over-alerting," the fight-or-flight response. Firm touch is usually well tolerated, and in fact can be modulating (moving you to the "middle," calming you down if you're sensory defensive or bringing you up if you're under-aroused, which can look like depression). This is a particularly important distinction during sexual activity. Several wives of returning service members reported to me that their husbands' sexual practices changed significantly after deployment: husbands could no longer tolerate light touch on themselves, as this alerted a fight-or-flight response, and because they couldn't tolerate light touch on themselves, they felt they couldn't give light touch to their partners. The thought of *giving* light touch made them feel the same aversion as they would if experiencing it themselves (remember that we judge others' sensory likes and dislikes from our own "personal sensory perspectives"). As they couldn't tolerate light touch, these husbands could not tolerate giving or receiving foreplay the same way they had in the past, but could tolerate the firm or heavy touch pressure of intercourse. (As mentioned above, firm or heavy pressure can at times modulate and reduce sensory defensiveness.) Significant difficulty with intimacy may result when a returning soldier's, first responder's, or frontline medical worker's changed sensitivity to touch is not understood. (The influence of sensory modulation challenges on interpersonal relationships and sexual intimacy is discussed in detail in Chapter 6.)

Touch sensitivity can also, unfortunately, negatively impact relationships with others—particularly with our children. Remember Jason, the service member just back from deployment who told me of a specific tactile issue he had with his teenaged daughter—she used to kiss him lightly on the cheek as part of their morning "goodbye" routine, but when he came home, he could no longer tolerate the light touch of her kiss and would pull away from her. She accused him of no longer loving her because he wouldn't let her kiss him, and this became a large family conflict. I explained to him that light touch alerted his fight-or-flight response, and he agreed that this was a problem. Then I asked him if he liked the heavy pressure of hugs, especially with an accompanying rub or pat on the back, and he replied, "Yes, a lot." When I asked if substituting the heavy touch of a hug for the light touch of the kiss would work for him, he answered, "Yes, we can do that! That solves the problem!" Several days later he happily reported that "It worked!!"

Takeaway Message

These are only a few examples of how sensory modulation challenges can affect veterans, first responders, and frontline medical workers. In later chapters, we'll discuss in more detail why these heightened reactions occur. And we'll discuss what types of sensory input *you can strategically use* to modulate your own reactions. As stated earlier, particular types of sensory input work well to positively affect modulation. Those sensory inputs are *body movement in a rhythmic way (head through space), heavy work with the joints and muscles,* and *deep touch pressure to the skin* (Wilbarger & Wilbarger, 2001). While a single, fast body movement may be alerting, repetitive, rhythmic movements like jumping on a rebounder (mini trampoline), doing jumping jacks, or running are modulating. While light touch is alerting, heavy touch pressure is modulating. Also modulating is heavy resistive work with joints and muscles, like pushups and lifting weights. Keep this in mind as we continue to look at varying reactions to different types of sensation from the environment, and the ways in which you can *choose* to include certain types of sensory input in your day with the simple Dial It Down process to improve your nervous system responses and your ability to participate fully in your preferred life activities.

CHAPTER 3:

"BATTLEMIND," "DIAL IT DOWN"

Now that you understand that soldiers', first responders', and frontline medical personnel's heightened reactions following active- and on-duty work may be related to sensory modulation challenges, let's look at how these reactions are described by one military program, Battlemind, and how Dial It Down works alongside that program. Note that while Battlemind is an older Army initiative, its concepts still apply to all branches of the military, as well as first responders, and can also be adapted as a framework for understanding the responses of medical personnel who've worked in sustained-threat situations.

Battlemind is a concept developed by the Walter Reed Army Institute of Research (WRAIR) based on research findings of the Land Combat Study (2003–2004). This concept was "designed to boost resilience before deployment" (Moore & Penk, 2011, p. 333) and to help veterans and service members understand their behaviors post-deployment. The Army then incorporated the original Battlemind concepts into its more extensive training program, the Comprehensive Soldier and Family Fitness Program (Amy Adler, Walter Reed Institute of Research, personal communication, March 4, 2015), and most recently, the Performance Triad P3 Program, which focuses on sleep, activity, and nutrition (see References for website).

Battlemind continues to provide a foundation for understanding the issues that affect military personnel when they return from active duty and serves as a conceptual grounding for this book. Battlemind is an acronym using the first letter of the first word in each phrase. Notice that each phrase has two parts: the first is the intended Battlemind part (combat mind-set) and describes a coping skill that helps service members survive and perform well in war. *These are all skills that are purposefully trained into military personnel as essential to keeping them alive.* The second part, after the word "versus," shows how that same skill *could become problematic* when carried over to life at home post-deployment or after leaving the military (Moore & Penk, 2011). When I first saw Battlemind in the course of my work with veterans, I was struck by how many of the concepts after the "versus" have a sensory modulation component and could be applied to members of any military branch and first responders (and now, additionally, to frontline medical personnel).

It is *crucial* to the process of understanding, healing, and "taking control" of your responses to life at home for you to understand that *the issues that are causing problems following active- or on-duty rotations are, during war and sustained-threat situations, essential tools that help to keep you alive and functioning in top form.* In the military, soldiers are specifically trained in these tools based on a long history of how best to prepare service members to survive and perform at peak levels during wartime. (I will discuss parallels to first responders and medical personnel below.)

The **Battlemind Training I** concepts are as follows (Moore & Penk, 2011, p. 334):

1. Buddies (cohesion) *versus* withdrawal

2. Accountability *versus* controlling

3. Targeted aggression *versus* inappropriate aggression

4. Tactical awareness *versus* hypervigilance

5. Lethally armed *versus* "locked and loaded" at home

6. Emotional control *versus* anger/detachment

7. Mission operational security *versus* secretiveness

8. Individual responsibility *versus* guilt

9. Non-defensive (combat) driving *versus* aggressive driving

10. Discipline and ordering *versus* conflict

Most of these concepts are self-explanatory for military personnel, but some need explanation for nonmilitary readers. For example, #4: military personnel know they cannot maintain *hypervigilance* for long periods of time. If they try to do so for too long, then "someone gets through the wire," and this is why guard duty rotates. And #5: *Lethally armed* means that you have a weapon and a clip on you, but the clip is not yet in the weapon; *locked and loaded* means that the clip is in the weapon, the round is in the chamber, and the safety is off. #7: *Mission operational security* means that everyone is responsible for the security of the operation; and *secretiveness*, according to one soldier, may be about not only the need to remain silent regarding the details of particular military operations but also a response to nonmilitary persons not understanding the military.

The training received by police and firefighters closely parallels these Battlemind concepts. The same is true of the training received by medical personnel, in the following ways: "buddies" (fellow medical personnel who understand their uniquely high-stress work situations) *versus* "withdrawal" from others; "accountability" to high professional standards for the safety and security of patients, *versus* the potential for these strict protocols to turn to "controlling" behavior outside of work; "targeted aggression," "tactical awareness," and "lethally armed" not, clearly, in the sense of using lethal force, but in the sense of needing to be intensely, life-or-death focused on patient-specific goals and protective gear, *versus* the potential for this sharp focus to turn to abruptness and hypervigilance in other contexts; "emotional control" as a huge component of medical training and practice, *versus* the potential for a type of emotional withdrawal or detachment that can baffle and distress nonmedical spouses and family; "mission operational security" in the sense of strict patient privacy laws, *versus* the potential for this acquired habit of secrecy to extend beyond patient-specific issues; and, most strikingly and tragically in the COVID-19 crisis, *individual responsibility* in the sense of the patient lives that medical personnel have been charged with saving (often without sufficient equipment and treatments) *versus* the "guilt" that high numbers of medical professionals report feeling over the unprecedented number of patient and colleague deaths that have happened "on their watch," as well as over sometimes having to decide who gets scarce treatment resources.

Look back again at the ten Battlemind concepts and notice that *the concepts after the* versus *may all be interpreted from a sensory modulation challenges viewpoint.* As a veteran, first responder, or frontline medical worker, you may be responding to life back home in ways that are perceived by yourself and/or others as hypervigilant, aggressive, angry or detached, guilty, secretive, or maintaining a "locked and loaded" (metaphorically speaking) trigger. And you may react to stressors by withdrawing or trying to control others' actions. *If you look at these behaviors from a sensory modulation challenges perspective, they take on a different meaning* that can make understanding and empowering yourself to take steps to change them much easier.

Check-In #1

Take a look at the ten Battlemind concepts and consider which of the words after the "versus" might apply to you, and how often you demonstrate these behaviors. Please check off the levels that apply to you on the following chart:

CHECK-IN #1: How Do BATTLEMIND Concepts Apply to You?

Level: Concepts:	Never	Occasionally	Sometimes	Often	Most of the Time
Withdrawal					
Controlling					
Aggression					
Hypervigilance					
Locked and loaded					
Anger/detachment					
Secretiveness					
Guilt					
Aggressive driving					
Conflict					

What does this tell you about your reactions to life "back home"? What, if anything, would you like to change?

_____

_____

_____

_____

_____

DIAL IT DOWN

Now that you've looked at your reactions in the Battlemind framework, please consider that at least some of these behaviors may be due to sensory modulation challenges. The Dial It Down framework is about intentionally decreasing your hyperarousal and other "versus" (post-deployment or post-sustained-threat) Battlemind issues so that you can participate more fully in your life. You actually already know a great deal about how to do this.

For soldiers, your excellent military training helped you "Dial It Down" in the past. The military's goal is to keep service members performing optimally, particularly in a war zone. (Police and firefighter recruits go through similar training programs; for frontline medical personnel equivalents, see "Frontline Personnel and 'Dialing It Down'" below.) For many of you, daily physical training kept you in top physical condition. But active-duty personnel also need to be in top *mental* condition. Training teaches you to control your fear responses, which are the mostly automatic fight-or-flight or "staying alive" responses: *the prime directive of your brain is to keep your body alive, so it alerts you to all possible danger.* As service members, you learn to be highly "functionally alert," and to respect and react to the alerting danger signals your body is sending you in the most appropriate way to preserve yourself and your squad or unit and to accomplish your mission. But *over*-alerting (as opposed to "functional" alerting) can lead to fear, disorganization, anxiety, poor decision-making, and lack of focus. So *how does training keep you in that "just right" mental space for optimal thinking and decision-making?*

Military, firefighter, and police training programs prepare you for numerous possibilities that you'll encounter in war zones or violent situations and teach you how to react through protocols and hands-on drills. But when the unexpected occurs, as it inevitably will in conflict situations, you must rely on *your own nervous system* to react appropriately. We know that a serious survival threat is handled best by a brain that, as stated above, is *functionally* alert but not *over*-alert. And we know that *the amount of sensory input that your brain has had recently establishes its current level of arousal.* We also know that heavy work with joints and muscles (e.g., heavy exercise like push-ups, carrying a heavy pack, carrying fire hoses) and rhythmic movement of the head through space (e.g., running, jumping jacks, marching) are the strongest ways to keep arousal levels (the fight-or-flight response) in the "just right" place for optimum action. Therefore, *the physical training that can be a very strong and regular part of active-duty life not only keeps you physically ready to react strongly but also keeps your brain at that "just right arousal level" so that you can act appropriately and make good decisions when in danger.* Now that you're off-duty or home from deployment, how are you going to keep your nervous system in that "just right place" given all the competing demands for your time and attention? By discovering how to Dial It Down.

Frontline Personnel and "Dialing it Down"

Frontline medical personnel are generally not given the same level of *physical* training and preparedness as military service members, police, and firefighters. But the difficult sleep-deprived schedules of medical residents and trainees tend to be viewed as a rite of passage, preparing personnel for an "in the trenches" mind-set of making life-and-death decisions under extreme duress and "training in" an ability to control fear or fight-or-flight responses. Strict protocols, drills, and hands-on experience are also key components of skilled medical training. Following clinical training, the more relaxed schedules and on–off shifts of many types of medical personnel tend to "cover" for the lack of physical training regimes: while ER and ICU shifts can be long and stressful, they have (prior to the COVID-19 crisis) generally been followed by "off" days for recovery (note that this differs greatly from the need for soldiers to operate for extended "on" periods during wartime). COVID-19 has pushed many frontline emergency response and medical workers into "wartime"-like conditions, in which personnel shortages have forced them to operate for periods of weeks, and in some cases months, with only limited if any "off" time, and frequently (for fear of spreading infection) in isolation from family and friends. For these professionals, both during *and* after their frontline work, learning physical techniques to "Dial It Down" (which do *not* require an extended investment of time) can be an essential support.

What is DIAL IT DOWN?

Dial It Down is an acronym in which the first letter of each phrase describes sensory-based strategies for understanding and taking control of your responses to life. You will notice below that the first letter in Dial It Down is "D" for "Defensiveness" (or hyperarousal/hyper-alertness), which we discussed in Chapter 1. This is because "sensory defensiveness" is the most prevalent type of sensory modulation challenge: Your body often has a hyper-alert or "defensive" reaction to sensory input as it tries to protect you from danger. In Chapter 2, we discussed the first "I," for the "Intensity" of your responses.

DIAL IT DOWN

1. **D**efensiveness (sensory modulation challenges): What are the sensory inputs from the environment that your body (nervous system) reacts to in a heightened or "sensory defensive" way? [**Chapter 1**]

2. **I**ntensity: How strong does a sensory input have to be before you react to it, and how intense are your reactions? Are your reactions appropriate to the stimulus (within the range of intensity that "most" people would show), or would they be considered over- or under-reactive? [**Chapter 2**]

3. **A**wareness: What does past and present research tell us about sensory modulation challenges? Can you recognize that sensory defensiveness/sensory modulation challenges might be an alternate explanation for some of your responses to input from your environment? How can you, and do you *want* to, use self-initiated wellness methods (like strong physical activities, which *are not* necessarily time-intensive) as tools to influence your nervous system to respond differently to these environmental inputs? *Knowledge is power*, and your "awareness" of sensory modulation challenges will change the way you view many situations. [**Chapters 3 and 4**]

4. **L**ikes/Dis**L**ikes: What sensory stimuli do you *dislike*, and how can this knowledge help you identify your individual sensory modulation challenges? What physical activities do you already *like* to do

that might help you modulate your nervous system's responses? How can these or similar activities (even if used for very short periods of time) be modified to influence your nervous system in a more positive way? [**Chapter 5**]

5. Intimacy/Interpersonal Relationships: How have sensory modulation challenges affected your relationships? How can understanding the role that sensory modulation challenges play in your responses to others, and in their responses to you, help you improve these relationships? [**Chapter 6**]

6. Transitions Through Trauma: Battlemind highlights the difficulty of making the transition to life back home after using military training to stay alive during war. Dial It Down offers a wellness method to help make that transition a success. How can the specific *sensory effects* of physical and psychological trauma on military, first responder, and frontline medical personnel be understood and evaluated as a crucial part of successfully facing the challenges involved in "coming home"? [**Chapter 7**]

7. Diet: Just as we need a diet of food to survive, we need a "sensory diet" to keep us feeling and functioning in top form. How can you combine modulating sensory experiences that you "like" into a daily "sensory diet" to keep your nervous system functioning evenly and optimally? [**Chapters 8, 9, and 10**]

8. Own It: It's important that you learn to understand your own unique sensory modulation challenges, develop your own sensory strategies to keep your nervous system in that just-right place for optimal functioning (modulated), and explain these challenges and strategies to others who can offer you support. How can you identify and talk about your sensory reactions and needs, especially to family members and close friends? [**Chapter 11**]

9. Win–Win: Sensory strategies can be a win–win for you, your family, and friends, as everyone needs these strategies. Sensory reactions are a part of daily life, but most people never pay attention to how they're responding to sensory input from others and the environment, or

how they may be affecting others' nervous systems by their sensory actions. Sensory strategies will also keep your nervous system in a better place so that you can benefit optimally from other strategies you may be using to treat issues such as post-traumatic stress (PTS), post-traumatic stress disorder (PTSD), or mild traumatic brain injury (mTBI). **Chapter 12** shows how one veteran put it all together for a win–win.

10. **New Solutions and Strategies**: The end result will be new strategies to keep your sensory systems functioning in a modulated range, so that you won't be negatively influenced by random sensory input and can therefore participate more fully in all the occupations of life as you choose to. **Chapter 13** shows how wellness interventions for sensory modulation challenges fit with other treatments for PTS, PTSD, and mTBI; **Chapter 14** offers new information to health professionals about sensory modulation challenges; and **Chapter 15** reviews what you have learned.

Appendices: The appendices go into more detail about issues of special interest to some readers:

I. The Science of How Modulation Works in the Nervous System: Additional Information

II. More About Interpersonal Relationships

III. Sensory Modulation Challenges at Different Ages

IV. Professional Treatment for SMC: The Wilbarger Therapressure Protocol™

The rest of this book will be dedicated to explaining the concepts underlying Dial It Down, and to helping you design your own wellness strategies so that you can "dial down" your sensory responses whenever you choose to.

CHAPTER 4:

What Do We Know About Sensory Modulation Challenges?

The "A" in DIAL IT DOWN: "Awareness"

Much of what we know about sensory modulation challenges (SMC) comes from research studies of and treatments applied to children, some born with sensory issues and some with a history of trauma. Adult sensory modulation challenges have been much less thoroughly studied, particularly in military, first responder, and frontline medical personnel who've been exposed to violent and/or traumatic situations—but this is beginning to change. This chapter is intended to help build your awareness of this new sensory-based model for thinking about the kinds of difficulties you may be experiencing following your active- or on-duty work in these situations. What is the history of our knowledge base about sensory modulation challenges? How have these concepts been developed, and what does current research show about them?

How Are Ways of Responding to Sensory Input Described by Health Professionals?

Labels for differences in responding to sensory input have evolved over time through research and greater understanding. Differences in sensory responsiveness were first identified by Dr. A. Jean Ayres in the 1970s (Ayres 1972a, 1972b, 1979) as over-alerting to tactile (touch) input, which she labeled "tactile defensiveness." Later, over-arousal responses in additional sensory areas were identified: auditory defensiveness, visual defensiveness, defensiveness to smells, etc. As occupational therapists and other professionals realized that *all* sensory systems could in fact be over-aroused, they began using the umbrella term of "sensory defensiveness," which is still used today. However, when different sensory challenges such as the previously mentioned *under*-arousal were discovered, health professionals—in the hope of making identification and research more consistent—began defining sensory defensiveness as one type of *SMC* (Greenspan, 2005, *Diagnostic Manual of the Interdisciplinary Council on Developmental and Learning Disorders* [ICDL]). A further refinement in labeling (and complexity!) occurred as different *kinds* of sensory issues were identified (for instance, difficulty in the brain's processing of sensory information involving sensory *discrimination* [e.g., difficulty with distinguishing by *touch* alone the difference between a dime and quarter in your pocket; difficulty with distinguishing by *hearing* alone the difference between the words "cat," "hat," and "pack"]). These differences *do* involve how the brain processes sensory information from the environment, but do *not* involve sensory over- or under- arousal. The *wider* umbrella term of "Sensory Processing Disorder" is sometimes used to encompass all sensory challenges, including sensory discrimination issues, sensory-based motor coordination challenges in children, and sensory over- and under-arousal. Adding even *more* complexity to this pyramid of labels, Sensory Processing Disorder itself is sometimes placed under the even *broader* umbrella term of "Sensory Integration Dysfunction."

Information on differences in sensory responses may be found under any or all of these varied terms, which can make it hard for people to easily track the research and treatment progress that's been made in one particular area. Given this book's intended focus on the sensory issues that most frequently and severely affect military, first responder, and frontline medical personnel, I have chosen to refer mainly to the sensory modulation challenges of sensory over-responsiveness (or sensory defensiveness) and sensory under-responsiveness.

How are Sensory Modulation Challenges Identified and Managed?

Sensory modulation challenges are actual, discernible *neurophysiological differences* in sensory systems that can be identified. For instance, children who demonstrate sensitivity to sound by being more bothered than most by loud or unexpected noises are now routinely referred by doctors and educators to occupational therapists for sensory modulation challenges evaluation and intervention. The same is true of children who feel physically uncomfortable at the touch of some types of clothes on their bodies (clothing tags, polyester clothes), and children who dislike the textures of certain foods in their mouths. Multiple books have been written to help the families of children with these issues develop ways of coping, growing, and thriving. But these issues are not yet fully understood in *adults*—both adults who may have been born with sensory modulation challenges or experienced traumas that weren't identified in childhood and have developed their own (sometimes maladaptive, e.g., through avoidance) ways of coping, and adults who have developed sensory sensitivities *as* adults through trauma.

Due to this lack of research and understanding, adults who experience sensory modulation challenges are more likely to be diagnosed with a mental health condition, as *some of the issues connected with sensory modulation challenges could be* misinterpreted *as mental health symptoms*. In some cases, addressing the underlying sensory modulation challenges can be a crucial addition to treatments aimed at improving an existing mental health condition, and in other cases the sensory modulation challenges model may offer a better explanation for apparent mental health symptoms. (As stated earlier, it is *essential* that if you are currently receiving treatment from a mental health professional, or are seeking to understand issues that haven't yet been diagnosed, you *always* check in with a health professional and never self-diagnose so that no part of your individual profile and path to better health and daily functioning is missed.)

Sensory modulation challenges in adults far too often go unrecognized. Patricia Wilbarger (1995) was the first to suggest a paradigm for the treatment of sensory modulation challenges in her work with children diagnosed with sensory defensiveness. The program includes extensive use of *sensory diets* at home and in school, and the *Wilbarger Therapressure Protocol™ (WTP)*, which remain the foundation for interventions with children to the present day (Wilbarger & Wilbarger, 2001, 2007).

In this book's new application of the paradigm to military veterans, first responders, and frontline medical workers, *sensory modulation challenges are proactively managed in four ways* (based on Wilbarger & Wilbarger, 1991):

1. The first is *knowledge.* **Knowledge is power.** Once you know about sensory modulation challenges, you begin to change the way you think about yourself and others and the way you view your own responses to the environment. You can understand why you may react in some of the ways you do, and you can help your family and friends change the ways in which they view this behavior. You can make *your own* decisions about how much you want to alter your sensory responses. If you react to sensation more than most people, you may choose to stay that way, as this can have positive effects (for example, the hyper-alertness needed to be a security guard). But if you or your family desires change, you can choose to *dial down* the hyperarousal w*hen you want to* (*you* control the *timing* of your wellness program) by doing simple activities to modulate your system.

2. Along with knowledge, you can **modify your environment** *by accommodating the environment to yourself and/or yourself to the environment* in order to avoid certain types of sensory input entirely, or to decrease the effects of over-alerting input on your nervous system. You're probably already doing this to some extent by avoiding situations that make you "stressed." Once you know that your behaviors are influenced by your changed responses to sensory input, you can more easily judge what types of sensory input you can tolerate and accommodate. *While you can accommodate by simply* avoiding *sensory-overloading environments, this may limit your participation in life events.* And no matter how carefully you structure your environment to avoid sensory stimulation, *stimulation levels can change unexpectedly at any time*, requiring you to have additional go-to strategies for coping with these challenges.

3. In addition to knowledge and modifying your environment, sensory modulation challenges can be handled through a self-administered wellness approach: a *"sensory diet"* (Wilbarger, 1995). As

mentioned earlier, we all need a certain level of sensory input to keep our nervous systems healthy and reacting in positive ways, just as we need food to keep our bodies healthy. But if we experience too much sensory input or too much intensity of input, we can become "overdone." A sensory diet keeps our nervous systems *modulated* so that increased sensory input doesn't have an over-alerting effect. *Sensory diet is the strongest, most flexible wellness option.* It involves providing yourself with specific types and schedules of sensory input to manage your own nervous system. This is best done through activities that *you* choose and like. These can be portable, can be done on a restricted time schedule that fits your life, can be done individually or with others (like family and friends), can change as your time and interests change, and, depending on the activities you pick, can be free or very low-cost. (The term *sensory break* is also used to indicate a time set aside for doing modulating sensory activities.) The three specific types of sensory activities that are most often used in sensory diets (I like to refer to them as "The Big Three") are: (a) rhythmic movement of your head through space (examples: running, jumping on a mini trampoline, jumping jacks, sitting and bouncing on a yoga ball); (b) resistive work with muscles and joints (examples: exercise bands, pushups, weights, wearing a weighted vest or backpack); and (c) firm pressure on the skin (examples: massage, pressure vest, sleeping under a weighted blanket). Additional activities will be discussed in Chapters 8, 9, and 10.

4. The fourth way the sensory defensiveness type of SMC may be managed is through a simple program guided by an occupational therapist, the *Wilbarger Therapressure Protocol™* (Wilbarger & Wilbarger, 2001, 2007). This program will be discussed in more detail in Appendix IV, but it involves a few minutes multiple times a day of specific deep touch pressure and firm proprioceptive sensory input aimed at modulating your nervous system. It must be taught to you and monitored by a specially trained occupational therapist.

How Is Sensory Modulation Accomplished by *Your* Nervous System?

Sensory modulation challenges apply to all age ranges and can be developmental (from birth) or acquired through trauma and extended survival/vigilance situations. As stated earlier, sensory defensiveness (over-arousal) is one form of sensory modulation challenges, with under-arousal being another. It's important to remember that sensory modulation is on a *continuum* from low to high arousal, and that while for many people sensory modulation usually isn't an issue, for some it's an occasional issue, and for others, it can be a constant struggle. Check-In #2 is intended to build your awareness of just how much of a struggle sensory modulation is for you.

Check-In #2: The Sensory Time Clock

1. How do you rate yourself on the Sensory Time Clock? Please fill out the clock pictured below for as "typical" a day as you can. If it makes a difference, do two clocks, one for a typical weekday and one for a typical weekend day.

    a. Are you aware of times when you were not able to control your responses to sensory input (sights, sounds, touch, etc.)?

    _____

    _____

    b. What was the result, and how did you respond when you realized that you weren't in control?

    _____

    _____

    c. What (if anything) have you done about it to this point?

    _____

    _____

    d. Where would your family members place you on the continuum from low to high stress/arousal?

_____

_____

2. Where would you place your family members on the Time Clock? Perhaps draw a clock for them or ask them to draw one for themselves.

a. Are you aware of times when they were not able to control their responses to sensory input?

_____

_____

b. What was the result, and how did you respond to the person and situation?

_____

_____

c. What (if anything) have you done about it to this point?

_____

_____

SENSORY TIME CLOCKS

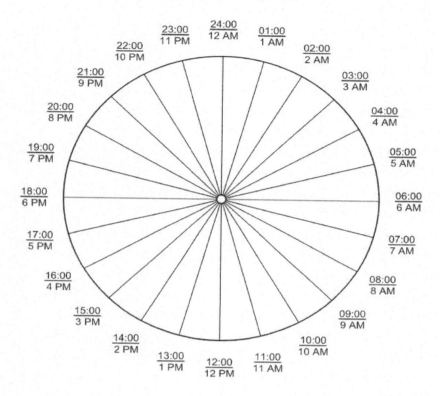

24 HOUR WEEKDAY SENSORY TIME CLOCK

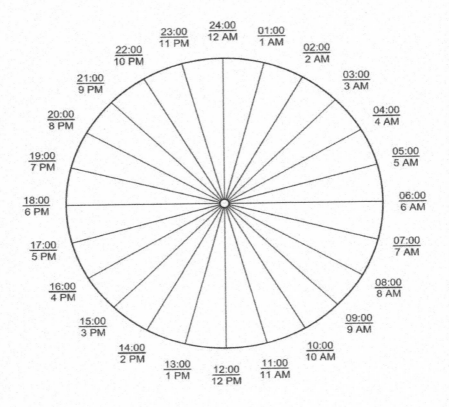

24 HOUR WEEKEND SENSORY TIME CLOCK

Color in time blocks (slices) on the sensory time clock based on your stress/arousal levels.

- Red: Very High Stress/Arousal (not in good control)

- Orange: Moderately High Arousal

- Yellow: Mildly High Arousal

- Green: "Just Right" Arousal

- Blue: Mildly Low Arousal

- Purple: Moderately Low Arousal

- Black: Very Low Arousal (asleep)

Hunting Mastodons: A Brief Fairy Tale about How Our Nervous Systems Still Have Caveperson Needs

Although the brain can and does make changes over time, this is usually a slow process. The lower brain centers that are responsible for our basic survival functions (heart rate, blood pressure, respiration, hormones) haven't changed much over the past two million-plus years. The human nervous system is designed for hunting and gathering. So how does this older part of the central nervous system work to keep us safe, and what does it respond to for modulation, and why? As we discussed earlier, the sympathetic part of the autonomic nervous system has as its primary purpose keeping us alive by alerting us to danger through the fight-or-flight response. Our nervous system is "used to" living in a much older time when it was responsible for helping the body do the very heavy work of daily life. Our nervous system cannot change (evolve) as fast as society does, so it has many important *residual* responses based on caveperson times.

Consider this short "fairy tale." Our nervous system is designed for very heavy work, for example, hunting mastodons. That nervous system would be very happy to track the beast for many days carrying a heavy load of "survival gear" (not the lightweight L.L. Bean kind), and then either set a trap (perhaps digging a deep hole and filling it with spikes) or drive the mastodon over a cliff so the creature could be caught and struck repeatedly with heavy spears (as mastodons were decidedly hard to kill). To get the mastodon back *to* the tribe then meant skinning the animal, chopping it up with knives and axes, and dragging it long distances. Finishing the hides to make clothing and shelter required lots of heavy work, and even eating the animal required heavy work as chewing the meat wasn't easy. Life then was all about very heavy work for muscles and joints.

Fast-forward to today: our nervous system still needs *very heavy work* to function optimally. But our "information" society does not reward heavy work: our jobs and schools require us to sit for large portions of the day. And at home, we're often in front of our TVs or computers, or using cell phones or tablets, so we don't move nearly as much as our ancestors did. Most of us don't do heavy work routinely. Those of us who feel the need to move, find it's often difficult to make the time to "exercise," which is seen as an add-on to our lives. And we often have a hard time finding activities with the intensity our bodies really need.

So "normal" nervous systems are already at a disadvantage in our society. Without routine heavy input, our nervous systems often remain on high arousal. Add on high stress, and we see compromises in our ability to pay attention, self-calm, and perform well in highly stimulating environments. The addition of any form of trauma can mean even more difficulty attending and staying modulated. In other words, not just those of us with sensory modulation challenges but *all* of us in our present society, need to go back to "hunting mastodons," that is, finding the time for heavy work and play.

CHAPTER 5:

Discovering If You Have a Sensory-Reactive Nervous System Resulting in Sensory Modulation Challenges

The "L" in DIAL IT DOWN: "Likes/Dislikes"

We are all reacting constantly to sensory input from our environments. What types of sensory input do you *like*, and what do you *dislike* or perhaps overreact to?

As stated previously, there is a *continuum of responsiveness* to sensory stimuli, and we as individuals don't always react in the same way to the same stimuli. Our reactions depend on several factors, one of which is the *underlying level of nervous system arousal at the time of the incoming stimuli*. Some of us are usually on high arousal, some of us are usually on low arousal, and some of us change easily. Most people spend most of the time reacting within a middle range; however, if you are tired, ill, stressed, or anxious, you may move out of your usual middle range. Some people's nervous systems function in an over-arousal range most of the time: as I've noted, their particular sensory modulation challenge is called "sensory defensiveness." For example, sirens are supposed to alert us to danger, but what if the clicking of a pen is highly alerting or annoying to you? What if your whole family wears turtleneck shirts in the winter, but you can't stand the touch of any material around your neck?

People with sensory modulation challenges/sensory defensiveness can have dislikes, or "pickiness," in just one or in many different areas. *No two people are alike in their patterns.* This is one of the main reasons why it can take time to evaluate and understand SMC. For example, one person may be bothered by some forms of light touch such as tags in shirts or synthetic materials, while someone else may not mind these things but may be bothered by being touched lightly by a loved one. A third person may dislike *visual* stimuli such as the busy mall at holiday times, bright lights, fabric patterns in sofa pillows, or the flickering of florescent lights (many people don't even realize that florescent lights flicker and also hum). A fourth may specifically dislike cooking smells, scented soaps, the smell of new clothes in a store, or perfume. Whereas a fifth person may have a few dislikes in each area. *The common unifying element is a reaction to sensory input that is out of scale with what a "usual" reaction to that particular input is expected to be for "most people," or even what the usual reaction is for that person when they are not "over-aroused" or "stressed out."* Remember that veterans, first responders, and frontline medical workers tend to react in particular to sounds, smells, light touch, and visual things that appear "out of place."

Check-In #3: Likes/Dislikes:
Might You Be Experiencing Sensory Modulation Challenges?

You may have decided by now that you experience some sensory modulation challenges. If so, you should also understand that you can make your *own* choices about what you want to do about this. To be able to make informed decisions, you'll first need to develop a more detailed understanding of how your nervous system reacts to different types of sensory input. To start, fill in short answers to the following sensory questions (please note, Check-In #4 at the end of this chapter will give you the chance to explore these questions in more detail):

1. Are there particular things that you react to strongly? Y/N. What are they?

    _____

    _____

2. Are there particular things that you under-react to (perhaps ask a friend or your partner what types of stimuli [e.g., sounds, sights] you seem to "tune out")? Y/N. What are they?

    _____

    _____

3. What do you do if you have these reactions?

    _____

    _____

4. Do any of your reactions make you or others uncomfortable? Y/N. What are those reactions?

    _____

    _____

5. What have you noticed about others' reactions to the same stimuli?

    _____

    _____

What Some Sensory Modulation Challenges Look Like in Adults

If you have a sensory-defensive nervous system, what does this look like? Learning the answer to this question will help you to *more specifically target* the areas that are most difficult for you. Adults are often able to rationalize or hide their sensory modulation challenges. If you were born with sensory modulation challenges or acquired them at a young age, and have never had them diagnosed or explained, your reactions are what you've always lived with. You probably know that others don't feel as you do, and you may have become adept at making excuses for your behaviors or at avoiding situations that might be too much for you. It's also not uncommon for persons who've had undiagnosed sensory modulation challenges since childhood to develop other (secondary) symptoms such as anxiety or depression.

If you're a veteran, service member, first responder, or frontline medical worker and acquired sensory modulation challenges later in life as a result of war, trauma, or sustained-threat situations, then you or others in your life have probably noted the *changes* in you. If these changes are upsetting enough, you or others may decide to refer you for evaluation. Sometimes a medical diagnosis of PTSD may follow. *Whether you have PTSD or not, separating out the sensory modulation challenges component from other PTSD or post-traumatic stress (PTS) symptoms involves understanding how your nervous system is reacting to the environment.* Though not all adults with PTSD or PTS show sensory modulation challenges, it appears from early research that this overlap in conditions is highly prevalent (Kimball, 2017, 2018, 2019, 2021, 2021a; Stroller et al., 2012; van der Kolk, 2014; Wilbarger & Cook, 2011).

Examples of Some Sensory Modulation Challenges in Veterans, First Responders, and Frontline Medical Workers

Remember that *each person is different and will be "bothered" by different sensory inputs.* No one is bothered by everything! The common denominator is that these inputs are frequently reported to influence alertness/arousal levels. This is by no means an exhaustive list. (I'll go into more detail about sensitivities related to specific sensory systems later in this chapter.) Please also note that while some of the spaces and activities listed below have been altered or curtailed for safety reasons during COVID-19, traditional (pre-COVID-19) interactions are described here, as looking back at past experiences will help you to better understand yourself and your sensory systems, and "normal" daily life will return.

You may be:

- Upset by crowds due to auditory, visual, tactile, and/or olfactory (smell) sensations.
- Avoiding places you would like to go to such as sporting events, parties, stores, big cities, or theme parks due to the possibility of too much sensory input (noise, lights, people in very close proximity, smells, too much movement, etc.).

- Upset by home noises: TV, children playing, cell phones, computer games, air conditioner/heater, etc. Some examples of resulting behaviors: often telling your children to be quiet, getting into an argument with a neighbor who hasn't fixed their noisy outside air conditioning compressor, always thinking the TV is too loud when others do not.

- Upset by visual "clutter" or things "out of place."

- Over-reactive to loud noises such as fireworks, cars backfiring, something falling.

- Upset by repetitive small noises such as water dripping, ticking clocks, people chewing, someone tapping a pencil.

- Waking often during sleep; difficulty sleeping.

- Sensitive to smells.

- Sensitive to light (might wear sunglasses indoors).

- Having difficulty with being touched lightly (this may affect intimacy, see Chapter 6).

- Experiencing worry, stress, anxiety.

- Disliking open staircases, sidewalk grates, or heights.

- Not liking "normal" changes in your environment such as rearranged furniture, moving, going on vacation to new places, a new job, a "renovated" store, etc.

- Feeling the need to control situations.

- Upset if routines or plans are not followed.

- Sitting with your back to the wall (preferably in a booth), and always plotting a way out (an escape route), in public places such as restaurants.

- Needing to be able to scan for danger.

- Having difficulty remembering things or making choices in sensory-rich environments. Example: buying tickets for the "right" movie at the "right" time from many choices and remembering what each family member wants from the snack bar.

- Difficulty sitting in a movie theater if there are people sitting behind you.

Examples in Each Sensory System

Now let's look at examples of sensory input in each sensory system that could cause reactions in people who experience sensory defensive (over-arousal) SMC—defined as "a constellation of symptoms related to aversive or defensive reactions to non-noxious stimuli across one or more sensory systems.... It is an over-reaction of our normal protective senses" (Wilbarger & Wilbarger, 2007, p. 5). Sensory defensive SMC has further been described as "a tendency to react negatively or with alarm to sensory input that is generally considered harmless or nonirritating" (Wilbarger & Wilbarger, 1991, p. 2). Wilbarger and Wilbarger (2001) discuss sensory processing as "resulting in a continuum of reactions from defensiveness and avoidant behaviors to the ability to joyfully and jubilantly explore sensation" (personal communications, Patricia Wilbarger, 1992). Ideally everyone should be able to experience joy as part of their sensory responses, but people with sensory defensiveness often need help in getting their nervous systems to this point.

Remember that veterans, service members, first responders, and frontline medical personnel react the most strongly to stimuli in four areas:

- Olfactory (smell)
- Visual
- Auditory
- Tactile

Other possible areas of sensory defensiveness not as commonly seen in these individuals are:

- Movement-based (Vestibular)
  - Gravitational insecurity (fear of gravity-challenging activities like those involving heights, but *not* balance-related)

- Sensitivity to movement (like car sickness)
- Proprioceptive (joint and muscle receptor) sensitivity
- Oral (mouth)
  - Textures of foods
  - Temperature of foods
- Interoception (ability to feel what's going on inside your body, such as hunger and fullness)

Each of these areas has individual indicators. The examples of defensive reactions listed below are only some of the possibilities, and *no one will have them all*. The *desired outcome* of looking at sensory modulation challenges/ sensory defensiveness is to help you understand your particular central nervous system responses, in order to help you *find functional ways to move your central nervous system responses toward a more "middle" or modulated range (if that is what you choose), and to develop natural and easy wellness strategies to keep your nervous system as modulated as possible.*

It is common for veterans, first responders, and frontline medical workers, as well as survivors of personal trauma, to have very strong responses to **specific selected sensory stimuli related to their trauma**, and to not react as strongly to other aspects of that same sensory category. For example, reacting to certain smells associated with the trauma, but not to other smells (reacting to the scent of gasoline or gunpowder, but not dirty diapers). This is different from the experience of people who were born with SMC, who usually react to most items in a category, such as many touch items or many visual items.

Types of Reactions

OLFACTION OR SMELL

The olfactory sensory system is unusual in its function and mechanisms in the brain. Smell sensations, *unlike all other sensations*, are *not* routed immediately to the thalamus by the central nervous system. The thalamus, which I like to refer to as the "major traffic cop" of the brain, receives all sensory signals *except for* smell and directs these sensory inputs to the parts of the brain they need to go to in order to be the most beneficial to the individual. Olfactory (smell) sensory inputs, however, do not go through the thalamus, but instead go *directly to the limbic (emotional) portion of the brain*, sometimes called the "smell brain." In the theory of brain development, this "smell brain" is a remnant of the old premammalian, reptilian brain (example, alligators) that wants to perform only the "three Fs"—feeding, fighting, and "reproducing" to perpetuate the species. The "old" limbic system is responsible for contributing to those functions of feeding, fighting, and reproducing even in our more advanced brains. This is why smells can have such a strong and immediate effect on us. *Smells are related to survival more directly and "unconsciously" than other sensory inputs.* We smell our food and decide whether it's safe to eat; our own smell changes when we're in danger, and we can even "smell danger" in the air or on others; and we also use smell (pheromones) as part of the decision-making process regarding who to have intercourse with (originally, to get us the best genetic outcome in our potential offspring).

So which smells have been known to trigger sensory-defensive reactions? Remember that this is not an exhaustive list, and that many people find some of these smells to be quite pleasant. It's only when you have a persistent negative response to *several things* in a category that this would be labeled a sensory-defensive response associated with that particular type of input, in this case, *olfactory defensiveness.*

SOME EXAMPLES

- New clothing smells
- Certain cooking smells
- Certain soaps, shampoos, and personal care products
- Gunpowder
- Soiled diapers
- Hospitals (disinfectant, alcohol swabs, etc.)
- Stores
- Spices

- Perfume or cologne

- Candles

- New carpets

- Adhesives, glue

- Body odor

- Detergent

- Nail polish remover

- Gasoline

- Others: fill in other smells that "bother" you

_____

_____

VISUAL

Visual defensive reactions center around things that are visually over-alerting. Most of the following examples of visual defensiveness are self-explanatory, with the exception of *gaze aversion*. We have all known people who will not look us in the eye. These people are sometimes thought to be "shifty" or not truthful. Gaze aversion is often seen in individuals with autism spectrum disorders, and tends to be viewed and treated through the lens of a behavioral symptom which interferes with the person's ability to relate socially (the person is therefore given "behavioral therapy" to address it). Gaze aversion, however, is frequently *not* a behavioral response, but is instead an example of visual defensiveness: the person finds it very uncomfortable to look at others due to sensory issues.

SOME EXAMPLES

Examples of "over-alert" responses associated with visual defensiveness:

- Gaze aversion (explained above)

- Bothered by bright lights

- Bothered by things out of place in the road

- Bothered by bright colors
- Avoids crowds due to too many visual inputs
- Continually wears sunglasses to decrease brightness and glare, even inside
- Dislikes flickering of florescent lights
- Dislikes clutter
- Experiences sun on snow as "too bright"
- Dislikes computer screens' flickering
- Bothered by hanging mobiles that move in the breeze
- Bothered by parades
- Bothered by shopping malls: movement of people, too many shapes and colors
- Disturbed by clutter: overloaded store shelves, as in grocery stores
- Disturbed by clutter in the home
- Dislikes 3-D movies
- Others: add others that "bother" you

_____

_____

AUDITORY

Auditory defensiveness is an overreaction to sounds. It is not specifically related to loud sounds, although these can be involved. Sometimes small sounds like a ticking clock, dripping water, or fingernails on a blackboard can be intolerable. Each person has sounds that are bothersome to them. Certain loud sounds are *meant* to alert a sympathetic nervous system "fight-or-flight response," as they are universal signals of danger—sounds such as sirens, weather warning horns, the TV warning alert beep, etc. Also, *people may make their own sounds to cover other sounds that bother them.* They may hum, whistle, sing, yell, stomp loudly, etc.

SOME EXAMPLES

People with auditory defensiveness may be over-alerted by:

- Ticking clocks

- The buzz of florescent lights

- The TV

- Sirens (by design)

- Beeping alarms, such as alerts on a cell phone, microwave timer or alarm clock (by design, but medical personnel may over-alert to any alarm with a pitch similar to hospital equipment, even when its source is an innocuous household device)

- Too-loud movies, concerts or conversation

- Whispering

- Babies' cries

- Voice pitches

- Environmental "background" noise (may need to wear earplugs)

- Sudden noises (may startle easily)

- Fireworks

- Other people's chewing

- Vacuums

- Mixers

- Verbal directions (may have difficulty with processing and following *spoken* instructions, but not with instructions given in written or other visual forms [charts, etc.])

- Others: add others you have experienced

  _____

  _____

TACTILE SYSTEM

The tactile system is the system that teaches us the most about sensory processing. The distribution of tactile (touch) sensory receptors in the body is very specific and is organized to alert us to the most dangerous life-threatening situations. The *most sensitive areas* are the chest, abdomen, face, and head. It makes sense that our nervous system would be organized in this way, given that *our vital organs are in the abdomen and chest, and vital sensory receptors are in the head (eyes, nose, mouth, and ears [which contain both hearing and balance centers]).* Every animal reacts with alertness when touched in these areas unless the animal is in a very safe situation. Think of your pet cats or dogs that will only let you stroke their stomachs when they're calm and trust you. To survive, we need to first protect those areas. Conversely, the least sensitive areas of the body are the back, and the backs of the arms and hands. (The back actually has more physical space between its tactile sensory receptors than any other part of the body.)

The skin is the largest organ in the body, and it is *constantly* receiving sensory input. The tactile system has two separate divisions that transport information from the periphery to the brain. The "*dorsal column medial lemniscal*" system is the discriminative track that carries touch pressure, pain, and temperature sensations to the thalamus for distribution to the appropriate parts of the brain for action. The "*spinal thalamic system*" carries alert/arousal information, and only 12% of its input goes to the thalamus. The rest (88%) goes to portions of the brain that directly alert us to danger, the *limbic system.* This is the *very fast* large track for immediate tactile danger/alert (for instance, the unexpected tickle you feel on your arm as you walk through the woods that you immediately swat as it could be a spider or mosquito).

A DEMONSTRATION OF HOW OUR TACTILE RECEPTORS WORK

For an example of how your tactile sensory receptors work, take your hand and lightly stroke your arm several times, but *only* touch the hairs. You will probably feel a tickling-type sensation. Next, rub your arm a few times applying very firm back and forth pressure with your hand. Now lightly stroke your arm hairs again. This time you probably feel much less sensation. *This is an example of how light touch alerts your nervous system to check things out because something "different" (and "possibly dangerous") is happening*, while heavy touch *cancels out* some of that light touch perception. We can use this phenomenon—that is, the ability of heavy touch pressure to reduce sensory sensitivity—as one way to keep our nervous systems modulated.

SOME EXAMPLES

Examples of tactile defensiveness include:

- Difficulty with intimacy (this can be a major problem for individuals suffering from post-traumatic stress and PTSD, as will be discussed in Chapter 6)
  - Dislikes kisses, especially on the cheek (but can tolerate heavy hugs)
  - Finds light-touch sexual foreplay upsetting rather than plea-surable, yet tolerates the heavy touch provided by intercourse
  - Dislikes unexpected touch, especially on the face
  - Dislikes public displays of affection
- Bothered by certain clothes (often *not* a problem for those with post-traumatic stress and PTSD, but is a problem for those born with SMC)
  - Tags in shirts
  - Manmade cloth (*not* natural fibers like cotton, linen, or silk). Manmade fibers break, and the broken fibers can "pick" at your skin
  - Turtleneck shirts
  - Socks (the seam inside is the most bothersome. Share the "sock secret" of wearing them inside-out to avoid the seam)
  - Belts: remember that the abdomen is a sensitive area

- Tight *or* baggy clothes

- Jeans

- Hoods, if they're loose and tickle the hair

- Pants worn at the waist, as again, the waist is a particularly sensitive area. (Hint: that is why some people wear their pants low)

- Hair cuts

- People touching you lightly

- People standing too close

- Having sticky substances on your hands

- Not feeling big cuts/bruises, yet over-reacting to small ones

- Must wear gloves when doing any messy work

- Bothered by certain textures of sheets

- Bothered by pets touching you unexpectedly, for example, the cat's tail

- Others: add others that you think of_____

_____

_____

OTHER SENSORY SYSTEMS

Defensiveness in the following sensory systems (movement, proprioception, oral, and interoception) is a less common problem for people with post-traumatic stress and PTSD, but it does occur, and so examples are included here. *These examples additionally contribute to our understanding that our nervous system will alert us to danger if there are* conflicting messages *coming from any two sensory systems at once.*

MOVEMENT/VESTIBULAR

(Not commonly a problem for military personnel and first responders in particular, as they get much physical/balance training to overcome issues in this area.)

The vestibular system governs our movement. It has two functions: one is responsibility for our balance and letting us know where we are in space in relation to gravity (the discriminative function), and the other is alerting us to danger (the modulation function). The system includes its receptor organ, the vestibular mechanism located in the inner ear (since we can't see this receptor like we can see the eyes, nose, or skin, we don't often consider how our balance comes about). The vestibular mechanism is made up of three small semicircular canals and two sack-like structures called the saccule and utricle. All are filled with a fluid (called "endolymph") that has the consistency of watery gelatin. Projecting into all five areas are hair cells of varying resistance (flexibility), which allows the system to grade its responses as the head moves through space. As the three semicircular canals are at right angles to each other and there is a set on each side of your head, they "triangulate" on movement *to let you know the direction you are moving in 3-D space* (think two gyroscopes).

Besides containing the endolymph and hair cells, the utricle and saccule also contain calcium carbonate crystals called "otoconia." *These very important tiny "rocks in your head" always fall (are pulled) down due to gravity.* So they constantly provide input to our brains, letting us know where our bodies are in relation to the ground. The *discriminative* function of the vestibular system works to keep us balanced at all times. *Balance problems do not result in sensory modulation challenges/sensory defensiveness*; rather, balance problems result in *movement* problems. In children, they can result in poor motor development, called Sensory-Based Motor Challenges, and in adults, in loss of movement ability due to disease or accident.

The sensory modulation challenges/*sensory defensive* responses related to the vestibular system are based on *over-alerting* to movement (interpreting "harmless" movements as dangerous). One is referred to as *gravitational insecurity*, which is a sudden fear brought on by a movement challenge or threat to movement security such as having to walk up a staircase with visible gaps between steps (e.g., a wrought-iron staircase offering views of the space below), or the fear or "weak-kneed" feeling when looking down from very high places. The other vestibular defensive reaction is *an aversive response to movement* such as disliking the falling feeling on a roller coaster or the spin of a Tilt-A-Whirl ride. (Don't worry if you no longer like these sensations but did as a child: our tolerance decreases as we age.)

Movement defensiveness is infrequent in veterans and first responders due to their intensive training (and is no more prevalent in frontline medical personnel than in the general population); however, fear of being in high places and "weakness" felt in knees when looking down from high places can occur (think of James Stewart in *Vertigo*, who develops his debilitating fear of heights following trauma as a police detective).

SOME EXAMPLES

Examples of vestibular defensiveness include:

- Gravitational insecurity: not fear of losing your balance, but fear of losing track of where you are in space. Some places where this may be experienced:
  - Open staircases/grates
  - Open balconies, high balconies
  - Falling/dropping amusement rides
  - Roller coasters
  - Escalators
  - Elevators
  - Any high places (looking out from the top floor of a skyscraper, etc.)
  - Being upside down, as in doing a somersault
  - Others: add others that you think of

    _____

    _____

- Adverse response to movement (may lead to a feeling of nausea)
- Seeing others move, as in watching others swinging or on a roller coaster, or feeling overwhelmed by movements in a 3-D movie

- Car or sea sickness. If you get car sick, this is an example of two sensory systems sending conflicting messages, resulting in an alert: your vestibular (balance) system tells you that you are seated firmly in the car, but your eyes say you are moving. Why do some people have this response, while others don't? Most people's eyes can repeatedly stop the action of the trees, buildings, and other things moving past them outside of the car, while others' eyes cannot do this fast enough and so it is interpreted by the brain as an "unexplained" dangerous movement. (Though again, note that you can have this *one* type of movement defensiveness but not SMC—an SMC diagnosis requires defensive reactions to more than one type of stimuli.)

- Dislikes changes in head position from neutral

- Dislikes initiating movement that is not "usual"

PROPRIOCEPTIVE SYSTEM

Closely tied to the vestibular system is the proprioceptive system. The discriminative part of this system provides feedback from your joints and muscles, which, at all times, lets you know where each part of your body is in space in relation to your whole body. This system is the one that lets you touch your nose with your finger when your eyes are closed, walk across your bedroom in the dark without bumping into things, and—to take a military example—feel through your combat boots the difference in the compactness of dirt surfaces that might indicate a buried explosive.

It is rare to have defensiveness in the proprioceptive system, but some people dislike pulling (traction) or pushing (compression) on their joints.

ORAL

Our mouths contain many sensory receptors, particularly on our tongues. Mouths are important in early childhood development, as babies learn about shapes and textures by putting things into their mouths. They also learn about the "safety" of potential food sources, for example, not wanting to swallow unfamiliar things as they may be "bad for the organism." In oral defensiveness, it is not the taste of a food that's the issue, but the food's *texture*

71

or temperature. Oral defensiveness is rare in people with post-traumatic stress or PTSD, but it is common in children and some adults born with SMC.

SOME EXAMPLES

- Textures of foods are bothersome (usually not tastes)
  - Slippery: oysters, clams
  - Jiggly: jello
  - Small pieces: coconut, chunky peanut butter
  - Lumpy: oatmeal, cottage cheese
  - Fuzzy: peach skins
  - Slimy: ripe bananas
- Temperature of foods: too cold, too hot
- Foods mixed together: casseroles, the peas touching the potatoes on the plate
- Utensils or aluminum foil touching teeth
- Popsicle sticks touching teeth/tongue
- Spices
- Strong flavors like onions, mint
- Dentists working in your mouth
- Food on the face
- Others: add others that you think of

  _____

  _____

Reactions to oral defensiveness:

- Gagging
- Licking or tasting nonfood items

- Preferring spicy, "hot," or sharp tastes such as pickle juice, hot peppers, or hot salsa

- Only eating a diet restricted to texture preferences (example: only eating mushy things like bananas, mashed potatoes, mac and cheese)

INTEROCEPTION

Interoception consists of the conscious and nonconscious perception of the current internal state of our bodies. All body tissues relay signals to the brain about their present conditions so that the brain can keep the body in a balanced state called homeostasis. With this information, the brain can make predictions to anticipate bodily needs and act to influence or resolve them before they arise. Interoceptive sensory discrimination issues may make it difficult for a person to tell what signals are coming from their body and where they're coming from (for instance, children with interoceptive discrimination issues may not realize when they're hungry or thirsty or need to go to the bathroom). And *modulation* issues can also affect the interoceptive system, resulting in over-arousal (defensiveness) or under-arousal.

SOME EXAMPLES

- Over-arousal
  - Feeling pain more intensely
  - Feeling pain for longer duration
  - Sensitive to feeling heart rate
  - Sensitive to feeling respiration rate
  - Feeling hotter or colder than others
- Under-arousal
  - Feeling pain less intensely
  - Not feeling full after eating

How Sensory Systems Work Together
to Alert Us to Danger

An important function of our sensory systems is to alert us to *subtle things that could actually threaten our survival*. All of us have experienced having a "feeling" that something wasn't right before we consciously figured out that we were in danger. If all of our sensory systems are signaling the same steady, "even" state, we feel safe, but if one system sends a message that is inconsistent or incongruent with the others, this triggers a fight-or-flight survival reaction.

An example of the vestibular and visual systems sending messages different enough to alert your sympathetic nervous system would be the following situation: You are stopped at a traffic light and a car has stopped next to you. The light is still red. But the car next to you suddenly rolls forward, and you stomp on your breaks, thinking that *you* are moving. Your vestibular system said that you were stationary, but your visual system was alerted and thought you were moving. Since the two messages were in conflict, your body reacted with arousal and a speedy action *to save you just in case*, because not reacting could be very dangerous.

Examples in other sensory systems are smelling smoke, but being unable at first to see that the source is your neighbor's fire pit: you will be alerted to danger until you reconcile the two sensory areas (olfactory/visual). Or a first responder answering a domestic violence call and "sensing" that the place doesn't "feel right": someone called for urgent help, but the address given is quiet and very dark, and looks locked up, an incongruity that alerts the responder auditorily and visually to possible danger.

Please note that alerting to differences in surfaces while walking, alerting to movement where there should be none and to items (such as medical equipment) being out of place, noting subtle differences in smells, and hearing subtle sounds are the types of skills that *kept you alive in war or as a first responder or were essential to your effectiveness as a frontline medical worker*. And turning off this "high alert" system when you are in a safe area or not involved in patient care is not easy. Understanding why your brain reacts the way it does gives *you* the power to intervene in the process and to reduce your hyperarousal when you want to.

Check-In #4: More Specifically Targeting Your Sensory Modulation Challenge/Sensory Defensive Levels: The "L" for "Likes/Dislikes" in DIAL IT DOWN

People with sensory modulation challenges/sensory defensiveness can feel different from others and/or be labeled as different by others. Are you seen as "overly picky" about sensory matters? Is this "pickiness" always with you to some degree, but worse when you feel stressed or tired? Has it developed or gotten worse since your deployment, active duty, or frontline work? Have you ever organized your life around your sensory comfort or missed things you wanted to do because you felt the need to control your sensory input?

CHECK-IN: WORKSHEET

On the following chart, write in the things that you are "picky" about or "bothered by." Place them at the level of their sensory sensitivity for you. Following the blank chart provided for you is a sample chart completed by a veteran.

SENSORY SYSTEMS, TYPES AND LEVELS OF SENSORY SENSITIVITY

Level:	Not at All	Mildly	Moderately	Severely
What I am sensitive to:				
Tactile: people touching me				
Tactile: things touching me				
Tactile: clothes touching me				
Smells				
Visual things				
Noises				
Movement of my body				
Temperature or textures of things in my mouth				
Internal body feelings				

Questions:

1. Are there areas in which you tend to be more sensitive to sensations?
    Yes _____ No ___

2. If so, which areas are they?

    _____

    _____

3. Describe an incident that may be related to a sensation that both-
    ered you.

    _____

    _____

    _____

    _____

Example of a chart filled out by a veteran (note: everyone's personal chart will differ, and yours may differ substantially from this; the point is to discover your *individual* sensory challenges):

This chart was filled out by a female Vietnam veteran who was a military nurse.

SENSORY SYSTEMS, TYPES AND LEVELS OF SENSORY SENSITIVITY

Level:	Not At All	Mildly	Moderately	Severely
What I am sensitive to:				
Tactile: people touching me	X			
Tactile: things touching me	X			
Tactile: clothes touching me	X			
Smells				X See below
Visual things				X See below
Noises				X See below
Movement of my body	X			
Temperature or textures of things in my mouth	X			
Internal body feelings	X			

Questions:

1. Are there areas in which you tend to be more sensitive to sensations?
    Yes __X__ No ___

2. If so, which areas are they? *Smells, visual, noises.*

3. Describe an incident that may be related to a sensation that bothered
    you. *The only sensory responses that are still automatic triggers are:
    Smells: Fresh tarmac paving. I was at Danang Air Force Base and there
    was always new paving ongoing for runways or roads. We (U.S. forces)
    paved a lot of roads and built many buildings. Visual: I still have a
    strong startle reflex when individuals appear in front of me without
    my hearing their approach, for example, appearing around a corner
    on a carpeted floor. Noises: Every helicopter overhead.*

Ed's Air Pillow Popping Example

Ed is a Vietnam-era veteran who never married. He was enjoying a Christmas
celebration with his extended family, which included several young children.
One child was given a gift wrapped in several layers of large-sized packing
"air pillows." Instead of playing with the gift, the children started stomping
on the air pillows, which created a loud sound even several rooms away. Ed
visibly jumped at the first loud sound and then angrily found the children
and demanded that they stop.

His siblings didn't understand his reaction and were not happy with
him for speaking sternly to their kids. Ed's auditory defensiveness, which had
started after his return from combat, had in this situation created a "sensory
mismatch" with his family. In the following chapters, we'll discuss proactive
strategies for managing sensory mismatches such as this one.

CHAPTER 6:

Interpersonal Relationships and Intimacy: How Sensory Modulation Challenges Affect Relationships and Sexual Functioning

The Second "I" in DIAL IT DOWN: "Intimacy and Interpersonal Relationships"

If you have read to this point, then you very likely believe that you or someone you love is experiencing sensory modulation challenges. How will this difference in the ways you tend to process sensory information affect your intimacy? In discussing the sensory side of relationships, it's essential first to remember that light touch alerts you to danger (think mosquitos and spiders), while heavy touch pressure on the skin *reduces* those alerts. Remember too that resistive work with muscles, joint compression, and rhythmic movement of the head through space can all help you modulate your nervous system to the middle range, bringing your senses down to a calmer, less "defensive" state, or up from an underaroused state.

Sensory Mismatches

A "sensory mismatch" in a relationship can lead to both physical and emotional problems. Remember, we generally judge others by our own sensory frame of reference. If both people in a relationship have sensory modulation challenges, then there is some understanding between them, as each can recognize their behaviors in the other: your military or first responder peers instantly "get it," for instance, when you don't want to go somewhere with large crowds or when you have a flashback, and your frontline medical colleagues instantly "get it" when you have heightened reactions to certain sounds or smells.

We usually don't *consciously* think about the effect that sensations have on us unless one sensation is strong enough to come to the forefront of our awareness: for example, if we're cold, hot, hungry, have to go to the bathroom, etc. We also tend not to recognize the *cumulative* effect of numerous varied sensations on our bodies; if we think about this at all, *we judge others' reactions by our own levels of tolerance for sensation.* If the other person is *not* like us, then sensory-based misunderstandings or even problems with living together may develop. If the other person has significant sensory modulation challenges that have not been identified, then *major* misunderstandings can occur.

Let's take a look at how sensory modulation challenges and sensory mismatches can cause problems in the different kinds of relationships in our lives, and conversely, how *understanding each other's sensory needs can make us feel recognized and validated.* Understanding these sensory mismatches can be the beginning of taking the initiative to talk about our own sensory needs with the people we care about, and to repairing, growing, and sustaining our relationships with them. (See Chapter 11 for more information on ways to "talk about it.")

Active- and On-Duty Work Provides Sensory Matches

As a veteran, service member, first responder, or frontline medical worker, you belong to an elite and exclusive club, and if you have served in a war zone, mass casualty situation, or COVID-19 hot spot, that club becomes even more exclusive. Your colleagues understand more about you than almost anyone else. This comes from sharing common experiences that are life-changing—some of which, as previously discussed, can actually *change the way your brain reacts* (see Appendix I). Your military, first responder, or frontline peers will understand if you react strongly to a car alarm or don't want to go to a crowded family reunion. Their sensory reactions match yours in many ways, and even if they don't match up exactly, they very likely know other peers who are going through what you're going through in adjusting to daily life. These sensory matches provide you with reassurance that you're not alone, and a place to find understanding. You don't have to be careful about how you react or watch what you say or do around these friends, as they will identify with you. They'll understand even if you "lose it." And the people who were in your squad or unit will always "have your back."

Adult Sensory Mismatches

But while military, first responder, and frontline peers understand your heightened sensitivity to sensory input, your family probably does not "get it," and your partner and/or children may regularly comment that you've "changed." So, what happens to relationships when there's a substantial sensory mismatch between us and others? Since *we and our family members are not used to looking for **sensory reasons** for our reactions*, our family members may come up with other explanations for our behaviors—which can include blaming us or attributing conscious motives to our actions (they may think, for instance, that you've started avoiding light touch or complaining about household clutter "on purpose" or because you "don't care enough" about them). If, on the other hand, you can help your family members to understand and interpret these differences *as sensory mismatches caused by sensory modulation challenges*, then your reactions can begin to make sense and the *blaming can stop*. What needs to be understood is that *you are not doing something intentionally, but that your changed behavior is connected to changes in how your brain interprets sensation.* Your nervous system is more likely to stay in a fight-or-flight mode (which your family members have probably experienced themselves from time to time, in situations like a near-miss car accident). With this new understanding, difficulties between you—a returning veteran, first responder, or frontline worker with sensory modulation challenges—and your family members are more easily recognized and addressed.

In Chapters 1 and 2, I discussed Jason, a veteran who told me about his sensory issues with his daughter: she liked to give him light kisses on his cheek, which after his deployment caused him a level of discomfort that led him to pull away from her. When she observed his behavior, she accused him of not loving her, and this painful dynamic became a family problem. I suggested that Jason tell her that while he didn't like the feel of a light kiss, he would welcome big hugs, especially with an accompanying back pat or back rub. I also suggested that he ask her to tell him in advance when she was about to hug him. So the solution to an issue that had previously had a "blame" component was a *sensory* one. The combat veteran *needed no surprises for his nervous system, so he needed to be warned before he was hugged.* And while he could *not* tolerate the light touch of the kiss on his cheek (as light touch, especially on the face, alerts us to danger), he *could tolerate and enjoy the heavy touch pressure of a bear hug* (because heavy pressure hugs are modulating).

Another (pre-COVID-19) example involves tolerating crowds. Emma and Nate, who lived in New York City, had different tolerances for noise and crowds. Emma had no sensory modulation challenges and spent much of her free time attending concerts and plays and going to restaurants. Nate had sensory modulation challenges that led him to become easily overstimulated and exhausted by all the noise and movement of the city. He would come home from his work, which involved 80–90 minutes of driving in heavy traffic, and immediately lie down for a nap—at the exact moment when Emma usually wanted to go out on the town with him. They needed to understand and discuss their sensory differences, and to make plans that allowed them *both* to feel supported and acknowledged (including spending some "date night" evenings at home and some of them out in restaurants, theaters, or other venues they'd researched ahead of time that would not put Nate's overstressed system on "high alert").

Sensory-based differences in tolerating clothing can also be an issue in some relationships. For example, Ellen couldn't tolerate synthetic fibers, tight clothing, and stockings, so she wore only loose cotton or linen. Her partner had a job that required regular attendance at formal events, and he accused her of sabotaging his career advancement when she wouldn't dress up for these events. With an increased understanding of differences in *sensory modulation*, many interpersonal problems can be seen from an alternative perspective, reducing frustration, blame, and misperceptions.

Parent/Child Sensory Mismatches

Parent/child sensory mismatches are common. Many books have been written to help the parents of children with sensory modulation challenges understand why their children often respond to sensations in ways they don't expect. However, as a veteran, first responder, or frontline medical worker, especially if you're reading this book, you as a parent are likely to be the one with sensory modulation challenges, and you may respond in ways your children don't expect. We've already discussed some of the stimuli that an adult with sensory issues might be bothered by, and many of these stimuli involve things that children like to do. Think of the exuberant ways in which many young kids greet a parent when you come in the door: they run toward you, throw their arms around you, kiss your cheek, yell out "Mommy" or "Daddy," and want to drag you off to see whatever they've been doing. And what if you add an excited dog to the mix, and the computer and TV are also making noise? Any or all of this may become *sensory overload* for you. Later, the children may argue with each other and call out loudly for you to take sides, or want to practically hang their bodies on yours, or leave toys scattered everywhere—and all the while you or your partner must prepare a meal with the varied sights and smells that this involves. *More* sensations to contribute to sensory overload!

Having a "coming home" routine and vocabulary will help. For example, you can discuss your sensory needs in age-appropriate ways (for very young kids, "Mom/Dad's body gets very tired after work—I *really* want to spend time and have fun with you, and to do this, I need some rest or recharge time first"), and make sure everyone understands that Dad or Mom gets to go to the bedroom first, close the door, and do some sensory diet activities or play music. Or maybe Mom or Dad first gets to go out for a run or a bike ride. It also could be possible to include your spouse or children in the run or bike ride *if* this would be modulating and enjoyable for you.

Ability to Engage in Intimate Touch

Sensory mismatches can lead to problems with physical intimacy, as in the previously discussed example of Jason's discomfort with his daughter's light kisses on the cheek. Another example involves intimate touch between a married couple. In this example, the wife was an occupational therapist and so knew about sensory modulation challenges. When her husband (who was not a veteran, but had experienced significant trauma) reacted negatively to light touch, she suggested that he might be "sensory defensive," to which he promptly replied, "No I'm not, I just don't like to be touched. And you're 'sensory offensive,' always touching me and wanting to be touched." He didn't like the term "sensory defensive"—but after further discussion, he agreed that the term "sensory modulation challenges" made sense to him. So, they talked about touch differences, and the touch rule they decided on for their marriage became the following: he could touch her as much as he could tolerate providing touch, and she would like as much touch as he could give, especially light touch. And she would never touch him unexpectedly but would ask permission or warn him when she wanted to hug him and would always give a heavy bear hug including patting or rubbing his back. Remember that besides not liking to receive light touch, people with sensory modulation challenges often don't like *giving* light touch (because what they experience as unpleasant, they assume the other person also feels is unpleasant, and just thinking about touching someone lightly can activate their own sensory issues). Even with an understanding of sensory modulation challenges, this couple had to *keep talking* and making accommodations and adjustments in order to meet each other's intimacy needs. They were committed to each other and they did so, happily and successfully over time.

Ability to Engage in All Types of Intimacy

WITH YOURSELF

If you have sensory modulation challenges, have you ever wondered why you can touch yourself and this doesn't bother you as much as someone else's touching you? For instance, it's almost impossible to tickle yourself. You can stroke the hairs on your arm and get a tickling sensation, but this doesn't cause you to jump or pull back. And you can't tickle yourself in the belly and cause a reaction. This is because you *know* how hard, where, and when you will be touching, and *your nervous system is in control.*

An important part of intimacy with yourself is knowing your sensory limits. Understanding what makes you escalate and what helps you "dial it down" are important for success in your daily life. This understanding will also expand your ability to explain your sensory responses and needs to others, opening up opportunities for successful intimacy in your private life.

WITH OTHERS: SENSORY RULES

Touching each other in our society follows many rules, including laws, spoken rules, unspoken rules, and cultural and family traditions. But *we almost never acknowledge or discuss **sensory rules***. *It's time to start!* For example, let's say you assign your son the chore of giving water to the dog and he just doesn't want to do it but can't tell you why. You observe what happens when he does give water to the dog, and see that the dog drinks, and then lifts its mouth out of the dish and shakes its head, splashing water and dog drool on your child. With your understanding of sensory modulation challenges, you now can see that your son may be upset by the tactile sensations of the water and dog drool landing on him (even if he doesn't mind the water, the dog drool is too much!).

Think about an office setting where the person in the next cubicle constantly snaps bubble gum, warms something foul-smelling (like day-old fish) in the microwave, or talks loudly as they work. While these things may not always bother you, on a day when you're more sensitive to sensory input, they would.

Think of the examples of children's spontaneous movements, noise-making, enthusiasm, constant use of beeping electronic devices, and ability to put everything out of place in a room in just a few minutes. All of this may bother you if you experience sensory modulation challenges. The intimate things that you do with your children like changing diapers, putting on sunscreen, bathing them, or letting them kiss you may challenge your sensory systems due to the tactile, smell, and surprise elements involved.

We can benefit from sensory rules in most situations. It's always preferable to discuss your sensory needs and thresholds *before* you're set off by the actions of others. *If you have sensory rules, they help to keep the "set point" of your nervous system down to a generally modulated level so that surprise sensory input does not push you over the edge.*

Sex and Sensory Modulation Challenges: What You Can Do About It

An intimate sexual relationship is something most adults want to establish and maintain. But sexual intimacy can be difficult for people with sensory modulation challenges, especially if the couple doesn't understand these challenges and how they can impact sexual responsiveness.

In 1966, William H. Masters and Virginia E. Johnson were the first to describe what they termed the *sexual response cycle* (Masters & Johnson, 1966). They delineated four phases: excitement, plateau, orgasm, and resolution. Phase one, the *excitement phase,* involves an increase in heart rate, breathing rate, and blood pressure, and erection of nipples. Blood flow increases to the genitals and lubrication begins. The skin may become flushed (called the sex flush) due to vasocongestion. Muscle tone (tension) also increases. During the second phase, the *plateau phase,* which extends until orgasm, all of the changes from phase one are intensified. *Orgasm* is phase three and involves the sudden release of sexual tension. Heart rate, breathing, and blood pressure are at their highest levels, and involuntary muscle contractions occur. During phase four, *resolution,* the body slows down, muscles relax, breathing, heart rate, and blood pressure decrease, and the person may feel a sense of well-being and fatigue.

People with sensory modulation challenges often experience problems with sexual response and functioning. These sexual problems *are not primarily about love or even the desire for sex.* First and foremost, *they're about the state of your nervous system and its ability to respond in a way that can allow you to participate fully in sex.* WebMD (2012) discusses the "Sex Drive Killers": stress, depression, alcohol, medications, poor body image, and too little sleep, among others. These are all issues that may be experienced by people with post-traumatic stress and PTSD. An additional crucial issue that is *not* listed above is *the importance of the state of your nervous system's responses to sensory input when you want to engage in sex, and what you can do about this.*

When you're experiencing sensory modulation challenges, the sympathetic part of your autonomic nervous system—your fight-or-flight mode—is usually over-reactive. While we do want some arousal to occur in the excitement phase of the sexual response cycle, we cannot have *so much* that our bodies interpret this as *danger* rather than pleasure. The excitement phase naturally results in the sympathetic nervous system responses of increased heart rate, breathing rate, blood pressure, and muscle tone—all the things you need to have to be able to flee from danger. But if your system *starts* at the danger level *before* sex, you actually have to *take steps to **dial down** your nervous system to a level of feeling safe* before you can successfully experience "excitement" and sexual pleasure. If you *start* at the danger level (with an over-reactive nervous system), you will find that you may not tolerate many of the things that are usually seen as pleasurable foreplay (these will instead push you "over the edge" into discomfort and/or cause you to shut down), for example, light touch, scented body creams, or scented candles. And remember, not only do *you* not want these things, but *you will also have difficulty giving them to your partner, as your nervous system reacts to your just thinking about how that would feel to your own body.* So foreplay can become a major problem. If you or your partner remembers what you could tolerate and provide before the development of your sensory modulation challenges, then significant guilt, anger, or sadness may result—emotions that will also affect your ability to engage successfully in sex.

For men with sensory modulation challenges, the other key issue in the excitement, plateau, and orgasm phases of sex is attaining and maintaining an erection. If your body is in the "staying alive" mode, it's very unlikely that this will happen the way you want it to. Please remember that this is *not* a setback based on a lack of emotional desire or physical capability, and that it's not your fault. It's *your nervous system sabotaging you.* Your nervous system is trying to "keep you alive" by diverting energy away from what it perceives as "nonessential" functions (like digestion and sex) toward being ready to fight or flee. Proactively reducing your fight-or-flight reactivity by using modulating sensory techniques both on a regular basis (through the "sensory diet" activities discussed in detail below) and shortly before engaging in sex should significantly help.

The final "resolution" phase of the sexual response cycle brings your nervous system into the "homeostatic" mode, the opposite of fight-or-flight, mediated by the parasympathetic portion of the nervous system: this mode is growth-promoting, modulated, calm, and "centered." We know that heavy touch pressure is one of the things that can lower the nervous system's over-reactivity and bring us toward parasympathetic equilibrium. The actual act of intercourse (as opposed to foreplay) is heavy touch pressure, so it's usually well tolerated even if you are sensory defensive. It will in fact make you feel more modulated (calmer if you are over-reactive, more energetic if you are under-reactive). This means that the act of intercourse may still feel "safe," but foreplay may not—which can easily put you in a dilemma with your partner. Intercourse without foreplay is often seen as nonloving or as not valuing your partner.

Several service members have told me that they felt so badly about the changed way they could tolerate sex after deployment that they sought sex outside of their marriages, with someone who did not remember how they could engage in foreplay before and so would not expect it, or with someone who would tolerate rougher sex. (The damaging emotional fallout of these actions is beyond the scope of this book; but some of these issues can proactively be addressed and prevented through understanding and communicating your sensory needs to your current partner and using the techniques outlined in the sections below.)

Resolving these Issues

Please don't despair! There are many positive steps you can take toward substantially improving your sexual functioning and intimacy. Remember that I've discussed some basic ways to keep your nervous system functioning well through particular types of sensory input. The types of sensation that have the strongest modulating impact on the nervous system are *rhythmic movement of your head through space (like running or rebounding), heavy work with joints and muscles, and deep pressure to the skin.* In Chapter 8, I'll teach you more specifically how to develop these "sensory diet" strategies and introduce other types of sensory inputs that can greatly change the level of your nervous system arousal. In the sections below, I'll discuss how to apply these basic principles to your sex life.

Foreplay

Certain foreplay techniques can be used to bring down levels of over-re-activity or over-arousal for you while still increasing the pleasure factor for both you and your partner, and to help men achieve and maintain an erection. The very first thing you need to do is open a dialogue with your partner about your sensory modulation challenges, and what works for you and why. It's most effective to talk with your partner at some nonstressful moment, when you have time to "just talk" (with no kids clamoring for attention, cell phones ringing, etc.). Start by explaining, or re-explaining, how sensory modulation challenges affect you in general, and then talk about which areas of *intimacy* you feel are affected by these challenges, and how you feel they're affected. Be as specific as you can be. While you may find it hard at first to initiate this conversation, please keep in mind that for most if not all of the many people I've discussed marriage and relationships with, *their spouse or partner has actually been* relieved *to hear the physical/ nervous system reasons for their difficulties with sex, and to hear how these differ from the psychological causes that most people tend to ascribe to these difficulties (like, "They just don't find me desirable anymore").* If your partner understands, then they can give you feedback on what also works for them within the parameters you set. You can then work together to come up with your *"rules of engagement,"* or the rules which guide your intimacy.

Many of us are not comfortable discussing sex with our partners, particularly talking *during* sex about what is working and what isn't, but it is important that you do so. *What works for you one day may not always work the next due to the state of your nervous system, which is based on the types of sensory input you've had that day.* If your nervous system is more reactive on a given day, then it would take more modulating types of sensory input to allow you to fully enjoy the experience of foreplay. So take steps to try to start sexual engagement with your nervous system as modulated as you can make it. This will involve things like pre-planning your sensory diet so that you do some "heavy work" (like running or rebounding) late in the day if you're planning evening sex, or planning sex earlier in the day soon after you've done a routine sensory diet activity. Enter this new phase with a sense of exploration with your partner, not with a feeling of restriction—a sense of learning new ways of loving each other.

Types of sensory diet activities which modulate your nervous system and are compatible with sex include (and remember, *you and your partner* can experiment and choose the ones that feel right for you, ignore the rest, and even invent new ones yourselves):

- Back rubs using heavy pressure: both giving and receiving back rubs require pressure that is modulating. Avoid using scented oils or lotions (as their scents may contribute to sensory overload).

- Doing some push-ups or jumping jacks together (nudity or partial nudity may add interest). Jumping jacks give you rhythmic movement of your head through space and heavy joint and muscle work, both of which are modulating.

- Having your partner just lie on top of you for a few minutes to provide you with heavy pressure.

- The person who has sensory modulation challenges might find keeping some clothing on in order to limit unexpected touch to be helpful, for example, wearing a T-shirt.

- Taking a hot, or very hot, shower may lower over-arousal and desensitize the skin slightly to light touch. (Remember that sensory modulation challenges really are *not about how sensitive your skin is, but how your nervous system adds up sensation to get to the "staying alive" level of reactivity.* You can change your environment to decrease the level of sensation that gets to you: for touch this could mean [as mentioned above] wearing clothing to cover your skin, or the hot shower to temporarily decrease your over-responsiveness to light touch.)

- Play-wrestling: actual physical wrestling with your partner, but with rules that there be no excessive force and that if either person says "stop," then it stops immediately.

- Pillow fights (which can both introduce a playful mode and provide you with the just-right heavy touch pressure of the pillow "hits" on your body [though again, remember to agree upon "rules" ahead of time, and be aware that falling down can be alerting rather than modulating]).

- Deep breathing (as in yoga-type breathing), or singing a song, which also requires deep breathing. Pick a song that has positive meaning for you and your partner. Some people find meditative chanting or drumming to be helpful.

- Using special modulating music like *Mozart for Modulation, More Mozart for Modulation*, and *Baroque for Modulation* (see References).

- Dancing without touching to something rhythmic; if you decide to touch, touch firmly.

- Leaving enough light on in the room so that there are no surprises: candles may be used if both parties feel safe with them, but don't use scented ones, as smells can contribute to sensory overload.

Things for a partner to remember during sex with someone who experiences sensory modulation challenges:

- Always ask permission before touching.

- Never touch or hug your partner from behind where they cannot see you approaching, as this may lead to a flight-or-flight-based increase in sensory reactivity.

- Always use firm touch pressure, never light touch, unless your partner specifically "okays" it. (And remember, their sensitivity to light touch is not "personal," it's an *unconscious* nervous system response that has nothing to do with you or with how much they desire intimacy with you. Most service members, first responders, and frontline personnel I've worked with crave intimacy with their partners—it's just that this intimacy must be attained through slightly altered methods, like that of heavy vs. light touch.)

- *Do not touch hair, face, chest, stomach, or genitals unless your partner gives permission.* These are the body areas most likely to evoke a "sensory defensive" response. (This is true of all mammals: remember, for instance, that your cat doesn't let you rub her stomach unless she's very relaxed and sees or senses that you're going to do this in advance and you start slowly.)

- As suggested previously, do not use scented lubricants, creams, or perfume, as strong or unusual smells can contribute to sensory overload.

- Never tickle, as tickling can be very upsetting for someone with sensory modulation challenges. (Many clients have expressed to me that "tickling is torture.")

Understand that people with sensory modulation challenges will tend to touch you with firmer pressure so that they don't increase their own over-alertness to light touch. This is actually a type of "empathy": remember that we tend to think/feel that others have the same sensory responses that we do, and so *giving* the kind of heavy touch they would like makes the person with sensory modulation challenges *feel* that they're reducing the possibility of a negative response that light touch might cause. When I discussed this with one wife, she had an "ah-ha" moment of understanding why her husband had changed since his deployment and now touched her nipples just a little harder than she liked them touched. And Beth, a former soldier, said, "Now I can explain why I don't like the [light] way my husband touches me since I've been back from Afghanistan." (Please note, if heavy touch is uncomfortable for you, it's important that you voice this to your sensory-defensive partner. Remember, heavy touch means touch with firm pressure but not hard enough to hurt. Incorporating awareness into sex with someone with sensory modulation challenges should always be a "two-way street" that is satisfying and pleasurable to *both* partners. It may take time to get there—but with mutual commitment and understanding, you will!)

Intercourse

Intercourse is usually better tolerated than foreplay by people with SMC, as it involves heavier touch pressure, and the normal human sexual cycle moves you to the calm, relaxed parasympathetic mode at orgasm. But there are still some ways to make the act of intercourse itself more pleasurable for someone with sensory modulation challenges:

- If the person with sensory modulation challenges is male, consider having him enter his partner from the back (kneeling on the bed, bending over, or spooning), as he would feel more control over the level of touch used, and his partner would not be as likely to touch him unexpectedly (though always remember and openly discuss the comfort level of *both* partners with different positions).

- Consider using additional (unscented) lubrication to prepare for the stronger movement that might be used by a partner with sensory modulation challenges.

Oral and Anal Sex

As with intercourse, have a frank discussion with your partner about what feels safe and comfortable for you and your sensory needs, and for theirs.

Sex Toys and Vibrators

Sex toys and vibrators can be helpful during foreplay and/or intercourse, as the person with sensory modulation challenges can independently experiment with their sensory qualities before use, and these items can be ways of providing firm touch to/from your partner.

Don't be shy about visiting your local sexual wellness center or sexuality resource store. If you are concerned about their customer service or their products, ask your physician for a suggestion about the best local resources. You will find that most staffs are very well-trained in providing nonjudgmental, private consultations about issues involving physical intimacy, and have extensive experience in helping to find solutions.

Masturbation

Since orgasm brings you into the parasympathetic (more modulated) state, some people use masturbation as a sensory modulator. Some may use multiple episodes of masturbation to calm themselves. Men often wonder why they can generally achieve an erection with ease during masturbation, yet sometimes have difficulty when they want to have intercourse. Remember that your brain *knows* that you (as opposed to a partner) will use "just the right" level of touch. Masturbation is extremely "sensory safe," as you can't activate your own sensory defensiveness. And you will tend to pick a location that's private, and that has the level of sensory stimulation that's just right for you. In addition, you don't have anxiety about being perceived by another person as "failing." If masturbation becomes a relationship issue, you can help your partner understand that masturbation is *not* a negative comment on the sex that they have with you, but it is about your own sexuality and basic sensory needs. Also, many couples choose to incorporate masturbation into their shared sexual intimacy.

Physical Disabilities

If you are a veteran with physical issues affecting your sexual functioning, many veterans' hospitals have medical programs specifically designed for you. Numerous veterans have faced and received guidance for these issues: Please don't hesitate to give healthcare professionals a chance to help. Not just veterans but anybody with physical disabilities can find guidance through their physicians and/or trained occupational therapists. Every person who craves physical intimacy *can* and should have it, and millions of people with disabilities have found satisfying ways to engage in intimacy with their partners—so do not count yourself out of enjoying this realm of experience.

Timing

For mutual enjoyment of sex, pick a time when both partners are as modulated as possible. As mentioned previously, doing sensory diet activities before sex, especially together, can be helpful. But sometimes the sex act itself can be used to modulate the nervous system. Since we know that orgasm brings us toward parasympathetic calmness, perhaps your partner would consider having sex to help you stay or become calm (using all of the modulating techniques that both of you know). One very perceptive wife told me that when she knew her husband would be seeing someone or something that usually triggered his nervous system into fight-or-flight mode, she would initiate sex with him the night or morning before, both to help modulate him, and also to let him feel her safe, loving touch and support. But not all partners would be willing and/or able to do this, and so as with all of the advice above, please remember that an ongoing dialogue between *both* partners about what is and is not "okay," comfortable, and validating to them is essential.

Check-In #5: How Have Sensory Modulation Challenges Affected Your Sexual Intimacy?

Now that you understand how sensory modulation challenges can affect relationships, think about issues in your sexual relationships that may have been caused by misunderstandings about sensory modulation challenges. What would you do now if these issues came up again? What can you do now to keep them from happening again?

Relationship _____

Issue/incident_____

How did you react?_____

What did you do about your reaction at that time?

_____

_____

Thinking about it now, was there a specific sensory "trigger" (unexpected light touch, etc.)?

_____

_____

With your new knowledge, how might you handle that sensory trigger differently?

_____

_____

How can you explain your trigger/s to your partner?

_____

_____

What could your partner do to help "deactivate" or "prevent" the trigger?

_____

_____

Are there other things you can do to prevent recurrence?

_____

_____

Check-In #6: How Have Sensory Modulation Challenges Affected Your Other Relationships?

Now that you understand how sensory modulation challenges can affect relationships in general, think about nonsexual relationship issues (for instance, misunderstandings around your nervous system's reactivity to your child's playing loud music) that might have been caused by sensory modulation challenges. What would you do now if these issues came up again? What can you do now to keep them from happening again?

Relationship _____

Issue _____

What Did You Do? _____

What Would You Do Now? _____

Things You Can Do to Prevent Recurrence

_____

_____

_____

_____

CHAPTER 7:

What is the Effect of Trauma on the Brain and How Does it Affect Modulation?

The "T" in DIAL IT DOWN: "Transitions Through Trauma"

What Types of Trauma Changes Do We See in Service Members, First Responders, and Frontline Medical Workers?

We have previously discussed some of the ways in which active-duty and medical personnel report feeling "different" after deployment and after facing sustained-threat situations. You may become more vigilant to sensory stimuli and often be unable to screen out "background" stimuli. You may overreact to things in your environment, have behavioral outbursts, have sleep disorders and problems with sexual intimacy, and perhaps even have digestive problems, as being on sympathetic arousal shuts down the gut to allow blood to flow to the muscles and brain for the fight-or-flight response.

Understanding your reactions is key to every part of the Dial It Down approach, and so in this chapter, we'll step back to give a more comprehensive overview of *why* you feel different—in particular, we'll look at what the trauma you've been exposed to (and what trauma in general) does to the brain. This will involve discussing what's currently known about both diagnosed and undiagnosed conditions related to trauma—like mTBI (mild traumatic brain injury), PTS (post-traumatic stress), and PTSD (post-traumatic stress disorder)—and the subtle psychological effects that you may potentially experience. All of these conditions connect to, and can be significantly improved by, self-treatment for sensory modulation challenges (in Chapter 13, we'll discuss in more detail how this self-treatment can also help to make other therapeutic interventions more effective). Almost *all* active-duty personnel who have been diagnosed with mTBI and/or PTSD experience some degree of sensory modulation challenges, and many active-duty personnel, first responders, and frontline healthcare workers who have *not* been diagnosed with these conditions will still experience sensory modulation challenges and may report post-traumatic stress.

What is the Effect of Mild Traumatic Brain Injury on Modulation?

The incidence of traumatic brain injury in military personnel is increasing substantially due to the types of weapons that are being used in war today. Many military service members have returned from deployment with diagnosed mTBI, and many others have returned with undiagnosed mTBI. We're also discovering that many active-duty personnel and first responders enter into their service with undiagnosed mTBI due to events in their pasts such as concussions from sports participation. Physical changes from moderate-to-severe traumatic brain injury are easier to observe and understand than the often-subtle behavioral changes that come with *mild* TBI, as mTBI leaves no outward physical scars. mTBI can cause many types of problems, but one in particular is often at the root of numerous other issues—*disinhibition*. Disinhibition means that the brain no longer has the level of ability it needs to "inhibit" or reduce the excitatory activity of some neurons. So, it has trouble filtering out the information it does *not* need as it sorts and prioritizes the huge number of pieces of sensory information coming into it every second of every day. Think about your eight sensory systems (touch, taste and texture in the mouth, smell, hearing, vision, balance and body awareness in space, muscle and joint awareness, and interoception) and how many pieces of information of each type you're responding to each second. If you then look around and observe the things you have *not* responded or attended to (for instance, sitting on your chair reading this, you're likely not fully attuned to the pressure of your body against the chair's surface, or the slight humming of the florescent lights, or the brushing of your clothing against your skin, or the lingering scent of laundry detergent, or the traffic going by outside, or the buzzing of the lawnmower at the end of the block), you'll get an idea of just how much inhibiting your brain *automatically* does for you. If you had to respond to all the things you usually filter out, you'd never be able to concentrate on any one task. Luckily, we don't have to worry about this if our brain is functioning in its intended manner, which is to "sort out" most information for us. However, if we experience something that changes our brain function like physical trauma, one of the primary effects may be *decreased inhibitory ability.*

The result of disinhibition is that we *react more* to sensory input of all types. We are not as able to inhibit some spontaneous responses such as reacting angrily to loud noises or unexpected touch, even though we "know better" cognitively. As disinhibition affects the prefrontal cortex (the "thinking part" of the brain), we may also have more difficulty inhibiting *thoughts* that come unbidden into our minds, like memories of trauma, anger at someone, or blaming ourselves for past issues. *Usually* we do not act on very many of the thoughts that originate in our brains, as we're able to evaluate their importance and relevance to our lives and to those around us. And we're able to pre-judge the reactions that others might have to our expression of certain thoughts. But *disinhibition from mTBI interferes with this ability to sort and screen out verbal and physical expressions of thoughts as well as reactions to sensory input.* This change in the level of a person's ability to inhibit sensory and other stimuli is one of the major issues seen in veterans and service members.

How Traumatic Stress Changes Your Brain

In addition to better understanding the effects of *physical* trauma from mTBI, we're also currently learning more about how *traumatic stress* from war and other sustained-threat situations can actually change the structure and function of our brains. In particular, *the production and re-uptake of neurotransmitters* can change due to traumatic stress. Neurotransmitters are the substances that are responsible for communication between brain cells (neurons): they either facilitate (excite) or inhibit signals between neurons in different parts of our brains. Weiss (2007) states that "exposure to traumatic stress is associated with changes in the limbic system, the hypothalamic–pituitary–adrenal axis, and key monoamine neurotransmitters" (p. 114). What is especially relevant is that "different neurobiological alterations can be linked to specific symptoms of hyperarousal, dissociation/numbing, and reexperiencing of trauma" (p. 114). (See Appendix I for a more in-depth discussion of the brain areas and neurotransmitters affected by traumatic stress.)

Changes in the effects of neurotransmitters related to traumatic stress can lead to the specific symptoms referenced above, and also (just as in mTBI) to less ability to inhibit incoming sensory stimuli. As Weiss (2007) states, "there appears to be a failure of higher brain regions to dampen amygdala arousal in PTSD … this deficiency in emotional regulation may result in hypervigilance to trauma cues, exaggerated startle, flashbacks, intrusive memories, and misinterpretation of innocuous stimuli as potential threats" (p.115). So, the result of physical trauma and/or traumatic stress can be that your brain more often stays in the *heightened state of arousal* we've discussed as the most common form of sensory modulation challenges, sensory defensiveness.

In addition, when we've experienced trauma, our brains actually store these trauma memories *differently* from regular memories. Rather than being stored in the narrative/storytelling memory parts of the brain (our episodic/autobiographical memories), they're stored as sensations in the body. Sometimes these sensations are the only "memory" of the trauma. As we have discussed before, sensations come into the brain through the thalamus, which I refer to as the brain's "major traffic cop," as it sends sensations where they need to go in the brain for further evaluation, analysis, and action. According to Bessel van der Kolk (2014), one of the leading researchers in trauma and post-traumatic stress, in his book *The Body Keeps the Score,* "breakdown in the thalamus explains why trauma is primarily remembered … as isolated sensory imprints: images, sounds, and physical sensations that are accompanied by intense emotions, usually terror and helplessness" (p. 70).

In typical (as opposed to trauma) memory formation, a part of the brain called the hippocampus is responsible for putting memory into chronological order and perspective. Then the memory is consolidated into narrative memory in the left frontal lobe of the brain so that we can explain and understand our experience. But trauma leaves "raw data memory" in the part of the brain called the amygdala, as *somatosensory* (body/sensory) experiences. Given that the amygdala regulates emotion, this different processing and storage of experience can result in *increased sensitivity to even subtle sensory associations with traumatic events* (Koomar, 2009). These associations are often experienced as flashbacks or triggers.

Trauma and traumatic stress can change people in varied ways. Some people may experience persistent intrusive thoughts or vivid sensory-based memories of the trauma. Some people may expose themselves to situations similar to the traumatic situation (one theory is that they do so in an attempt to "normalize" and/or process the event). Violence toward others can come from the reenactment of victimization, as can self-destructive acts such as suicide.

Conversely, some people may actively avoid all potential "triggers" of the emotions related to the trauma, and even emotions in general. In this psychological or emotional "numbing," a person avoids emotions because their over-reactions to stimuli are difficult for them to understand, and they can't express how they're feeling or figure out what to do about it. Some people may "self-medicate" with drugs or alcohol.

Although emotional numbing looks like under-arousal, it can actually be a state of hyperarousal that has depleted neurotransmitters and psychological resources. This depletion can then lead to a state like sensory deprivation that is referred to as "shut down." The brain is overworked and "shuts itself down" for a time from reacting to immediate sensory input as a self-preservation measure (Kimball, 1993 pp. 99–100, 166; 1999 pp. 130–131, 158; van der Kolk, 2014; Kimball, clinical examples, 1976, 1977). One study showed that emotional numbing was the primary issue that veterans' partners wished they could change in order to increase their shared intimacy (LaMotte et al., 2015).

To help get their nervous systems out of "shutdown" and back to a more "normal" level, people with sensory issues can use a heavy-work sensory diet that moves them to a more modulated state. This is why some veterans and first responders, for instance, may find themselves "self-treating" by engaging in high-intensity sports involving heavy work with their joints and muscles, or prolonged rhythmic moving of their heads through space—like riding "Harleys," fast skiing, and "murder ball." I've even worked with people with a history of trauma who've revealed that they felt the need to "cut themselves" when in a shutdown state to be sure that they could still feel *something*, and as a way (even though they knew it was maladaptive) to "get back" from feeling numb.

Trauma survivors need to work through the trauma. They need to regain a feeling of safety in their own bodies. Van der Kolk (2014) states that "more than anything else, being able to feel safe with other people defines mental health: safe connections are fundamental to meaningful and satisfying lives" (p. 352). Trauma may be held, in part, as tension/stress in particular areas of the body: for example, some people always get headaches or a sore neck or back when stressed. This bodily tension can be worked on through various forms of psychological counseling (discussed in depth in Chapter 13), and also physically, through occupational or physical therapy. Some occupational and physical therapists (as well as some osteopathic physicians and massage therapists) have specific training in a form of manual therapy called cranial sacral therapy that can facilitate reductions in both physical and emotional tension.

Post-Traumatic Stress and Post-Traumatic Stress Disorder

As we have seen in discussing the Battlemind program (Chapter 3), military personnel, first responders, and frontline medical personnel are all trained to be able to deal with and make decisions in highly stressful situations. They are trained in using their own fear/alert responses as warning signals for danger (medical personnel, for instance, are trained in being hyper-conscious of safety protocols, and also hyper-alert to subtle shifts in a patient's appearance, behavior, and vital signs). Members of the military and first responders are additionally trained in using tactical abilities and discipline to maintain emotional control over fear and anger while at the same time being aggressive toward "the enemy," including being prepared to use lethal force. If military and first responders don't use all of their training at every moment in wartime or active shooting situations, they may not survive; if medical personnel don't use all of their training at every moment in a COVID-19 ward, they risk losing patients, and risk endangering their own lives and the lives of colleagues (if they're still living at home, they've carried the added burden that any lapse in hypervigilance while at work could also endanger their families).

The military in particular has learned how to "train in" hypervigilant reactions and abilities, and how to maintain in its soldiers the level of cognitive alertness needed to sustain these abilities over extended periods of time. One way the Army keeps its personnel sharp is with 75 or more minutes of strenuous daily physical training. These workouts not only keep soldiers *physically* strong, but also *mentally* in that "just right place" of nervous system modulation so that they can make good decisions to keep themselves and their fellow soldiers alive and achieve their missions.

But when military personnel, first responders, and frontline medical personnel return home from active- or on-duty work, their trained "heightened" reactions may not fit in well with "regular" life. The nervous system reactions that were honed to the level of saving their lives and those of others while on duty don't need to be maintained at that high level in most of daily life. For some, the transition is very difficult to make. This, combined with the traumas that many such personnel experience, may lead them to experience some symptoms of post-traumatic stress and even PTSD, like "having repeated, disturbing, and unwanted memories of the stressful experience"; "irritable behavior, angry outbursts, or acting aggressively"; "being 'super alert' or watchful or on guard"; and "feeling jumpy or easily startled" (PTSD Checklist, *DSM-5,* 2013). (Even if they don't meet all the criteria for a formal PTSD diagnosis, personnel with these symptoms are likely experiencing post-traumatic stress, or PTS.) So *what was formally necessary for survival and was required behavior while on duty, may now be looked at as a mental health problem or as maladaptive in a different environment.* It is not known which active-duty or frontline medical personnel are more likely to develop PTS or PTSD, and what factors make others more able to adapt, but *all* such personnel are changed by their experiences of trauma.

Behavioral and mental health issues are not black and white like physical injuries, and so it's difficult to make a definitive diagnosis of them, and even more difficult to know what causes them in some people, but not to the same degree in others. Future research on brain functioning may shed more light on this issue

Is Sensory Processing Involved in Trauma?

As discussed above, the nervous systems of trauma survivors are often dys-regulated, usually "stuck" on sympathetic arousal (fight-or-flight), although trauma survivors can also be under-aroused and may dissociate (splitting off "memories" of the trauma from their conscious awareness and storing them as raw, unprocessed sensations instead). Van der Kolk (2014) stated that "in PTSD the sympathetic and parasympathetic nervous systems are out of sync. Failure to keep this system in balance is … why traumatized people … are so vulnerable to overrespond to relatively minor stresses" (p. 267).

And Clancy et al. (2017) found evidence for "intrinsic sensory hyper-activity and disinhibition … a unique sensory pathology of PTSD … moti-vating new interventions targeting sensory processing and the sensory brain in these patients" (p. 2041). At this point, my research (Kimball, 2018, 2021, 2021a) indicates that the specific *hyperarousal* components of PTS and PTSD exactly match symptoms of SMC and can be addressed by using sensory techniques.

Two studies by this author (Kimball, 2021; Kimball, 2021a) revealed that veterans with a diagnosis of PTSD had significantly more issues with SMC when compared to veterans without a PTSD diagnosis. Using the Adolescent/Adult Sensory Profile (Brown & Dunn, 2002), Kimball (2021) showed that veterans with a medical diagnosis of PTSD demonstrated increased Sensory Sensitivity, Low Registration, and Sensation Avoiding (types of sensory modulation challenges). On an unpublished Sensory Over-Responsivity Inventory for Adults, used with the generous permission of its authors, Miller and Schoen (2008), the PTSD group also showed significantly higher scores.

Kimball (2021a) again used Miller and Schoen's (2008) unpublished Sensory Over-Responsivity Inventory for Adults (SensOR) and their unpublished Sensory Under-Responsivity Inventory for Adults (SensUR) (Miller & Schoen, 2008) to compare the sensory responses of six groups. The raw score means (averages) were compared, with higher scores indicating more sensory issues. Both veterans with diagnosed PTSD and nonveterans with a trauma history but no diagnosis of PTSD showed significantly higher SensOR scores when compared with "normal" individuals. And veterans with PTSD showed significantly higher SensUR scores when compared with "normal" individuals. (See Appendix I for more information on these studies.)

In 2018, Kimball et al. studied treatment for sensory modulation challenges in four women with PTSD from personal trauma who self-treated with the Wilbarger Therapressure Protocol™ (see Appendix IV). After following this sensory modulation treatment protocol, one woman who was found to have PTSD from repeated blast injuries, and therefore, had a suspected mTBI, only made a slight positive change in her SensOR. However, the other three showed significantly decreased stress, increased concentration, improvements in their sensory processing inventory (via Miller & Schoen's SensOR), and participation in their lives, and showed modulation in their cortisol levels (the stress hormone). The modulation of cortisol levels after self-treatment with the Wilbarger Therapressure Protocol™ is particularly noteworthy, as previous research had shown that eight weeks of treatment for PTSD using psychotherapy or pharmacotherapy (Sertraline) did not result in changes in total cortisol output, even when the treatment was successful enough to allow removal of the PTSD label (Pacella et al., 2014).

Van der Kolk (2014) suggested that new approaches to healing trauma should "focus on strengthening the body's system for regulating arousal" (p.78); found that "talk therapy" in isolation (without additional sensory-based interventions) generally does not work well for trauma patients; and suggested reducing hyperarousal through yoga, body work, breathing, and meditation—all of which readers of this book will recognize as sensory diet strategies. In the following chapters, I will help you develop an individual sensory diet that's strong enough to modulate your nervous system, works with your daily schedule, and is based around activities that you like.

If You Acquired Sensory Modulation Challenges Through Trauma, How Can This Be Evaluated?

Most of the methods for determining whether a person is experiencing sensory modulation challenges involve taking sensory histories. A number of Check-Ins are included throughout this book to help you analyze your sensory responses. Standardized assessments for sensory modulation challenges have been available only since 1999, and most of the work on evaluating sensory modulation challenges has been done by occupational therapists. Brown and Dunn (2002) were the first to publish a sensory profile for adults, the Adolescent/Adult Sensory Profile, a self-assessment asking you questions about your reactions to different sensory events in your life. (See Appendix I.)

Accessing Evaluations

If you wish to access the Adolescent/Adult Sensory Profile, it is usually available through occupational therapists. These profiles are self-administered and can be self-scored, but it is helpful to have a therapist interpret them and discuss the results with you. If you don't have access to an occupational therapist, a general sensory inventory can help you understand whether you may be experiencing sensory modulation challenges. Please note that, as stated earlier in this book, PTS and PTSD involve psychological as well as physical and sensory components, and it's important that you do not self-diagnose. Dial It Down is intended to empower you to understand, take charge of, and implement your own wellness regime—and it *will* make other interventions more effective—but it is not intended to *replace* these other interventions if they're indicated, or act as a substitute for the individual advice of trained medical and occupational therapy personnel. A crucial part of self-empowerment in facing an mTBI, PTS, or PTSD diagnosis is understanding that *you should not be alone* in your diagnosis and treatment.

Miller and Schoen (2008) have unpublished Inventories for Sensory Over-Responsivity, Sensory Under-Responsivity, and Sensory Craving in children. They are also in the process of standardizing an examiner-administered scale (in conjunction with Western Psychological Services) for adults and children called the Sensory Processing 3-Dimensions Scale (Miller, Schoen & Mulligan, 2018). They have allowed me to apply their scales in their preliminary research form in the studies discussed earlier in this chapter (Kimball, 2018, 2021, 2021a), and I have observed that the Sensory Over-Responsivity Inventory for Adults (SensOR) and the Sensory Under-Responsivity Inventory for Adults (SensUR) are very well-suited for use by persons with mTBI, PTS, or PTSD. They are, in addition, extremely helpful as a pre- and post-assessment to measure changes that occur through wellness self-treatment and professional treatment. In the previously mentioned study of four women with PTSD (Kimball, 2018), the Sensory Over-Responsivity Inventory for Adults (SensOR) was the main sensory scale that showed change after the women engaged in treatment for sensory modulation challenges using the Wilbarger Therapressure Protocol™ (see Appendix IV). Miller and Schoen have graciously allowed me to use the prepublication version of their inventories in this book so that readers can conduct a self-analysis of their Over-Responsivity (sensory defensiveness) and Under-Responsivity. Although not all possible sensations that might bother you are listed on these inventories, many of those that are common to service members, first responders, and frontline medical personnel are included. (Note: some of these items may repeat items that were mentioned in previous chapters; those chapters provided an overview, while this chapter and these inventories will help you to more comprehensively identify and note changes in potential problem areas.) These inventories can indicate if you have tendencies to be Over-Responsive and/or Under-Responsive to sensory input and can help you see which types of sensations your nervous system is the most responsive to. You are asked to fill out the inventories below as a pre-assessment of your sensory modulation challenges. If you then decide to develop your own sensory diet and use it for several months (Chapters 8, 9, and 10), you can do a post-assessment using these same inventories to review the changes that using the sensory diet (along with any other interventions) have made in your responsiveness to sensation (Chapter 9).

Check-In #7: The Sensory Over-Responsivity Inventory for Adults and The Sensory Under-Responsivity Inventory for Adults

THE SENSORY OVER-RESPONSIVITY INVENTORY FOR ADULTS (MILLER AND SCHOEN, 2008, UNPUBLISHED MANUSCRIPT). PRINTED BY PERMISSION.

Directions: Check each description that applies to you.

These garments bother me:

_____1 seams in clothing

_____2 tags in clothing

_____3 socks

_____4 changing from long to short pants

_____5 accessories (e.g., watch, jewelry, scarf, hats)

_____6 elastic on clothing

_____7 fuzzy or furry textured clothes (e.g., sweaters, collars, etc.)

_____8 wool clothes

_____ *Subtotal*

These aspects of self-care bother me:

_____9 washing or wiping face

_____10 cutting toenails or fingernails

_____11 having haircut or hair clipped

_____12 hair washing or drying

_____13 hair brushing or combing

_____14 getting dressed

_____15 brushing teeth

_____16 getting dirty

_____17 having crumbs around my mouth

_____18 having messy hands

_____19 having a messy mouth

_____*Subtotal*

These tactile sensations bother me:

_____20 mud

_____21 finger paint

_____22 glue

_____23 play dough

_____24 foods

_____25 hair care products (greasy/sticky)

_____26 kissing

_____27 coarse carpet

_____28 light stroking touch

_____*Subtotal*

These visual sensations bother me:

_____29 brightly colored or patterned materials (e.g., clothes, upholstery, drapes, wallpaper)

_____30 florescent lights

_____31 fast-moving images in movies or TV

_____32 visually cluttered environments

_____33 busy pictures in books or complex and busy images in artwork

_____*Subtotal*

These smells bother me:

_____34 perfume/cologne

_____35 cleaners/disinfectants

_____36 bath products

_____37 soaps

_____38 air fresheners

_____*Subtotal*

These aspects of food and eating bother me:

_____39 salty foods (e.g., nuts or chips)

_____40 soft foods

_____41 lumpy foods

_____42 slimy foods

_____43 soup with vegetables or meat pieces

_____45 eating bread crust

_____46 food preparation/cooking

_____47 new unfamiliar foods

_____*Subtotal*

These sounds bother me:

_____48 sound of utensils against each other (e.g., spoon in bowl, knife on plate)

_____49 clothing that makes noise (e.g., swishing cloth, accessories)

_____50 doorbell ringing

_____51 dog barking

_____52 sirens

_____53 alarms

_____54 radio or TV in the background

_____55 florescent lights

_____56 someone talking when I am trying to concentrate

_____57 clock ticking

_____58 construction or landscaping equipment

_____59 water running or dripping in the background

_____*Subtotal*

Sounds in these places bother me:

_____60 toilet flushing in the bathroom

_____61 appliances/small motor noises (e.g., blender, vacuum, hair dryer, electric shaver) at home

_____62 concerts

_____63 large gatherings

_____64 restaurants

_____65 parades

_____66 malls

_____67 gymnasium

_____*Subtotal*

These aspects related to movement bother me:

_____68 climbing activities

_____69 walking or climbing up open stairs

_____70 experiencing heights

_____71 walking or standing on moving surfaces

_____72 playing on the playground jungle gym

_____73 playing on the playground swings or slides

_____74 going on amusement park rides

_____75 going up or down escalators

_____76 chewing foods

_____*Subtotal*

_____*Grand Total*

THE SENSORY UNDER-RESPONSIVITY INVENTORY FOR ADULTS (MILLER AND SCHOEN, 2008, UNPUBLISHED MANUSCRIPT). PRINTED BY PERMISSION.

Directions: Check each description that applies to you.

Typically, I have a less intense response than others to:

_____1 the doctor giving me a shot

_____2 bruises or cuts

_____3 hurting self

_____4 being touched on the arm or back (e.g., unaware)

_____5 wet or dirty clothes

_____6 dirt on myself

_____7 objects that are too hot or too cold to touch

_____8 bumping into things or falling over objects

Typically, I do not notice:

_____9 food or liquid left on lips

_____10 hands or face that are messy/dirty

_____11 drooling or food that has fallen out of mouth

_____12 the need to use the toilet

_____13 feelings of hunger (does not seek food when hungry)

_____14 over-filling mouth when eating

_____15 feelings of being "full" (must intervene to stop overeating)

_____16 strong or noxious odors

Typically, I do not notice:

_____17 activity within a busy environment

_____18 an object coming toward eyes quickly

_____19 someone entering or leaving the room

_____20 materials or people in the room needed to complete an activity

Typically, I do not respond:

_____21 when name is called or has to be touched to gain attention (hearing is OK)

_____22 when a new sound is introduced

_____23 to unexpected loud sounds (e.g., fire drills, hall bells or other loud noises)

_____24 when given directions or instructions only once

_____25 to a normal volume speaking voice (e.g., others speak loudly to gain his/her attention)

I:

_____26 perform movement in a slow and plodding fashion

_____27 give little indication of like or dislike from movement

_____28 appear to be in my own world (tuned out)

_____29 do not visually scan the environment (look around)

_____30 leave clothing twisted on body

_____Total

Please remember as you complete these inventories that there are no "judgments" or "right/wrong answers" attached to them: you may have many intense responses in several categories or only a few in some categories. The purpose of these inventories is simply to identify your areas of sensory sensitivity in the interest of helping you to better understand your responses to life, and (if you choose) to take steps toward change.

The following chapters will help you to identify these potential steps toward change, and will discuss many easy, practical ways for you to incorporate them into your daily life.

CHAPTER 8:

How Are Sensory Modulation Challenges Self-Treated: Accessing Wellness Through a Sensory Diet

The Second "D" in DIAL IT DOWN: Sensory "Diet"

Key Points in Using Sensory Diet as a Wellness Tool

A sensory diet is the number-one way for you to take control of and influence your own nervous system's responses. As mentioned earlier, the decades of research and clinical work that developed our understanding of how to treat sensory modulation challenges in children are now being successfully applied to adults. Four concepts guide the treatment of SMC, and only one of these four requires professional help. The other three are wellness methods that you can carry out yourself through many activities you already do and enjoy.

The four ways to influence sensory modulation challenges, which were introduced in Chapter 4 (Wilbarger & Wilbarger, 2001, 2007), will be discussed in more detail here so that you can start to incorporate them into your daily life:

1. The *first* and most important self-treatment is *knowledge*, knowing that sensory modulation challenges exist. This knowledge gives you the power to change the way you view your responses to the environment, and to change the way your family and friends view your behavior. Earlier chapters have given you information about alternative ways of thinking about yourself or your family members; initiating conversations about SMC challenges with others;

and making small changes (like developing a "coming home from work" routine with your family or substituting deep-pressure hugs for light-touch "goodbye" kisses from your kids). We've also discussed how this knowledge applies to some of the issues involved in post-traumatic stress and PTSD, and the importance of incorporating sensory wellness techniques to improve the effectiveness of your existing treatments if you have been diagnosed with PTSD (and, if you have not been diagnosed, of using sensory wellness techniques in addition to seeking guidance from a health professional).

2. The second self-treatment for sensory modulation challenges is *accommodating the environment* to yourself, and yourself to the environment. Once you know that your behaviors are influenced by your changed responses to sensory input, you can more easily judge what *types* of sensory input you can tolerate and accommodate, and what types you may need to modify or (when possible) avoid in order to manage your over-arousal. For instance, it makes sense for some veterans and first responders to avoid fireworks shows as these are a powerful sensory and trauma trigger, and to do what they can to dial their sensory systems down to as modulated a setpoint as possible before going with their families to crowded and unpredictable venues like malls or concerts (and/or to limit their time in these venues). It makes sense for some frontline medical personnel to consider asking their spouses to take the kids to routine medical checkups, as certain smells (alcohol wipes, disinfectant, etc.) may push them toward sensory hypervigilance/overload, and, as with sensory-defensive veterans, to do what they can to dial down their sensory systems before going with family to crowded and unpredictable places. When you incorporate accommodation with knowledge and have open conversations with your family about your sensory challenges as they relate to your environment, you'll be taking powerful steps toward limiting misunderstandings and creating a more comfortable, understanding, and accepting *home* environment for everyone.

Skipping ahead for a moment, to point 4. As mentioned previously, the *fourth* treatment concept is a program that is professionally guided by a trained occupational therapist, called the Wilbarger Therapressure Protocol™ (Wilbarger & Wilbarger, 2001, 2007). We will discuss how it is done, who can teach it to you, and the research behind it in Appendix IV.

3. The *third* self-treatment, and the strongest, most flexible wellness option, is a **sensory diet**. This is *the* major wellness self-treatment for sensory modulation challenges, and so we'll discuss sensory diet concepts in detail throughout the rest of this chapter, as well as in chapters 9 and 10. (Though please always keep in mind that a combination of techniques—in particular, points 1 and 2 above with 3—will be the best practice and yield the best results as you work to Dial It Down.)

Sensory Diets

A sensory diet can be carried out by anyone. Our previous discussions about sensory modulation challenges, including both over-arousal and under-arousal, outlined the basis for sensory diets. Sensory diets are used to modulate the nervous system, that is, *to bring your nervous system into the middle, "centered" range* of responding to input. (See Appendix I for more information on the science of SMC.)

A sensory diet is a *self-directed* wellness approach, and it can be carried out in the natural environment. *It changes the "set point" of the nervous system—moving it away from the sympathetic fight/flight response if the person is over-alert, or toward more arousal if the person is under-alert.* This will, again, allow other treatments you may be using for PTS, PTSD, anxiety, or depression to work better, because a more centered nervous system will help you "take in" therapeutic information more fully.

When developing sensory diets, we try to discover activities that we *already do* as well as new ones that will allow us to get the most out of our time—always aiming for those types of sensory input that will have *the strongest, longest-lasting modulating influence*. Once you've gained an understanding of the *sensory qualities* of each activity that are modulating, it will be easier for you to plan a sensory diet or sensory breaks to fit your specific needs. The following are categories of modulating activities (we have briefly discussed these before):

1. The strongest form of modulating input comes from activities that involve *rhythmic movement of the head through space*. Rhythmic movement engages the vestibular/balance system. Examples are running, skiing, jumping jacks, or jumping on a rebounder. "Working out" even for as short a time as 10 minutes using rhythmic movement can have the longest modulating effect on the nervous system—an effect that appears to last from *4 hours to as long as 24 hours*.

2. *Heavy work with joints and muscles* (proprioception) is the next most modulating type of input. Any type of pushing or pulling activity *with resistance* works the joints and muscles in a heavy way. And any type of "load" on a joint that results in joint traction or compression (push-ups, lifting weights, walking with a weighted vest or backpack) is "heavy" work. Using heavy work has a modulating effect on the nervous system that lasts approximately *2 hours to 4 hours*.

3. *Firm pressure on the skin* is modulating. Firm touch pressure on the skin, such as during a massage, being wrapped tightly in a blanket, or bathing using a loofah sponge, is modulating. Using firm pressure on the skin can have the next longest modulating effect, in the range of about *1 hour to 2 hours*.

I refer to the three types of input above as "the big three" because they usually have an observable influence on modulation. Other sensory strategies that can contribute to modulation include:

4. *Vibration:* Try a vibrating chair, vibrating back cushion, or a handheld vibrating back/body massager such as those you can find at most drugstores (though avoid using massagers on your stomach, chest, or face, as these areas can be easily overstimulated).

5. Our *mouths* can add sensory modulation in a number of different ways:

a. The mouth muscles can be used to provide heavy work to the nervous system through resistive chewing and tugging activities (this is why many people use chewing gum to "calm their nerves").

b. Sucking and blowing activities can be modulating; for example, sucking thick liquids through a straw, or playing a brass or woodwind instrument.

c. Certain sensory qualities of food items can be modulating; for example, tastes such as sour, sharp, and spicy. Everyone will differ as to what they find modulating, so this may require some experimentation on your part.

6. Certain *auditory* inputs can be modulating; for example, certain classical music, especially Mozart and baroque, and some drumming music is modulating. Auditory input using popular music usually is not as modulating because of the way popular music is processed. With the rise of streaming services, file size (mp3) became more important than fidelity (wav files). To have a long-lasting modulating effect, music must include a full range of sounds, especially the high-frequency sounds and overtones that the mp3 format cuts out. While you don't need the full overtone series for basic hearing, you do need it to influence modulation (Emily Kimball, personal communications, 2021). For several examples of modulated music that includes a wider range of sounds, see *Mozart for Modulation, More Mozart for Modulation*, and *Baroque for Modulation* in the References.

7. *Breathing*: Deep breathing, from the belly not the chest, is modulating; for example, yoga breathing or military 4-4-4-4 breathing.

8. *Neutral warmth*: We have all experienced the perfect temperature that our bed gets to just before the alarm goes off in the morning. I define this as "neutral warmth," and it is very modulating. Other examples are wearing a coat or putting your hood up when it isn't cold out just because it *feels* more comfortable, or wrapping up in a blanket while watching TV.

Some of the Science Behind Sensory Diets
(More in Appendix I)

To understand how using sensory input, especially the "big three," influences our nervous systems, we'll take a brief look at some neuroscience. Rhythmic movements of the head through space like jumping and running activate the *vestibular system*, which is responsible for our balance, basic background muscle tone (not gym-rat "buff" tone, but the *readiness* of our muscles however firm or flabby to respond to sensory input and demands), and the ability to use certain muscle groups together to stabilize our body parts for *action*. The vestibular system is crucial to survival, and as such it is powerfully "hard-wired" into all of the other sensory systems in a way that you can—through sensory diet—use to your advantage.

Unlike most of the other "sensing" organs like our eyes or skin, we can't see the vestibular receptors, as they're located next to the inner ear. As discussed in Chapter 5, the vestibular mechanism consists of three semicircular canals at right angles to each other, along with two "sacks" called the utricle and saccule. All of its structures (the canals and sacks) are filled with "endolymph," which has the consistency of a watery gelatin, and they contain hair cells called cilia that send signals concerning direction of movement when they're displaced within the endolymph by head motion. With one such mechanism located in each ear, the vestibular system as a whole allows us to accurately "triangulate" in on our movements. The utricle and saccule also contain calcium carbonate crystals called "otoliths," or the proverbial "rocks in your head," which are always pulled "down" and therefore perform the very important, at times *life-or-death*, function of detecting gravity. For example, when we slip on ice, a definite *vestibular* response occurs as we try to catch our balance: we are not at that time *consciously* discriminating how our arms or legs move to protect us and (hopefully!) prevent a fractured skull or broken limb. Our reaction instead is mostly automatic (unless we're trained like a pro-athlete or performer in how to fall safely, and then only if we have time to react). To take another, "caveperson," example revisiting Chapter 4, think of all of the automatic vestibular actions needed to scramble away just in time from the wooly mammoth we've led to the edge of a trap.

The vestibular system, both figuratively and literally (through its calcium carbonate crystals), rocks!

And this extraordinary system hooks into *every other* sensory system: if we're running and suddenly come to the edge of a cliff, for instance, information from our eyes ("Whoa, that's a long way down!") instantly activates our vestibular system along with our proprioceptive system to keep our balance and to move our muscles in order to jerk away before we've even *consciously* had time to process the threat (the actual thought "Whoa!" comes afterward). In combat and active shooter situations, the *sound* of incoming fire activates a "drop and take cover" or fast escape movement (vestibular and proprioceptive response) before we've consciously processed and located the threat. In frontline medical situations, the *sound* of a patient alarm bell activates a rapid muscle response (grabbing for equipment, running, etc.) before we've consciously zeroed in on the specifics of the danger.

While it's uncommon for veterans, first responders, and frontline medical workers to have sensory modulation challenges originating *from* their vestibular systems (vestibular challenges are mainly seen in children born with SMC), the vestibular system is "hard-wired" into all of our other sensory systems including the most common problem areas for these personnel (vision, hearing, touch, and smell) *in the interest of survival itself,* and this hard-wiring is the reason for its primacy as a positive "modulator" in sensory diets. Any action that has a *modulating* effect on the *vestibular system,* like the steady, rhythmic movements of running or rebounding and the types of gentle adjustments to gravity inherent in activities like swimming or horseback riding, gives our brains (unconscious) input that we're safe and "okay." This general "A-okay" in turn gives *every other sensory system* "permission" (through neurochemical changes) to "stand down" and move to a more centered place. And it is this more centered place—the place, for military and first responders, that your physical training (running, jumping jacks, etc.) kept you in during active duty—that allows you to make the best judgments of and responses to *actual* danger, without the clouding effect caused by constant over-alert.

The next-strongest type of sensory input comes from the proprioceptive system, which functionally works closely with the vestibular system. Proprioception is the automatic understanding from our joints and muscles of where we are in space. It's the sense that keeps us from crushing a paper cup we're holding by guiding us to automatically adjust our pressure to account for the amount of liquid that's in it, and that allows us to touch our nose with our finger while our eyes are closed. Proprioceptors are found in muscles, tendons, joints, and skin, and are sensitive to changes in tension and pressure, which provide information to the brain on body position and how we're moving. All muscles and joints are involved; however, the neck and back joints, shoulders, and hips give the most feedback to the nervous system. *Any firm pushing or pulling activity, especially against resistance, involves proprioception that is modulating to the nervous system.* In other words, proprioceptive input, like vestibular input, gives a (slightly weaker) "A-okay" signal to the brain that helps to modulate all other sensory systems.

The tactile or "touch" system is the last of the "big three" systems used in sensory diets. We have already discussed the sympathetic fight-or-flight response, but we have not discussed in as much detail the *mechanisms that lead us to **either** react with alarm to a sensory input **or** to just discriminate what it is*. Each of our eight sensory systems has *both* an alert/arousal function and a discriminating function.

If a bug lands on you, for instance, you *alert* to it and swat it automatically before determining its danger level. The dual nature of each sensory system is the most apparent in the tactile system, which, unlike the other seven systems, actually has *two completely different sensory pathways* for alert/arousal information and discriminative information. The dorsal column medial lemniscal system carries *discriminative* touch (two-point discrimination, conscious proprioception, touch pressure, and vibration). Of the two tactile systems, it's the newer one in brain evolution and plays a role in the development of coordination. This is the system you use (along with the vestibular and proprioceptive systems) when you're learning a new movement routine such as an exercise or dance.

The other tactile system, the "anterolateral system," is a nonspecific *protective* system that can produce sympathetic arousal. It's also called the "evaluative system" (see Appendix I), as it evaluates the level of threat that's produced by incoming touch. It's a diffuse system that can send sensory input quickly to the reticular formation (part of the brain's danger arousal network), and is responsible for the body sensations of pain, temperature, and crude touch (tickle and itch). It plays a major role in tactile defensiveness such as aversion to light touch. Heavy touch pressure (from a massage, etc.) by contrast gives an "A-okay" signal to the brain (saying: "There's no light and fast, unpredictable tactile threat like a spider here!"), thus *modulating the nervous system and reducing its set-point to keep it from reacting strongly to light touch input which could otherwise activate a fight-or-flight response.*

Key Points in Discovering and Designing Sensory Diets

Now that you know more about the science and relative strengths of different sensory inputs to the nervous system, you can use this information to design *your unique sensory diet* to help keep your nervous system modulated. The overall strength of a sensory diet is important. We need to be able to analyze each activity for *power*: for *how long this activity will affect the nervous system.* It's important to design the best schedule to *maintain* that power. For this, *timing* is crucial, that is, realistically taking into account both *how long* each activity will influence your nervous system, and *when* you can do your sensory diet activities throughout the day. You should also try to steadily maintain the routines of daily living (e.g., when you go to bed, when you wake up, and when you eat), as these routines in themselves are organizing to the nervous system. And remember to adapt the environment around you to reduce disorganizing input whenever possible (always accepting that, for large portions of the day for most of us, it's not always possible to do so).

KEY POINTS FOR DEVELOPING SENSORY DIETS

1. To get the most out of your sensory diet, *use "the big three"*: vestibular (rhythmic head movement), proprioception (heavy work with muscles and joints), and tactile (firm touch pressure).

You will want to make the best use of your time by choosing the strongest, most modulating, longest-acting sensory inputs available. Research has shown that *combining different types* increases the overall strength of the inputs. *Vestibular combined with proprioceptive activity* (for instance, rebounding on a mini trampoline, which both moves the head through space and compresses joints) is the strongest. Adding hand weights or a weighted vest to a rebounding or running routine makes the proprioceptive component and the combined effect even stronger.

2. Find ways to *increase the modulating input of activities you already like.* If you like walking, again add a weighted vest (not a *pressure* vest, which may trigger flashbacks in veterans due to its being too much like a flak jacket, but a loose-fitting fishing or hunting vest with weights or rocks in the pockets), a backpack, or wrist weights. If you have favorite TV programs, place a mini trampoline (rebounder) or yoga ball in front of the TV and bounce through your show. Or sit on a yoga ball while playing video games or working on your computer. Many activities can be adapted in this way.

3. Analyze the sensory qualities of your favorite or usual activities, and *then amp them up* in any or all of the following ways:

    a. Increase Intensity (for instance, increase muscular intensity by adding some sprints into your run, or by increasing your pace or resistance levels when walking or biking)

        •   Increase the proprioceptive/joint compression component (as with adding a backpack to walking, mentioned above, or adding wrist weights when you run)

        •   Match the intensity to your personal and physical needs (many people can do more, and their bodies *need* more, intense physical work than they may think; but on the flip side, you should always check in with a physician if you have any underlying health conditions like heart disease, diabetes, or back or neck issues that may make increasing workout intensity a challenge, in which case, it's possible to substitute increasing frequency and/or duration instead [see Increase Frequency and Increase Duration sections below])

b. Increase Frequency

- Add sensory diet activities in more often (for instance, don't just go for one long run only on weekends; go for a short run once a day, and/or add 10 minutes of walking with a weighted vest or wrist weights daily at lunchtime, or a 10-minute rebounding session while streaming your favorite show right when you get home in the evening). Remember that short, frequent sessions spread throughout the day can often be more effective that one long session.

c. Increase Duration

- Although frequent short activities work well, you may find that lengthening a short workout fits better in your day. Adding even small increments can be highly effective. A 30-minute run can be increased to 35 minutes, with significant positive sensory impact; a 10-minute rebounding session can be increased to 12 and then 15 minutes.

d. Change the Rhythm

- Change the novelty-to-repetition ratio to match your personal needs. Some people need repetition to feel modulated, while others need novelty. For instance, some people find that biking the same route each time adds to their modulation as they prefer not to be surprised by unexpected occurrences, while others like to try different routes so that all of their senses can be more engaged.

Remember to *always adapt these sensory qualities to fit **your specific needs***. For example, if it isn't possible for you to do very *intense* activity (like heavy work) due to physical restrictions, try less intense but more frequent activity, or less intense activity for a longer period of time.

4. If you want to change or add activities, look for *activities that will be easy for you to access on a regular basis.*

   Look for activities that don't cost too much, do not require travel (unless you want to), can be done alone or with others based on your personal preference, can be done in varying environments, and can be fitted into varying time periods (both length, and time of day). Examples might include outdoor activities such as running, biking, hiking, swimming, or higher-intensity activities such as rock climbing, skiing, windsurfing, surfing, and skateboarding. Indoor activities can include weightlifting, chair pushups, theratubing exercises (resistance stretching with a rubber tube or band), and online classes such as yoga, Zumba, body fitness with hand weights, and basic exercise classes. Since they are online you can start and stop them to get just the right time and strength fit. Many people are finding that a home gym provides varying "just right challenges" for sensory diet. An exercise bike, universal gym, or treadmill can allow you to do a short or long workout any time you need it. Again, activities that *you actually like to do* will work the best as you are more likely to do them consistently. Find the *"just right challenge"* for yourself.

5. *Timing is everything!*

   Analyze your day. Find opportunities for sensory inputs spaced throughout the day. How can you fit modulating activities in regularly so that they influence your nervous system all day long? You do *not* need large amounts of time for this. More frequent, short sensory diet activities work even better than one long workout. For example, a 1-hour workout would be helpful and may be what you're used to, but you might find that six 10-minute workouts *spaced throughout the day* would be more beneficial in keeping your nervous system modulated, and also may be a better fit for your life. *Or*, as mentioned above, you might choose to keep your long run or workout but also add a few 5- to 10-minute activities at different points throughout the day. Please note that if you tend to work out later in the day, you might find that adding a sensory workout of as little as 10 minutes in the morning *before* you go to work will be the most crucial "timing" adjustment in helping you enter your day in a more modulated state.

6. *It's individual*

   Everyone's sensory needs are different. If you are in a relatively calm state, a few light sensory diet activities will work to get your arousal level to that "just right place" for what you want to do. But if you are stressed, anxious, or angry (high arousal), or depressed (low arousal), it will take more sensory exercises to change your arousal level.

7. *When do you need modulating activities?*

   Structure your day so that you can do sensory diet activities **before** *your most difficult activity or most challenging tasks.* For instance, if you have a stressful team review meeting right after lunch on Tuesdays, plan to add in 10 minutes of walking with wrist weights or a comparable activity at lunchtime.

8. *The goal is to modulate your system **before** it is out of control.* Adding sensory diet activities *throughout your day* is your best bet in taking proactive action to Dial It Down, as is flexibly adding activities as needed before stressful events that you know are coming (like the difficult team meeting mentioned above). Keep some activities "in your pocket" for *unanticipated* meetings or events (like an unexpected call from the school asking you to meet with the principal about your child at 3 p.m., or a call that concerns you from the boss asking for a meeting in 2 hours). Though 5–10 minutes is optimal, *even as brief an activity as 3 minutes* of calming sensory input like wall pushups against a bathroom stall can help to keep you modulated. Not every stressful event can be anticipated (like a near-miss on the highway, or a child's having a tantrum), but if you stick to the sensory diet basics outlined here, your nervous system will be

in the best place it can be in order for you, rather than your fight-or-flight response, to be in control.

9. *It is important to have a **sensory intervention plan** in place for times when you find yourself about to "lose it."*

   We don't always have advance warning regarding "losing it," and this is one of the things that all people with sensory modulation challenges need to learn to accept (and forgive) in themselves. But by paying attention to your sensory responses and incorporating the knowledge that you've gained so far in this book, you may find yourself becoming *more aware of the earliest changes in your body* that a fight-or-flight response produces right before you "blow"—like muscle tension and increased breathing rate. Keep a few small helpful items in your backpack, briefcase, or car, like some resistive tubing for a quick stretching exercise when you feel these earliest changes, and remember *"anywhere" modulating basics* (which can be done very discreetly) like pushing the heels of your hands together rhythmically, chair pullups or chair pushups (see p. 164), and yoga breathing. It is harder to get yourself back to modulation once you have "lost it" than it is to do a quick sensory diet activity beforehand to help you lower your set point. Sometimes just lowering your set point a *small* amount can be enough to keep you in control in difficult sensory-stimulating situations.

10. Find a *"sensory diet buddy"* to work out with. Introduce a friend, especially another veteran, first responder, or medical colleague, to these concepts and work together to help each other stay modulated.

11. *"Sensory Snacks."* We have discussed the "big three" (the vestibular, proprioceptive, and tactile systems), but other sensory systems can also add modulating input, as can a less intense use of the big three. Little tune-ups called "sensory snacks" can add up to help you stay modulated (but remember, they do not take the place of a regular sensory diet as they are low power and have far less of a modulating effect). Keep small sensory tune-ups in a backpack, purse, desk drawer, or uniform pocket. They can include:

a. Hand squishies

b. Fidget toys

c. Mouth items. The mouth can provide modulating input through working the muscles in strong chewing. Use activities like chewing gum, or add resistive chewing to meals or snacks with items like apples, carrots, celery, or jerky. (If you don't like regular gum, Spry Gum is designed to be good for teeth and has more resistance that most sugarless gum.)

d. Certain tastes have also been found to be modulating: these include sour, bitter, sharp, or salty-tasting items.

e. Exercise tubing: This is easy to carry, and its ends can be tied together so it can be looped over chair arms or legs for many varieties of stretching exercises.

12. *Consider your environment.*

The first rule of sensory diets is to do what *can* be done, which may include having to do your exercises in an indoor space during the workday or work week. But before and after work (or during your lunch break, if you're fortunate enough to get sufficient time and to be close to a natural setting), consider that sensory diet activities are often enhanced when you do them in an *outdoor, natural environment* like a park, woods, seashore, or quiet backyard. Nature sounds like water running over rocks, waves, birds singing, or the wind rustling tree leaves can be very modulating.

13. *Be responsible for your own nervous system.*

To sum up all of the above, *learn about your own body and what works for you.* Discover which activities are the most modulating for your unique sensory system, *and* which activities are the most practical for you as an individual given your daily routines and environment (where you live and work). No matter how cramped your schedule or physical space, you *can* find sensory diet activities that will work for you, and doing so is a must if you want to take control of your sensory responses and participate as fully as possible in your life.

In addition to knowing what *works* for you, learn to recognize the signs when things *aren't* working: What does your body do to alert you that your arousal level is escalating? Preplan your de-escalation. As stated above, bring "sensory snack" items with you that can help, or plan things you can do in different situations. For example, while in a meeting, at a musical performance or at a play, or any time when you have no choice but to sit for an extended period of time, do chair pull-ups or lean slightly forward with your hands on your knees and push downward on your knees toward the floor. If you can, push in a pulsating way without calling attention to yourself, which is better than using constant pressure, but both will work. Can you leave the room where the over-alerting is occurring and do a little bouncing on your heels with your knees straight (which gives modulating proprioception up your legs and spine) or do wall pushups in the restroom? If you're driving, can you push firmly on the inside of the roof of your car with one hand while steering with the other, or alternately, grip the steering wheel harder and then lighter?

Summary

You have now been introduced to many potential components of sensory diets. In the following two chapters, I'll help you work more specifically to discover activities in *your* life that you can use to create your own sensory diet—activities that you like to do, and that fit and reflect both your sensory needs and your available time.

CHAPTER 9:

Discovering Your Own Sensory Diet

The Second "D" in DIAL IT DOWN: *Your* Sensory "Diet"

To discover which activities will work the best for your personal sensory diet, you first need to look at the activities you *already* do and enjoy. If you enjoy and "voluntarily" participate in them, then you'll be more likely to keep doing them and build them into a regular routine. Remember that to increase modulating input to our nervous systems, we can take our normal activities and *increase their intensity, frequency, or duration, or change their rhythm.* Also remember that *the strongest activities are those that involve the rhythmic movement of the head through space (vestibular), heavy work with the joints and muscles (pulling and pushing - proprioceptive), and heavy pressure on the skin (tactile).* Other sensory experiences give lesser levels of modulating input, but can still be used to add to the effectiveness of your sensory diet.

Check-In #8

What does a typical weekday or a typical weekend day look like for your sensory system? To find out, you can complete the steps outlined below. To help clarify these steps, we'll explore them as they relate to a veteran named Bob in the chart that follows.

1. Chart your usual activities, including any modulating sensory activities that you already do.

2. Chart the current stress level of each activity.

3. Decide *when* you need to be more modulated.

4. List things that you like to do:

    a. Rate the *sensory power* of each activity (remember the "big three"). How powerful is the activity as a modulator in your life?

    b. How much time does each activity usually take?

    c. Is the activity versatile enough to fit into other time frames? What is the minimum time needed for it?

5. Where and how could you add some short sensory activities into your day? (Remember: timing is everything!)

6. Think of ways to amp the modulating "sensory power" that each experience can give you. (Remember: intensity, frequency, duration, rhythm.)

Example: Bob

Bob was active duty in the Army's 10th Mountain Division and was deployed to a combat zone. He later left the military and started an office job. Let's look at a typical day for Bob and analyze the stress levels of his activities to illustrate how to develop a sensory diet:

CHART #1: WEEKDAY CURRENT ACTIVITIES: BOB

Time of Day: Mark how long	Your Activities	Current sensory Stress Level: Mark high, med, low	Where Do You Need More Modulation?
12 am	Sleep, sleeps poorly	Medium	X
1 am			
2 am			
3 am			
4 am			
5 am			
6 am	Gets up Showers Dresses	Low	
6:30 am	Gets 2 kids up, feeds and dresses them	High	X
7:30 am	Drives them to school and day care. Drives to work, 40 minutes in heavy traffic	Med	X
8:30 am	Desk job in finance, much time on phone with customers	Medium to high depending on time and activities	X
10 am	Office		X
11 am	Office		X
12 pm	Lunch	Low	
1 pm	Meetings	High, depending on activities	X
2 pm	Office		X
3 pm	Office		X
4:30 pm	Drives home, 40 minutes in heavy traffic	High	X
5 pm	Takes kids to after-school activities: swimming, baseball, ballet, etc.	Med	X
6:30 pm	Arrives home		X
7 pm	Plays with kids, likes active outdoor games	Low to med	
8 pm	Dinner	Low, eats after kids, after playing outside	
8:30 pm	Supervises kids' homework, etc.	Med	X
9:30 pm	Kids to bath, bed	Med	X
11 pm	Facebook Video games	Low Med	

Note that the chart above addresses steps 1, 2, and 3 on our list: usual activities and current stress levels, and where more modulation is needed.

We'll address the next steps below:

Step 4. What does Bob *like* to do? Can these activities be modulating?

- Military-style exercises
- Mountain biking
- Kayaking
- Running
- Active games with his kids: ball games, running, water games
- Gardening: mowing, digging, planting, creating and maintaining gardens
- Facebook, computer searches
- Video games
- Golf
- Hunting
- Tennis

CHART #2: BOB'S FAVORITE ACTIVITIES
AND THEIR RATINGS (SENSORY MODULATION POWER,
TIME NEEDED, AND VERSATILITY)

Activities Bob Likes	Sensory Modulation Power Level: Rate High, Med, Low	Usual Time	Minimum Time
Military-style exercises	High	30 min	10 min
Mountain biking	High	1–2 hours	30 min
Kayaking	High	2–3 hours	2–3 hours
Running	High	45 min	15 min
Active games with his kids: ball games, running, water games	Med to high	1–2 hours	15 min
Gardening: mowing, digging, planting, creating and maintaining gardens	Med to high	1–2 hours	15 min
Facebook	Low	1 hour	15 min
Video games	Negative, can be over-alerting	1 hour	Do not do right before bed
Golf	Med	1 hour for driving or putting practice, 2–3 hours for a game	Try putting in backyard, 20 min
Hunting	Med to high	Several days, only in the fall. Is the sensory advantage stalking an animal, or hiking in the woods?	Try walking/hiking in local wooded areas and trails to get into the natural environment more frequently, 20 min
Tennis	High	1–2 hours	1 hour

Steps 5 and 6:

CHART #3: WEEKDAY CURRENT ACTIVITIES: BOB (WITH SENSORY DIET MODULATION ACTIVITIES ADDED AND "AMPED")

Note that the sensory stress levels of each activity are significantly *lowered* by adding sensory diet, though not completely *erased*: the goal of sensory diet isn't a perfectly modulated day (very few people with or without SMC ever experience that), it's a day with *lower* stress levels that will allow you to participate more fully in, and feel more in charge of, your life.

Time of Day: Mark how long	Your Activities	Current Sensory Stress Level: Mark high, med, low	Where Do You Need More Modulation?	Modulation Changes You Can Make
12 am	Sleep	Low	X	Sleep with a weighted blanket.
1 am				
2 am				
3 am				
4 am				
5 am				
6 am	Gets up Showers Dresses (clothes not bothersome)	Low	X: Lower your nervous system set-point proactively, *before* it becomes an issue	Shower: warm water, modulating. Add 10-minute core workout with medicine ball.
6:30 am	Gets 2 kids up. Feeds and dresses them	Low to med	X	Involve kids in another 10 minutes of exercise—mini trampoline, jumping jacks (the benefits are such that you *can* use 10 minutes of a favorite show to motivate this). BONUS: this sensory work will help them concentrate in school.

7:30 am	Drives kids to school and day care. Drives to work, 40 minutes in heavy traffic	Low to med	X	Possible car calisthenics (see explanation directly below this chart). Try classical music, nature sounds or drumming music.
8:30 am	Desk job in finance and customer service	Medium depending on time and activities	X	Park away from the office and carry a backpack with several full water bottles in it. If possible, sit on a yoga ball instead of a desk chair.
10 am				Always take the stairs at work, wearing wrist weights if possible, or a weighted vest.
11 am				
12 pm	Lunch	Low		If office has a gym, work out at lunch, or walk outside with a weighted vest, or do "stairs." If you're lucky enough to have a private office, work out there.
1 pm	Meetings	Medium depending on activities	X	Schedule the most stressful meetings right after lunch workout.
2 pm				
3 pm				
4:30 pm	Drives home, 40 minutes in heavy traffic	Low to med	X	Drive a less stressful route if possible. Listen to calming music.
5 pm	Takes kids to after school activities: swimming, baseball, ballet, etc.	Low to med	X	Possible car calisthenics. Have kids do it too! While the kids are doing their activities, don't just surf your iPhone, but add a 10-plus-minute walk with weights or a mini-run or do "portable" military-style activities like jumping jacks and pushups.

6:30 pm	Arrives home	Medium	X	The modulation from activities above will carry over here.
7 pm	Plays with kids, likes active outdoor games	Low		- Go for run or bike ride, take kids with you. - Or split the time by going for a 30-minute run and spend 30 minutes in active games with the kids. - Or spend whole time with kids in active games. - Wear a weighted vest for as many activities as possible.
8 pm	Dinner	Low, eats after kids, after playing outside		
8:30 pm	Supervises kids' homework, etc.	Med	X	Playing classical music will help Bob and kids concentrate.
9:30 pm	Kids to bath, bed	Low to med	X	Design a routine and stick to it. Routines are modulating for Bob and the kids. Will get them to bed more easily.
11 pm	Facebook Video games	Low Med	X	Try to avoid these activities *right* before bed; do them earlier in the evening, possibly while the kids are doing homework.

Explanation of "car calisthenics" mentioned in chart above:

1. Alternate heavy gripping and relaxed grip on the steering wheel.

2. Heavy pushing with one hand on the ceiling inside the car.

3. When stopped, push the heels of your hands together rhythmically.

4. For passengers, keep exercise tubing in the car for stretching/ heavy work.

CHARTS #3A AND 3B: BOB'S WEEKEND CURRENT ACTIVITIES WITH MODULATION ACTIVITIES ADDED

CHART #3A: SATURDAY

Time of Day: Mark how long	Activity	Current Sensory Stress Level: Mark high, med, low	Where Do You Need More Modulation	Modulation Changes You Can Make
12 am	Sleep	Low	X	Weighted blanket
1 am				
2 am				
3 am				
4 am				
5 am				
6 am				
7 am	Tennis with group of friends	Low	Activity provides modulation	Good modulating activity
8 am	Tennis			
9 am	Tennis			
10 am				
11 am	Work in the yard	Low	Activity provides modulation	Good modulating activity
12 pm	Work in the yard			
1 pm				
2 pm	Play with kids in yard or go to playground, pool, bike ride, etc.	Low	Activity provides modulation	Good modulating activity
3 pm	With kids			
4 pm	With kids			
5 pm	Nap	Low		
6 pm	Nap			
7 pm	Dinner	Med		
8 pm	Family movie night	Low		
9 pm				
10 pm	Kids to bath, bed	Low to med	X	Design a routine and stick to it. Routines are modulating for Bob and the kids. Will get them to bed more easily.
11 pm	Facebook Video games	Low Med	X	Try to avoid these activities *right* before bed; do them earlier in the evening.

CHART #3B: SUNDAY

Time of Day: Mark how long	Activity	Current Sensory Stress Level: Mark high, med, low	Where Do You Need More Modulation?	Modulation Changes You Can Make
12 am	Sleep	Low	X	Weighted blanket
1 am				
2 am				
3 am				
4 am				
5 am				
6 am				
7 am				
8 am	Breakfast	Low to med		Do the cooking for family; routines are modulating.
9 am	Dress, drive to church	Med	X	Organize clothes the night before; play classical or drumming music in car.
10 am	Church	Low	Activity provides modulation	Church can be very modulating due to prayer and singing (deep breathing).
11 am				
12 pm	Brunch at church	Low		
1 pm	Mountain biking, golf or kayaking	Low	Activity provides modulation	Involve family
2 pm	Same			
3 pm	Same			
4 pm	Play with kids, active games	Low	Activity provides modulation	
5 pm				
6 pm				
7 pm	Dinner	Low		
8 pm	Whole family preparing for week ahead	Med	X	Might use a checklist or specific routine to keep whole family modulated.
9:30 pm	Kids to bath, bed	Low to med	X	Design a routine and stick to it. Routines are modulating for Bob and the kids. Will get them to bed more easily.
11 pm	Facebook Video games	Low Med	X	Try to avoid these activities *right* before bed; do them earlier in the evening.

SUMMARY

Bob needed to add modulating activities to his *weekdays*, but he was already aware of what he needed to do on weekends to keep himself modulated. He was struggling to find the amount of time needed for his very "active" activities on weekends, as his wife wanted him to spend more time with her and the kids. Once sensory modulation challenges were explained to the couple, they were able to openly discuss *both* of their needs and to look in particular at the amount of heavy sensory input that Bob needed to stay regulated. He began including his children in his activities more, and they really enjoyed doing many strong sensory activities with their dad. Bob was amazed at how well his children did at many of these activities – and at how much more quickly they did their homework when they had been active with him beforehand instead of playing video games, playing on the computer, or watching a movie.

His "sensory diet" turned into a win–win for the whole family, as they also benefited from sensory diet activities. He and his son had more time together as his son really enjoyed learning golf and playing baseball, and both his son and daughter enjoyed doing "military style" workouts with Dad (modified for their ages) and learning tennis. After working on his sensory diet, Bob decided to "train for something important"—trying to qualify for the "Tough Ruck," a separate portion of the Boston Marathon for active-duty military, veterans, first responders, and some civilians, which requires them to run (or march) 26 miles carrying a backpack (rucksack) wearing the name of a fallen servicemember or first responder. All participants pledge to raise funds for the Military Friends Foundation which supports military families and families of fallen heroes. *Update*: Recently Bob successfully ran it for the fourth time!

Check-In #9: Your Turn: Charting Your Current Sensory Diet

Now it's your turn to follow the steps to develop your own sensory diet.

What do a typical weekday and typical weekend day look like in your life?

On Chart #1 below, record your usual activities for both a typical weekday, and Saturday and Sunday, adding any sensory experiences you usually include.

- Chart the current stress level of each activity.

- Decide *when* you need to be more modulated

- **Leave the last column blank** *until you have filled in Chart #2.*

CHART #1 WEEKDAY CURRENT ACTIVITIES

Fill this in, leaving the last column *blank* until after you have filled in Chart #2. (Refer back to Bob's chart as needed for guidance on format.)

Time of Day: Mark how long	Activity	Current Intensity: Mark high, med, low	Where Do You Need More Modulation?	Power Additions: Modulation Changes You Can Make
12 am				
1 am				
2 am				
3 am				
4 am				
5 am				
6 am				
7 am				
8 am				
9 am				
10 am				
11 am				
12 pm				
1 pm				
2 pm				
3 pm				
4 pm				
5 pm				
6 pm				
7 pm				
8 pm				
9 pm				
10 pm				
11 pm				

CHART #1A: SATURDAY CURRENT ACTIVITIES

Leave the last column blank until you have filled in Chart #2.

Time of Day: Mark how long	Activity	Current Intensity: Mark high, med, low	Where Do You Need More Modulation?	Power Additions: Modulation Changes You Can Make
12 am				
1 am				
2 am				
3 am				
4 am				
5 am				
6 am				
7 am				
8 am				
9 am				
10 am				
11 am				
12 pm				
1 pm				
2 pm				
3 pm				
4 pm				
5 pm				
6 pm				
7 pm				
8 pm				
9 pm				
10 pm				
11 pm				

CHART #1B: SUNDAY CURRENT ACTIVITIES

Leave the last column blank until you have filled in Chart #2.

Time of Day: Mark how long	Activity	Current Intensity: Mark high, med, low	Where Do You Need More Modulation?	Power Additions: Modulation Changes You Can Make
12 am				
1 am				
2 am				
3 am				
4 am				
5 am				
6 am				
7 am				
8 am				
9 am				
10 am				
11 am				
12 pm				
1 pm				
2 pm				
3 pm				
4 pm				
5 pm				
6 pm				
7 pm				
8 pm				
9 pm				
10 pm				
11 pm				

CHECK-IN #10: Rating Your Favorite Activities for Sensory Power

CHART #2: YOUR FAVORITE ACTIVITIES AND THEIR RATINGS: WHAT DO YOU LIKE TO DO?

1. Rate the sensory power level that each activity can potentially add to your modulation (remember the "big three": rhythmic movement, heavy joint and muscle work, and heavy touch pressure).

2. How much time does each activity usually take?

3. What is the minimum time needed? Is the activity versatile enough to fit into other time frames?

Please list all activities that you like to do and rate what you think the sensory power level of each is for you, and the usual time and minimum time needed for each activity:

Activities	Sensory Modulation Power Level: Rate high, med, low	Usual Time	Minimum Time

Check-In #11: Adding Power to Your Present Sensory Diet

1. Now go back to your Chart #1 (look back to Bob's charts for guidance on format and creative ideas):

    a. Where and how could you add more sensory diet work into your day from your favorite activities in Chart #2?

    b. Remember: Timing is everything!

    c. Put in more power *before* stressful events. It's much easier to lower your nervous system "set point" before it gets too high (once you're in the fight-or-flight mode, it takes more effort to get back down to a modulated state).

2. Think of ways to amp the modulating "sensory power" that each experience can give you.

    a. Remember: change intensity, frequency, duration, and/ or rhythm.

YOU DID IT! When you have finished Chart #2 and placed your modulation changes in the last column of Chart #1 for a typical weekday and both weekend days, *you will have created your first comprehensive sensory diet!* Understand that *this is an evolving and changing plan.* Every day will be different, and you'll have to adapt your sensory diet depending on life events. But now you know how to make changes to help keep your nervous system modulated.

Check-In #12: Adapting Your Sensory Diet to Include Others

Now that you have a *personal* sensory diet, go back to see how you might incorporate family and friends into your sensory diet plan. Consider finding "sensory diet buddies" to do activities with.

Creative Sensory Diet Activities Discovered by Veterans, First Responders, and Frontline Medical Workers

*   A game invented by a veteran's dog: the veteran lies on top of a blanket in bed, then the dog burrows under the blanket and tries to push its owner out of bed as the owner resists.

- Several large dogs sleep on top of the veteran, providing weight and neutral warmth, both of which are modulating (this brings new meaning to the old saying, "It's so cold, it's a three-dog night"!).

- One first responder liked to mow grass (the heavy work of pushing and the vibration of the power mower are modulating), and was disturbed by the visual distraction of unmown grass on her street, so she performed "random acts of kindness" by secretly mowing elderly neighbors' lawns when they weren't home. This gave her a big boost in her sensory diet, while also modifying her visual sensory environment, which lowered her overall arousal. One person caught her at it, and it turned out that person was too ill to do it herself and was very thankful for the help. A big win–win!

- In Chapter 12, you'll meet Sydney, a female veteran who would wake from a daily afternoon nap on the couch disoriented, upset, angry, and scared. Her sensory diet solution was to keep two closed milk jugs partially filled with water next to the couch, and *before opening her eyes* or leaving the couch, she would do ten biceps curls with each hand. The result was modulation (a feeling of calmness) when she opened her eyes.

- Several veterans, first responders, and frontline medical personnel have commented that their sensory diet activities seem to work better if they're done outside in a natural environment. One even became a "Certified Forest Therapy Guide" to introduce his peers to the healing power of nature.

- Several veterans, first responders, and frontline medical workers have commented that learning to play a musical instrument, or taking up a long-abandoned instrument, has added to their sensory diets. Most popular and easiest to learn are guitar and drums (both "band" drums and Native American or ethnic drumming), but other string instruments and anything that requires blowing, such as a flute or brass instrument, are also good.

- On the *Today* show on 4/17/19, Marine veteran Mica Herndon was being interviewed after he crossed the finish line of the Boston

Marathon. He stated, "I run to deal with daily life. I have PTSD. My release is running!"

Comments Made by Veterans, First Responders, and Frontline Medical Workers Who Discover Sensory Diets

- "So *that's* why I really feel good when I'm out in the woods cutting trees and clearing brush!" (Army veteran)
- "After my one morning a week doing farm work, I feel great and have energy to get lots of things done the rest of the day." (Navy veteran)
- "My wife understands now and encourages me to run after work." (Frontline medical worker)
- "My husband gets it that I need the clutter picked up." (Army veteran)
- "When I work out hard at the gym, I have a real goal for my body and that feels great, especially as I get older." (Vietnam veteran)
- "Lifting weights doesn't do it; I need high-intensity core work like in the military." (10th Mountain Division veteran: Bosnia)
- "We want to go back to being superheroes, and the feeling and strength I get from this [sensory] work helps." (Retired first responder)
- "In the Army it's all about movement, communication and shooting straight. This stuff reminds me about how important movement is." (10th Mountain Division veteran)
- "I feel great when I'm mountain biking over rough terrain." (Army veteran)
- "It seems that when we get our bodies back into shape, people look at us differently – not because of how we *look* but how we *feel*." (Army veteran)
- "I'm glad my husband now understands about how I respond when he touches me." (OIF/OEF Army veteran)
- "This is so empowering. It's the first time in 20 years that my family has been able to discuss and understand my PTSD!" (Army veteran)

Horseback Riding Programs

I have been privileged to be involved as an occupational therapy consultant with numerous horseback riding and other equine-based programs for veterans, helping plan these programs and assess what working with horses has meant to these individuals. While these programs are specifically aimed at military veterans, horseback riding is an excellent sensory activity for anyone with post-traumatic stress or PTSD, and first responders and frontline medical workers should consider whether adding scheduled riding or lesson time at a local stable to their sensory diets might work for them (even places like New York City often have accessible stables and therapeutic riding programs). Horseback riding provides a unique combination of vestibular and proprioceptive work, along with exposure to the outdoors, tactile input, and emotional ties to the horse. Other equine activities and barn/farm work are also good sensory diet activities. Here are just a few comments:

- "I feel the best after my riding session. Both riding and grooming the horses is great!" (Vietnam veteran)

- "When working with horses, it's not just physical. It's about the relationship with the horse, the feeling of connection." (Vietnam veteran)

- "When I've done several hours with the horses, I'm good to go for the rest of the day from a physical pain standpoint. I'm good to go for several days from a mental PTSD standpoint." (Navy SEAL, Vietnam veteran)

- A barn owner told me that the veterans were very good at working with wild mustangs, as the horses and vets seemed to understand each other.

Dave's Story: Dave's Life Story Reflects His Need for a Strong Sensory Diet and How He Created It for Himself

Since serving in Vietnam, Dave has created numerous ways to keep himself modulated so that he can be successfully involved in his life. He is very active, friendly, and enthusiastic. When I first met him, Dave was 71, an Army Ranger veteran with two purple hearts. He described himself as having a "significantly changed personality" when he came back from Vietnam. He said he'd been very outgoing growing up, but changed to being more reserved. He had been on his own since his parents died when he was 16. He had lived with several other men in an apartment and had a large group of outgoing friends. But when he came back from Vietnam, he found that he couldn't handle crowds, and in addition:

- He would walk out of restaurants if he couldn't sit with his back to the wall.

- He only went to movies in the early morning because if someone sat anywhere behind him, he would walk out (he still does this).

- He still jumps at loud noises 50 years after his service.

- He is still bothered by the smell of mud.

- He won't touch a gun.

- He once reflexively threw his fiancée to the ground in Times Square to "protect" her when a nearby truck backfired.

- He doesn't like anyone close to him in the water even though he's always been a scuba diver.

So how does Dave handle his hyperarousal? When he first came back from Vietnam, Dave bought a one-way ticket to London and explored England and France for four months. Later, he married his fiancée and had one child. When his wife died of cancer, he left his son with his grandparents and rode a motorcycle around the country for six months (note: vibration is very modulating). He married again and had two more sons. When he got custody of them in a divorce proceeding, he quit his international high-tech job which required much travel to devote his time to being a single father. As a dad, he owned a karate studio and did active things like baseball and scouting with his kids. When his sons graduated from high school, he bought an RV and "took off again." He stated: "The trips cleared my head."

Now that Dave is retired from work and raising children, he lives in a Florida retirement community that provides the opportunity for numerous exercise programs. He has found that heavy physical exercise keeps both his body and mind fit. He engages in heavy physical training several times each day. His regimen includes 70 minutes of cardio including 10-pound weights 7 days a week, 3 yoga classes a week, and he just started Zumba classes. His hobbies include pickleball and racquetball, and he is a master diver working on dry suit certification. He enjoys massages, he travels a lot, and is very involved with friends in his community.

Dave realized early on that very heavy exercise made him feel physically and emotionally fit and helped him to function better in most situations. He has discovered the perfect sensory diet for himself, including building a home yoga studio "for more serenity."

While Dave's sensory diet is perfect for him, it is not necessary to do modulating activities as many hours a day as he does. Everyone has their own needed levels, but extended sessions are not required for the full effect of sensory diet. Short sessions several times per day will also work.

Check-In #13: Assessing the Effectiveness of Your Sensory Diet: Post-Assessment with the Sensory Over-Responsivity Inventory for Adults and the Sensory Under-Responsivity Inventory for Adults (Miller and Schoen, 2008)

The effectiveness of your sensory diet depends on its strength and on how well you stick with it. Sensory diets work immediately, but *need to be done consistently.* Give yourself 4–8 weeks of doing your sensory diet before you complete the post-assessment. You can also reassess after using your sensory diet for a longer period of time.

POST-ASSESSMENT INVENTORIES

THE SENSORY OVER-RESPONSIVITY INVENTORY FOR ADULTS (MILLER AND SCHOEN, 2008, UNPUBLISHED MANUSCRIPT). PRINTED BY PERMISSION.

Directions: Check each description that applies to you.

These garments bother me:

_____1 seams in clothing

_____2 tags in clothing

_____3 socks

_____4 changing from long to short pants

_____5 accessories (e.g., watch, jewelry, scarf, hats)

_____6 elastic on clothing

_____7 fuzzy or furry textured clothes (e.g., sweaters, collars, etc.)

_____8 wool clothes

_____ *Subtotal*

These aspects of self-care bother me:

_____9 washing or wiping face

_____10 cutting toenails or fingernails

_____11 having haircut or hair clipped

_____12 hair washing or drying

_____13 hair brushing or combing

_____14 getting dressed

_____15 brushing teeth

_____16 getting dirty

_____17 having crumbs around my mouth

_____18 having messy hands

_____19 having a messy mouth

_____*Subtotal*

These tactile sensations bother me:

_____20 mud

_____21 finger paint

_____22 glue

_____23 play dough

_____24 foods

_____25 hair care products (greasy/sticky)

_____26 kissing

_____27 coarse carpet

_____28 light stroking touch

_____*Subtotal*

These visual sensations bother me:

_____29 brightly colored or patterned materials (e.g., clothes, upholstery, drapes, wallpaper)

_____30 florescent lights

_____31 fast moving images in movies or TV

_____32 visually cluttered environments

_____33 busy pictures in books or complex and busy images in artwork

_____*Subtotal*

These smells bother me:

_____34 perfume/cologne

_____35 cleaners/disinfectants

_____36 bath products

_____37 soaps

_____38 air fresheners

_____*Subtotal*

These aspects of food and eating bother me:

_____39 salty foods (e.g., nuts or chips)

_____40 soft foods

_____41 lumpy foods

_____42 slimy foods

_____43 soup with vegetables or meat pieces

_____45 eating bread crust

_____46 food preparation/cooking

_____47 new unfamiliar foods

_____*Subtotal*

These sounds bother me:

_____48 sound of utensils against each other (e.g., spoon in bowl, knife on plate)

_____49 clothing that makes noise (e.g., swishing cloth, accessories)

_____50 doorbell ringing

_____51 dog barking

_____52 sirens

_____53 alarms

_____54 radio or TV in the background

_____55 florescent lights

_____56 someone talking when I am trying to concentrate

_____57 clock ticking

_____58 construction or landscaping equipment

_____59 water running or dripping in the background

_____*Subtotal*

Sounds in these places bother me:

_____60 toilet flushing in the bathroom

_____61 appliances/small motor noises (e.g., blender, vacuum, hair dryer, electric shaver) at home

_____62 concerts

_____63 large gatherings

_____64 restaurants

_____65 parades

_____66 malls

_____67 gymnasium

_____Subtotal

These aspects related to movement bother me:

_____68 climbing activities

_____69 walking or climbing up open stairs

_____70 experiencing heights

_____71 walking or standing on moving surfaces

_____72 playing on the playground jungle gym

_____73 playing on the playground swings or slides

_____74 going on amusement park rides

_____75 going up or down escalators

_____76 chewing foods

_____Subtotal

_____Grand Total

SENSORY UNDER-RESPONSIVITY INVENTORY FOR ADULTS (MILLER AND SCHOEN, 2008, UNPUBLISHED MANUSCRIPT). PRINTED BY PERMISSION.

Directions: Check each description that applies to you.

Typically, I have a less intense response than others to:

_____1 the doctor giving me a shot

_____2 bruises or cuts

_____3 hurting self

_____4 being touched on the arm or back (e.g., unaware)

_____5 wet or dirty clothes

_____6 dirt on myself

_____7 objects that are too hot or too cold to touch

_____8 bumping into things or falling over objects

Typically, I do not notice:

_____9 food or liquid left on lips

_____10 hands or face that are messy/dirty

_____11 drooling or food that has fallen out of mouth

_____12 the need to use the toilet

_____13 feelings of hunger (does not seek food when hungry)

_____14 over-filling mouth when eating

_____15 feelings of being "full" (must intervene to stop overeating)

_____16 strong or noxious odors

Typically, I do not notice:

_____17 activity within a busy environment

_____18 an object coming toward eyes quickly

_____19 someone entering or leaving the room

_____20 materials or people in the room needed to complete an activity

Typically, I do not respond:

_____21 when name is called or has to be touched to gain attention (hearing is OK)

_____22 when a new sound is introduced

_____23 to unexpected loud sounds (e.g., fire drills, hall bells or other loud noises)

_____24 when given directions or instructions only once

_____25 to a normal volume speaking voice (e.g., others speak loudly to gain his/her attention)

I:

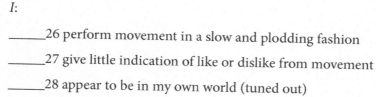

_____26 perform movement in a slow and plodding fashion

_____27 give little indication of like or dislike from movement

_____28 appear to be in my own world (tuned out)

_____29 do not visually scan the environment (look around)

_____30 leave clothing twisted on body

_____*Total*

Please note that sensory diet does not eliminate all your SMC. It should help to modulate and "even out" your nervous system's reactions so that they are not so bothersome, but when you retake the inventories, you may still have some of the same check marks. Since these inventories do not ask you to rank the *intensity* of your responses, you might find it helpful to check your responses to see how many areas have *decreased* in intensity and now bother you less. If you find that you have not made as much progress as you might desire, don't despair, keep going! Consider modifying your sensory diet by increasing the intensity, frequency, duration, and/or novelty of your plan (Chapter 8). Remember that each sensory diet component influences your nervous system for a certain length of time, and that during high-stress days, you might need stronger or more frequent activities. You may also consider finding an occupational therapist trained in the Wilbarger Therapressure Protocol™ which has the potential to decrease or eliminate some symptoms (see Appendix IV).

CHAPTER 10:

Sensory Diet Activities for Military, First Responder, and Frontline Medical Personnel

More on the Second "D" in DIAL IT DOWN: Sensory "Diet" Additional Activities to Consider Including in Your Sensory Diet

In past chapters, we've discussed SMC (sensory modulation challenges) and the wellness self-treatments for it. In Chapter 9, we looked at ways to build a sensory diet from activities you already enjoy doing. *The goal of this chapter is to review an additional range of activities you may choose to incorporate into your personal sensory diet.* Though you will already be familiar with some of these activities, we'll discuss different ways to both "amp up" the familiar and consider venturing into the unfamiliar. Some activities will appeal to you and others will not. Look at them as possibilities *for yourself.* If you don't like them, you're less likely to do them, so feel free to cross them off your list. In considering new activities, please remember that in order for sensory diets (and sensory breaks) to work well, they have to actually *be a mental and physical break from your normal daily activities* like work and taking care of children; if they're not, your nervous system will simply keep functioning at its present level. If you try an activity that doesn't seem at first to change your modulation level, you can experiment with changing its intensity, frequency, duration, and/or rhythm for added sensory power.

Also remember that *everyone's sensory needs are different and may change by the day or even the minute, depending on what types of sensory inputs are "bombarding" your nervous system.* If you're in a relatively calm place when disruptive sensory inputs reach you, a few light sensory diet activities may work to get your arousal level to that "just right place" for what you want to do. But if you're stressed, anxious, or angry (high arousal), or depressed (low arousal), it will take stronger sensory diet activities to change your arousal level.

Finally, please remember, as has been said before, that *it's all in the timing. Sensory breaks work the best when they're spread throughout the day and are done **before** your nervous system becomes overloaded* (you *can* use sensory activities to help yourself come back "down" from an overload, but this will take much more time and effort than prevention).

Each type of activity ("heavy work," "head-through-space" vestibular, firm touch pressure, etc.) has a different *duration* of impact on the nervous system and may take a different amount of time to "start working." It usually takes a minimum of 5 *minutes* of an activity to alter the nervous system, and it may take longer. I often suggest a 20-to-30-minute heavy workout once a day (or even twice if possible) with "mini-workout" sensory diet activities of 5 to 10 minutes spaced throughout the remainder of the day as often as you need them (generally, at least 90 minutes to 2 hours apart). Some people need much more sensory input to keep their brains calmly alert. Others may only need a few 10-minute sessions spaced throughout the day. *The point is to pick activities that you like to do, will continue to do, and that you feel change **your** alertness and stress levels.* It's important to be as realistic as you can about your schedule: sensory diet activities *must fit in with your other life responsibilities.* Involving your children and/or other family members, friends, and colleagues with you in sensory diet activities can be very rewarding. If you have a job with intermittent high stress, try to plan sensory diet activities during your "down" times. If you are a healthcare worker with prolonged high stress during a shift, you will find that even a 3-5-minute sensory break will help keep you modulated and focused (see the list of specific "emergency break" activities at the end of this chapter).

Sensory Diet/ Sensory Break Activity Suggestions for Veterans, First Responders, and Medical Workers

Once you are aware of the sensory qualities you're looking for in modulating activities, it's easy to discover activities that fit your preferences and needs. Most of the following activities can be done at home with little equipment.

1. Vestibular or rhythmic movement of head through space activities (these also include heavy work):

   a. Jumping jacks

   b. Jumping/skipping rope

   c. Running of all types, especially carrying extra weight (see 4b below)

   d. Jumping on a rebounder (mini trampoline)

   e. Skiing (water and snow), snow boarding

2. Proprioceptive or heavy work with the joints and muscles (heavier varieties):

   a. Pushups

   b. Wear a weighted vest. (Caution: if you're a veteran, be careful about using the pressure vests sold for athletes to wear under clothing as these may trigger flashbacks due to their similarity to flak jackets. As suggested earlier, for an inexpensive version that should feel safer, you can make your own loose-fitting weighted vest using a fishing or hunting vest from a discount store. Fill the pockets with stones or fishing weights or take apart 5-pound adjustable weights and use the individual weight sleeves in your vest.)

   c. Chinning bar (door frame bars are inexpensive and easy to install)

   d. Marching (cross country or in place, particularly with a heavy step, and wearing a backpack or wrist and/or ankle weights: judge ankle weight carefully so as not to strain your back)

e. Walking up and down stairs wearing a backpack, wrist and/or ankle weights

f. Biking, especially off-road biking (note that both biking and swimming include strong vestibular input)

g. Swimming laps, especially outdoors or in a quiet pool. Indoor pools are often very noisy, and they echo. You can always wear earplugs to reduce noise (be sure to use *silicone* earplugs in the water, not foam): they have the added benefit of keeping water out of your ears if that is an issue for you.

h. Water games: water polo, water volleyball, Marco Polo (with your kids)

i. Surfing

j. Yoga

k. Dance classes: Zumba, Tap, Hip-Hop, Ballet, Ballroom, Rock-and-Roll (both the music and movement are modulating)

l. Rowing

m. Weight training, using slow repetitions

n. Any gymnastics workout

o. Play wrestling: can be done with two adults or two children or one adult and one child. The idea is to playfully wrestle on the floor using heavy work. There is *no tickling allowed*, as that can be torture for someone with sensory modulation challenges. And there is a strict rule that if one person says "Stop," the wrestling stops immediately.

3. Proprioceptive or heavy work with joints and muscles (lighter versions than above that can be done in many environments; some can be done without others even being aware that you're doing them):

a. Bouncing, so that your heels strike the ground with your knees straight to get a slight jarring through the body (this also adds vestibular/movement of head)

b. Firmly pushing the heels of your hands together, alternately pushing and releasing

c. Curling your fingers, hooking your hands together with your elbows horizontal and then pulling against your fingers for resistance, alternately pulling and releasing

d. Placing your hands on the top of your head and then alternately pushing down toward the floor and releasing (be careful to keep the neck perfectly straight so as not to aggravate neck issues, and use light to medium pressure only)

e. Holding your hands up near your shoulders, with your elbows bent near your waist, and rapidly shaking your hands back and forth (feel the effect of traction on your wrist, hand and finger joints)

f. Chair pushups: sit on a chair, place your hands on the seat and push your bottom off the seat several times (if your arms are short, you may need to lean forward to do this)

g. Carrying heavy objects (groceries, books): this works best if you carry them close to the body to reduce back strain

h. Carrying a heavy backpack

i. Chair pull-ups: sit on a chair, curl your fingers or place your hands under the seat of the chair, and pull your bottom down firmly into the seat (you will feel strong resistance in your arms and core); repeat several times. This works well anywhere as it is not distracting, and most people will not notice that you're doing it.

j. Wall push-ups: can be done at work, in restrooms, or stairwells during breaks

k. Clapping in rhythms: make up various rhythms, or clap in time to your favorite song

l. While seated on a chair, push down on your knees in a rhythmic manner (off-on)

m. Vibration: mowing the lawn, vibrating seat cushions or chairs

4. The strongest activities combine rhythmic movement of the head and heavy work. Be sure to follow all safety rules.

For example:

a. Jumping rope on a mini tramp

b. Running with additional weight on your body (backpack or weighted vest)

c. High-impact or extreme sports like downhill skiing (particularly fast or over moguls), mountain biking, rock climbing, marathons, Ironman competitions, etc.

d. Participating in sports like football, running, tennis, and kayaking

e. Motor sports also add vibration: riding motorcycles, dirt bikes, ATVs, snowmobiles (remember helmets)

5. Heavy (firm) pressure on the skin:

a. The classic backrub. Have someone give you a heavy (firm) rub on your back, *as the back is the least sensory-defensive area to touch*. Remember that light touch alerts us to danger, *so be sure they touch you firmly*. Also, state your preference for the strength of the rub (very hard, hard, medium), and know that you can direct the backrub at all times.

b. Take your hand and, firmly and quickly, rub your arms (on your skin or through your clothing; both will work). You also can rub the tops of your thighs through clothing while remaining seated (if you have your own office or access to an empty employee break room, you can do this at work).

c. While bathing, rub yourself with a bath sponge (loofah) or a face cloth.

6. Things for the mouth that give short-acting "sensory snacks" (not called that because they're food, but because they contribute a small, snack-like amount of modulating sensation to the nervous system):

a. Resistive chewing and tugging activities

    i. Gum: all real gum and some sugarless gums provide resistance and therefore heavy work for the jaw. Two or three pieces of "Double Bubble" or similar gum work very well. Resistive sugar-free gum includes Spry, which is good for the teeth.

    ii. Other resistive candies include Tootsie Rolls, Gummy Bears, Swedish Fish, and Twizzlers

    iii. Resistive chewing also includes crunchy items, like heavy pretzel rods, apples, carrots, and jerky

    iv. A water bottle that requires strong sucking (like some types with built-in straws) rather than sipping

b. Sour, sharp, or spicy foods have been found to be modulating

    i. Sour Patch Kids, Sour Gummy Bears (at the movies, I overheard a couple discussing whether they'd "bought enough sour candy to keep the kids paying attention through the movie")

    ii. Atomic Fireballs candy

    iii. Lemon hard candy

    iv. Spicy salsa with heavy corn chips for crunch (heavy mouth work)

7. Listening to music:

Why do live music and some recordings help modulate our nervous systems while other recordings do not? Recordings such as *Mozart for Modulation, Baroque for Modulation,* and *More Mozart for Modulation* (see References) are recorded in full spectrum and are *specially mastered to intensify the high-frequency sounds and overtones that are thought to influence modulation.* They can be played at a low background level or through headphones. Certain chants and drumming also work, as does music at live concerts if you can tolerate the crowds. Regular classical recordings also can be helpful. It is suggested that you vary the types of music you listen to in order to see which types actually help you concentrate. The hard part is differentiating between music you like to listen to emotionally, and music that doesn't distract you and actually helps you focus. As noted previously, most popular music (Rock, Country, etc.) recordings do not work as well for modulation due to the way they're processed to fit the download file size.

8. Playing music:

Playing music by yourself on instruments like the guitar, piano, or string instruments adds modulated sound as well as vibration. Playing wind and brass instruments requires deep breathing, another modulating component. Drumming of any type is modulating.

9. Deep breathing:

Place one hand on the top of your upper chest and one on your stomach. See where most of your breathing comes from. Stressed people tend to breathe from their chests with a shallow and rapid pattern, which is the pattern we use if we're at an increased fight-or-flight (sympathetic arousal) level. Try to breathe so that the hand on your *stomach* moves. Take a few deep breaths moving your stomach hand; this helps to shift your nervous system toward homeostasis (parasympathetic response).

10. Meditation:

There are many different types of meditation, and all are aimed at lowering our arousal levels so that we can feel calmer and more in control. Many people feel that Transcendental meditation is particularly effective in helping them to achieve this state, although it involves an intensive training program. Mindfulness meditation is becoming very popular and can be done anywhere. It involves keeping your mind focused on being in the "present moment," consciously observing and "staying fully present" in that moment. Even if it is not an easy or pleasant moment, it is observed and accepted for what it is without blame or judgment. Research on meditation has shown that it can lower anxiety, frequency of panic attacks, and blood pressure, as well as help with insomnia (Goldin & Gross, 2010; Walsh & Shapiro, 2006).

11. Prayer and other spiritual practices:

    The spiritual practices of many different faiths have been shown to lower blood pressure and reduce anxiety.

12. Routines: We know that routines can contribute to modulation by lowering anxiety. The only caution is to make sure that these routines don't become so rigidly, inflexibly followed that they interfere with relationships or become obsessive/compulsive behaviors.

13. Spending time in a natural environment:

    Being outdoors in an environment with trees and other vegetation, water, natural views, and natural sounds is modulating. Decreasing the manmade "noise" around us helps, but more than that, the sounds of nature are modulating in themselves. The variety of high-frequency and other natural sounds acts on our brains to influence modulation: birds singing, water rippling in a brook, waves on the beach, the wind blowing, and leaves rustling in trees all help to reduce over-arousal.

    Additional modulating aspects of nature include visual input without "clutter" and without the fast, random movements that occur in a city: think of scenes such as sitting on a beach watching the waves, seeing the view from on top of a mountain, or walking through a forest looking at the moss underfoot and at how the sunlight plays through the trees. Some people feel that being in natural environments is a form of meditation. For example, some hunters report that they go hunting mainly because it gives them a chance to spend hours in the woods sitting in one spot just observing the natural world.

    All of the above places also have natural *smells* (salt in the ocean air; decomposing leaves in the forest; pine pitch) which can be very modulating to the powerful olfactory region of our brains (the reptile "smell brain") discussed in Chapter 5.

14. Self-medicating:

Some people may drink excessively or use street drugs as a way to "take the edge off" of the anxiety caused by sensory modulation challenges. This is not your best option, and in fact, may lead to the opposite outcome, as drugs and excess alcohol come with the steep "price tag" of a rebound effect (your system may become edgy after the initial mellowness of alcohol wears off; your system may become jittery and depressed as you come off of any "high"; and these ups and downs get in the way of building the steady calm state we've discussed as the goal of sensory modulation). If this is the way you have been coping with your sensory modulation issues and/or anxiety, please consider the alternative ways offered in this book, as well as other treatments for PTS and PTSD. And please seek help for any addiction issues you may have developed. Help is available through trained therapists and/or through attending programs like Alcoholics Anonymous.

15. Others:

Now that you know the key ingredients in sensory diets and sensory breaks, you can add ideas of your own. If you factor in the sensory guidelines we've discussed, are honest with yourself about what works for you and what doesn't, and take reasonable safety precautions, anything—from skydiving to scuba diving—is possible.

Existing Programs That Can Be Incorporated Into a Sensory Diet Program

Please note: While many of the programs listed below were specifically developed for military veterans and service members, these programs additionally offer valuable models of modulating sensory input that can be adapted to fit the needs of first responders and frontline medical workers experiencing PTS and PTSD.

Numerous programs have been developed to help veterans and service members dealing with the trauma of war. These programs include intense physical activities which you now know are sensory diet activities. But they also incorporate many military skill-sets, and are usually done with other military personnel for "unit" or "squad" identity. Many are provided over a special weekend, sometimes including activities for partners and children. Some occur once a week. The special weekend programs provide an intensity of physical and psychological work that's designed to show participants what can be possible in their lives. Often, however, daily follow-up using the same activities may not be practical (for example, rock climbing or skiing), so sustaining the gains you've made at the level you attained during the weekend will require you to problem-solve possible alternative activities after you're back home. The one-day-a-week programs can add consistent sensory input and coping skills, but again, for the results to carry over into your life for more than a day or two will require planning.

These programs can be an important part of healing if you can get to one, and they can certainly jump-start your sensory diet program or move it forward. But sensory diet needs to be done throughout *each* day. Therefore, these programs can only be *part* of your sensory diet. Remember, *timing is everything!* It's important for you and your family to understand that it's possible to maintain the gains from these programs only if you add in sensory diet practices once you return home.

PATH International Equine Services for Heroes

PATH is the Professional Association of Therapeutic Horsemanship International (pathintl.org). It provides veterans who were active duty since 9/11 with free riding sessions at PATH-approved barns. (As noted in Chapter 9, first responders and frontline medical personnel with sensory modulation challenges, PTS, and PTSD can also greatly benefit from horseback riding.) Why does riding work as part of a sensory diet (some of these benefits were briefly mentioned in Chapter 9)?

- Rhythmic movement of the horse moves your head through space (vestibular)

- Your hips, back, and legs are in the perfect position to support muscle tone and develop core and leg muscles

- Every movement adds proprioception (joint and muscle work)

- "Neutral warmth" from the horse's body is modulating

- The emotional component is very strong: the rider's connection to the horse, and the horse's attentiveness to the rider

- The ability to work successfully with a large animal is empowering

- Being in a large, generally outdoor, space is modulating

- Currying (brushing) the animal is heavy work

See the award-winning video about one special veteran (Rob Foley) and horses: "A Different Journey-Full Circle," a 2017 EQUUS Film Festival #1 National Award winner (D'Apice & Foley, 2017), listed in the References section.

Artists for Peace and Freedom

This is a unique art therapy program ("action painting") in which veterans vigorously "throw" paint onto a large canvas that's placed outside in a natural setting. Each veteran picks their colors to physically "throw away" some aspect of their pain. They then discuss the meaning of the abstract painting they've created with other veterans. This program was started and brought to Maine by a veteran from Denmark. The program's founders are now looking for ways to expand it to other states. A video about this program is available on Vimeo (see the References section [D'Apice & Foley, 2018]).

Sensory Enhanced Yoga

Many types of yoga have been self-reported as beneficial by veterans, first responders, and frontline medical personnel who suffer from PTS and PTSD. Research on the effectiveness of yoga is ongoing, but one peer-reviewed study in particular looked at 70 military personnel who'd been deployed to Iraq (Stroller et al., 2012). They were randomized into two groups, the sensory-enhanced yoga group and a control group. 35 received sensory-enhanced hatha yoga for nine sessions or more and 35 received no yoga. Each yoga participant attended a minimum of two sessions per week and a total of nine sessions for a 3-week period. The sensory-enhanced yoga group was provided with yoga classes to which increased heavy sensory input was added. The results showed that yoga reduced state and trait anxiety, and that there was significant improvement in 16 of 18 measured mental health and quality-of-life factors. (The Adolescent/Adult Sensory Profile, which is used to measure sensory modulation issues, did not show change, but the authors felt that this may have been due to random grouping factors that did not equally distribute service members with higher sensory needs into both groups.) The conclusions from the study were that "a sensory enhanced hatha yoga program successfully reduced symptoms of combat stress and improved occupational performance in deployed military personnel" (Stroller et al., 2012, p. 67).

Extreme Sports

Extreme sports adventures work as sensory diet input for individuals who are extreme sensory seekers. *XSports4vets* in Montana provides white water rafting and other "extreme" activities. The *Warrior Adventure Quest Program,* run by the Army at Ft. Benning, Georgia, is another "extreme" program designed for the reintegration of returning soldiers. It uses "high-adventure, adrenaline-boosting outdoor activities such as whitewater rafting, skiing, paintball, rock climbing and scuba diving" (Molinaro, 2009).

These activities are widely available through clubs and companies throughout the country, and should be considered as sensory diet additions by any first responders and medical personnel who enjoy extreme sports.

Maine Adaptive Sports and Recreation:
No Boundaries Program

This program is free to any veteran with a disability. In the winter, it provides adapted downhill skiing, cross-country skiing, snowboarding, and snowshoeing. In the summer, it offers kayaking, canoeing, golf, fishing, hiking, and cycling. Spouses or significant others can also attend for free. For those "from away" (not from Maine), lodging and air fare can be provided.

Weekend programs also include family members and time to bond with other participants. (See https://www.maineadaptive.org for further information.)

The *Adaptive Sports Center* in Colorado offers scholarships and discounted rates to veterans and first responders with disabilities, and many other "adaptive sports" programs throughout the country do as well. These programs should also be considered by any frontline medical personnel with disabilities who are seeking to expand their range of potential sensory diet activities.

Wounded Warrior Project

The Wounded Warrior Project provides free programs for mind, body, and social engagement to "veterans and service members who incurred a physical or mental injury, illness, or wound while serving in the military on or after September 11, 2001" (https://woundedwarriorproject.org). Their Project Odyssey Veterans Retreat program provides a retreat and then continuing services aimed at helping veterans work through combat stress and mental health issues. "Activities include horseback riding, canoeing, whitewater rafting, kayaking, rock climbing, a high ropes course, fishing, skeet shooting, sled hockey, and skiing at retreats held in various locations across the country" (https://www.woundedwarriorproject.org/programs/combat-stress-recovery-program/project-odyssey).

Surfing Programs

The *Jimmy Miller Memorial Foundation* provides a free Ocean Therapy adaptive surfing program which assists "individuals coping with mental and physical illness in accessing the ocean environment" (http://jimmymiller-foundation.org/). The program is available to Marines at Camp Pendleton and to veterans through the West Los Angeles VA Hospital at Manhattan Beach, CA. Research on the program shows that veterans who attended it "reported meaningful improvement in PTSD symptom severity...and in depressive symptoms" (Rogers et al., 2014, p. 395).

First responders and frontline medical personnel who have an interest in surfing should research surfing programs in their areas: surfing can provide strong vestibular and proprioceptive as well as heavy touch input as part of a sensory diet.

"Not-So-Extreme" Sports

Family-friendly activities like:

- Hikes
- Swimming
- Bike riding
- Mountain biking
- Play wrestling
- Football
- Running

Participation Activities

- Yard work
- Cleaning
- Gardening
- Cutting brush and trees
- Moving furniture
- Volunteering for agencies that need "heavy work" like *Habitat for Humanity*

Dogs

Many organizations provide companion and service dogs for veterans and first responders. Dogs offer the following benefits:

- Unconditional love: the human-animal bond has been shown in many studies to lessen stress and anxiety and reduce feelings of isolation
- Dogs get their humans outside for walks – giving the sensory benefits of movement and the outdoors

- Dogs demand that their humans develop routines (routines are modulating)

- Dogs provide "neutral warmth," which is modulating, with their bodies by sitting or sleeping on or with you

- Dogs provide "heavy work" in many ways: tugging on leashes, play-wrestling

- Dogs alert their humans to approaching people, potentially offsetting the perceived need for hyper-alertness

- Dogs buffer their humans from unwanted touch from others

- Dogs provide heavy touch/pressure

- Dogs provide a nonthreatening way to interact with others

- Large dogs are the best for sensory diet (they provide heavier pressure, and it's heavier work to walk them)

- In choosing a dog, be mindful of the pitch of the dog's bark, as some small dogs have "annoying" high-pitched barks that are difficult to stop and may exacerbate existing auditory sensory challenges

Music as Sensory Input

In addition to the special recordings for modulation discussed in earlier chapters, there are also listening therapy programs which can help with modulation. Some of these can be bought online, but most are first prescribed and carried out in an occupational therapy setting so that the best program and music can be selected to address the person's specific listening/auditory issues. They include:

- Tomatis Method

- Therapeutic Listening (Sheila Frick)

- Auditory Integration Training (Berard)

- The Listening Program

- Integrated Listening Systems

Common Features:

- Listening programs are used with adults with anxiety, sound hyper-sensitivity (including auditory sensory defensiveness), and attention issues

- They train the brain to process sound more efficiently

- Auditory processing problems may develop in adulthood as a component of many types of central nervous system processing issues, including PTS, PTSD, and mTBI

- The music in these listening programs is electronically filtered so that the listener's focus can be on specific frequencies known to be therapeutic

- Right and left ear sound balance is varied to engage both sides of the brain

Summary

This is just a glimpse of the near-limitless array of activities that can be included in your sensory diet. Pick the ones you like, try various durations, times of day, and intensity levels, and enjoy the benefits as your nervous system modulation improves. Consider inviting your family and friends to participate with you.

Reproducible Handout

What can you do if you get overloaded when you have no time to do your usual sensory diet, for example, a sensory overload at work or in a store? Consider photocopying this handout and keeping it available as a "go-to" in your wallet:

The 3-to-5-minute "Emergency" Sensory Snack

Here is a list of activities that are easy, take little time, and can tide you over until you can do more sensory work:

- Wall pushups in a stairwell or restroom

- Jumping jacks in the hall or break room

- With your knees straight, bounce heavily on your heels

- Chair push-ups (put both hands on your chair next to your bottom and push it off the chair)

- Chair pull-ups (hook all your fingers under your chair and pull your bottom down into the seat)

- Put the heels of your hands together, elbows out to the side and alternately push and release

- Hook your fingers together, elbows out to the side and alternately *pull* and release

- Leave an exercise band or tube in your desk, purse, or backpack to do a few arm or leg exercises

- Walk up and down several flights of stairs

- Have someone else stand behind you and alternately push firmly on your shoulders in a downward direction and release

CHAPTER 11:

Talking About It

The "O" in DIAL IT DOWN: "Own" It

How to Begin the Conversation

Now that you know about sensory modulation challenges and have evaluated yourself through numerous Check-Ins, it's time to share your understanding with others. If you are the person with sensory modulation challenges, it would be helpful to show another person in your life the portions of this book that you feel specifically apply to you. If you are the spouse or friend of a person you think has SMC, it would be helpful to show that person the parts of the book that you feel apply to them. Pick a quiet time without the possibility of interruptions for your discussion. You might want to mark the portions of the book that you feel they should read, leave the book with them, and agree to meet again at a later time. Remember that this is a *new way* of looking at what may be going on in your lives, and so it might take time for them to understand and get used to this different point of view.

Discussing sensory modulation challenges and agreeing that they are present in your lives are key steps toward "owning" or taking responsibility for these issues – but please keep in mind that this agreement might not come easily, or all at once, as in the example of the occupational therapist and her spouse with SMC in Chapter 6. Remember to *leave time* for your partner or spouse to process this new information; and if hurt feelings or misunderstandings persist, you might consider seeking the help of a trained therapist to facilitate communication. Occupational therapists have the most training in sensory issues; and some couples counselors are also beginning to understand them. If you are the spouse or partner of someone with SMC, it's important for you to understand that none of us likes to be "labeled": labels are valuable as "toolkits" to help address issues with daily life and functioning, but you also need to communicate that you don't view any label as definitive of the whole person whom you love. Please see the "Communication Strategies" section below for more information about ways to discuss the effects of sensory modulation challenges on your lives.

When and if your partner or spouse does accept that these issues are present, you'll be ready to move on to the next step, that of jointly addressing how to *deal with* these challenges. You will need to reach accommodations concerning finding time for sensory diet activities, and you may wish to discuss whether family members would like to get involved in doing sensory diet activities together. You should also discuss what can be done *if*—in spite of the best sensory wellness plan—at times, sensations become too much and cause a defensive reaction (like "losing it" or "shutting down"). If you're the person with sensory modulation challenges, having a shared "emergency plan" can be very helpful to family and friends who may feel powerless to help you and may even react in a hurt or angry way, both because of their sense of powerlessness, and/or because they don't fully understand the intense impact that environmental sensations can have on you. (As discussed in earlier chapters, we tend to judge others' sensory responses by our own responses, and if you haven't talked to family and friends about your SMC, they may unconsciously make assumptions like, "This noise [or touch, or smell, or clutter] doesn't bother me, so why should it bother you?") Making accommodations like suddenly having to leave a "fun" event will be easier for a partner to accept and understand if you've discussed beforehand the possibility of your senses being overloaded by the noise, crowds, etc. Your partner can even help you brainstorm preplanned alternatives to "dial it down" during crowded events: for example, you can make a plan to go sit out in the car if you're starting to feel your stress level rising and do some breathing and resistance stretching with an exercise band for ten minutes. Or if you are at an event where you're seated, you can place your feet flat on the floor and just push down hard on your knees, alternating between pushing and releasing for a few minutes. Even if you don't *feel* your stress level rising, you can proactively plan to do these things after a certain number of minutes (defined by you) of participating in the event, in order to keep yourself more modulated for the remainder of it.

Of course, simply knowing about sensory modulation challenges will not solve all of your sensory communication issues: situations, responses, and feelings change over time, and so *ongoing* communication about your and your partner's different responses to life is essential. The following sections offer some optional strategies to help with communication. Please remember that everyone, not just people with SMC, could use guidance and help with communication at one time or another.

Communication Strategies

"*I* STATEMENTS"

What is your normal way of communicating with others if you're not totally happy about what they're doing? If you are like most people, you probably use "*you* statements," and "always" and "never" statements. These are assertions like: "You always forget to carry out the garbage!" and "You're always spending time with your buddies; what about our family time?" and "Why do you always react negatively to everything I suggest?" and "You never listen to me!" For most people on the receiving end, "*you* statements" feel like blame, as others are telling them what they did wrong or what they failed to do. This is especially true of people with sensory modulation challenges: these accusations can evoke feelings that are much stronger than the speaker intended or than what most people without sensory modulation challenges would feel, as they often bridge into that sensitive area of the different, *intensified* responses that people with SMC have to the environment around them, including the family/home environment with all of its noise, clutter, touch, and strong expectations to be fully *present* at all times. For instance, "You never take out the garbage" could connect to the listener's sensory defensiveness around strong smells; "You never help the kids with homework" could connect to the listener's sensory defensiveness around sound and visual clutter, if homework tends to be done at a crowded table with lots of background noise; and "You always turn away when the kids try to kiss you" could connect to the listener's tactile sensitivity to light touch and sticky mouths. Each individual with SMC is different and each home environment is different: this is why effective, open communication about feelings and challenges is so important.

One way to communicate without blame that's commonly taught in therapeutic settings is using "*I* statements." "*I* statements" shift the focus away from the person who's being "blamed" and back to the person who's making the statement. Therefore, the person making the statement takes responsibility for *their own* feelings about the issue and changes the "blaming *you*" statement to an "*I* feel this way" statement. The "*I* statement" traditionally has four parts:

1. When _____

2. I feel _____

3. Because _____

4. What I would like (or want) is _____

The "when" is about a *specific behavior* that the speaker is responding to.

The "I feel" is the *emotion* that the speaker feels about this behavior.

The "because" is about *the speaker's unmet need* and their *thoughts about* that unmet need.

The "what I would like or want" is *behavior that would meet* the speaker's expressed need.

Note that the *"you"* **has to stay out of** *all parts* **of an "*I* statement,"** or it goes right back to being a "*you* [blaming] statement." This isn't about who did what to whom; instead, it's about how one person *feels* about what happened and how these feelings or the misunderstandings surrounding them *can be resolved.*

EXAMPLES OF "I STATEMENTS"

1. When the garbage isn't carried out, I feel anxious because I hate the smell, and I worry about mice. What I really need is for the garbage

to be outside in the garbage can. (Notice that there is no "you" here, and the possibility that someone else [like the speaker] could take out the garbage is left open – therefore no blame is attached.)

2.   When I think I'm not being listened to, I feel like I'm not important, because that's what I've experienced from my family growing up and my relationships in the past. That makes me feel hurt and upset. What I need is for the person I'm speaking to, to in some way, acknowledge that they heard me.

3.   When I'm home alone with the kids on Saturday, I feel angry because my idea of a family has always been spending time together. What I need is to find a way to have more family time.

Try converting some of your "*you* statements" to "*I* statements." It will be hard at first, as "*you* statements" are *a habit that we all fall into*. But keep trying, and maybe even laugh with your partner at your first (probably as awkward as learning to ride a bike!) attempts. This learning curve is natural. Be sure to celebrate your successes, too!

LISTENING AS A PARTNERSHIP EXPERIENCE

One of the things we all want in life is *to be heard*. When our friends or partner appear not to "hear" us, this can evoke many strong emotions, and can often lay the groundwork for misunderstandings and arguments. For example, we have probably all experienced coming home tired from our day at work and being met by several people wanting to talk to us at the same time. This can feel like an "attack" or "overload" for anyone, but for a person with sensory modulation challenges it definitely *is* a *sensory* attack. One way of dealing with this is to set up a "coming home routine" like those which were mentioned in Chapter 6 (an additional example will be shown in a personal story in Chapter 12), with all family members understanding that you need some "sensory break" time before you can fully take in what they're saying.

Another way to be sure that you are both *listening* and *being heard* in a partner dynamic is to set aside time to talk and respond. We all know that in practice this often doesn't work, as one person may tend to dominate the "conversation," but there are ways to organize conversations so that each person *is* heard.

1. First, agree that you will have an organized communication time.

2. Pick a time that will be free from interruption.

3. Pick a length of time that is doable for you and your partner and will allow you to cover the specific issue at hand (8 minutes, 12 minutes, 20 minutes).

4. Divide the time in half so that each of you has your own time.

Here is the first script:

5. The first person, the talker, talks for the designated length of time **without** *the other person interrupting or commenting in any way* (example: 2 minutes each).

6. The second person, the listener, listens intently to the first person, concentrating only on what the first person is saying and *not* on anything the second person wants to say in rebuttal. In fact, *there is **no** rebuttal as this is about **just listening** intently*.

7. When the first person, the talker, is finished talking for the designated length of time, the second person *summarizes* what was said, *without adding commentary*. They say, "What I heard you say was_____."

8. When the second person, the listener, has finished summarizing, the first person may correct any misunderstanding of their initial statement, but again, there is *no* discussion of the points.

9. Now it is the second person's opportunity to be heard by reversing the roles.

The second script:

After trying out the first script several times, you may if you wish move on to the second script, which is essentially the same as the first, except that now you can offer some affirmative head nods, "ahs," etc., though again, *no discussion* during the listening or "what I heard you say" times. *This is still about really **paying attention** to the other person, listening and letting them know you've heard them fully.* It is not the time for you to be thinking about what *you* want to say or how you are feeling about or responding to the information they're sharing with you.

When you have tried this several times, you may find yourself *asking clarifying questions during your listening*, but again, do *not* get into a discussion during the sharing time. If you want to engage in a back-and-forth discussion, save this step until after each person has had a turn to speak.

(If you are interested in reading a very short book about the basis for this method, look at Jackson, H. (1978), *The Human Side of Human Beings: The Theory of Re-Evaluation Counseling*, Rational Island Publishers.)

Please note that if you have sensory modulation challenges, doing a short (10-minute) sensory workout *before* sitting down to listen will be extremely helpful in moving you toward being modulated and receptive, rather than defensive. (The point is not that you *agree* with what's being said by your partner – it is that you keep your mind [with its powerful connections to your sensory system!] open to *hearing* what's being said.)

Nonverbal Communication

The need and ability to communicate verbally, which requires good listening skills, goes hand-in-hand with the need to communicate **nonverbally**, which requires good *observational* skills. We've all experienced uncomfortable moments when a person's words didn't match their body language. Numerous books have been written about the meanings of different body movements or positions. The key "takeaway" for partner dynamics isn't what textbooks say about the significance of any given gesture, but rather that you *ask* the person what they may be feeling if you notice that their words and body language don't match. Say something like, "I know what you just said, but I get the feeling that there's more to this conversation. Can you help me understand this better?"

The Principles and Skills of Loving

Underlying our need to be heard is our need to be loved. Just saying that you love someone is not enough. Outside the bounds of Hollywood mythology, you don't just "fall" in love. Jerry Jud, as reported by Jim Hession (2003), believes that "love is an intention...that there are skills in learning how to love and there are skills in doing it" (p. 4). Jerry Jud came up with the Principles and Skills of Loving, quoted below:

LOVE IS AN INTENTION

Principles of Loving

More than anything else, we want to love and be loved.

Love is a gift.

Love is good will in action.

Love is a response to need.

Skills of Loving

Seeing: I do not look over or through you. I see you in your uniqueness.

Hearing: I listen to what you are saying.

Honoring of Feelings and Ideas: I recognize your right to feel and think as you do.

Having Good Will: I will you good and not evil.

Responding to Need: If you let me know what your needs are, within the limits of my value system, I will not run away. I will be there for you (Hession, 2003, p. 25).

Jud goes on to further explain the Skills of Loving, in the following passage:

LOVE IS AN INTENTION

SEEING

I do not look over you, under you, through you. I see you in your uniqueness.

I need to be seen. I want to be seen. SEE ME!

HEARING

I listen for the meaning behind your words.

I need you to hear me, not just my words. I need you to help me say what I intend and to hear the message behind my words.

FEELINGS AND IDEAS

I recognize your right to feel and think as you do. I may not agree with your feelings and ideas but you are entitled to them because you are human.

Only when I fully acknowledge my feelings and ideas can I grow. If in your presence I can be honest and open about my feelings and ideas, then I can be honest, open and can grow.

GOOD WILL

I HAVE GOOD WILL FOR YOU. I will you good and not evil. I care about you.

I need your good will, your help and understanding, in order to develop my potential. Alone I cannot grow. I need your caring.

NEEDS

YOU HAVE NEEDS. If you disclose them to me, within the limits of my value system, I will not run away. I will be there for you.

If I am left alone with my needs, where shall I turn? I can only deny having them, stuff them down or pretend they do not exist – or seek to have them fulfilled in some devious way. I need to believe that when I share my needs with you, you will not run away (Hession, 2003, pp. 27-28).

From: Hession, J. *Love is an Intention: An Interview with Jerry Jud about the Principles and Skills of Loving* (see References).

CHECK-IN #14: Talk about it.

This is the "O" for "Own It" in Dial It Down. Truly "own" your sensory issues and their emotional effects on you and on the people you love by *talking* about these issues.

Now that you know about sensory modulation challenges, are you ready to take the next step of "owning it" and talking about these challenges with someone you care about? Yes_____ No_____

If "No," what do you believe to be your main barriers to doing so? How might you overcome them? (Some possibilities to consider if you answer "No" to this or any of the Check-In questions below would be taking more time to understand your own issues, and/or working privately with a trained occupational therapist, and/or seeking out a therapist to talk to first in a "neutral" space outside of family dynamics. Remember that *understanding is key*, both for your emotional wellbeing and the emotional wellbeing of the people you love; so do reach out to a professional for support in taking this step if needed.)

_____

_____

If "Yes," who will you talk to? _____

What specifically will you reveal about your sensory modulation challenges and how they affect your functioning and participation in life activities?

_____

_____

Are you willing to explain some of the concepts in Dial It Down?
Yes_____ No _____

If "No," please see the possibilities listed above.
If "Yes," what are the most important concepts to you?

_____

_____

Can you ask the person to understand you and help you?
Yes _____ No _____

If "Yes," what can you ask them to do (be specific)?

_____

_____

_____

Are you willing to hear the other person's reactions to your sharing?

Yes _____ No _____

If "Yes," what did they say that surprised you?

_____

_____

_____

What did they say that might be helpful to you?

_____

_____

_____

CHAPTER 12:

A Life Story Illustrating the Use of
Sensory Modulation Methods

The "W" in DIAL IT DOWN: "Win-Win"

The following is the story of a veteran who, after learning about sensory modulation challenges, very successfully developed her own sensory diet program and then in addition decided to be treated using the Wilbarger Therapressure Protocol™. Her use of strategies to "Dial It Down" became a win for her *and* a win for her family and friends, as she was able to participate more fully in all areas of her life. She has graciously allowed me to report her story to help others with SMC.

"Sydney's" Story

Sydney was a participant in a research study I conducted on sensory processing styles in military veterans with PTSD. After the study was completed, she participated in several optional individual feedback sessions where she became interested in having her story told, as she wanted to support others with SMC.

Sydney was assaulted while serving in the military 20 years ago, and was subsequently diagnosed with PTSD. She is married and has two adult children. In addition to her PTSD diagnosis, over the years, she has also been diagnosed with lupus, polymyositis, possible fibromyalgia due to severe pain, seizures, and more recently, possible scleroderma. Sydney finds any touch to be painful, but heavier pressure is more tolerable for her. The treatment history for her pain has been very complicated as Sydney is allergic to most pain medications. Chemotherapy drugs were tried at one point, but had no effect on her pain levels. Deep tissue massage was also tried, but exhausted her, although it did help slightly by decreasing lactic acid build-up in her muscles. Pool therapy was attempted, but Sydney was fatigued for days after any session of targeted movement in the water. It took years for her necessary seizure medications to be correctly titrated to stabilize her seizure disorder.

Sydney filled out several sensory history forms and also completed an oral sensory history as part of the research study's feedback sessions. The sensory symptoms she reported are as follows:

- Touch
  - Even touching herself is painful
  - The sensation of her legs touching a chair is painful
  - She takes very hot showers
- Clothing that is painful
  - Tags
  - Buttons
  - Jeans
  - Certain materials
- Sounds that are bothersome
  - Noise of the TV
  - Squeaky rocking chair
  - Her own jacket sleeves rubbing against her jacket
  - Women's vinyl boots rubbing together
- Smells that are bothersome
  - Perfumes and men's cologne can cause seizures
  - Soaps, body wash
  - Hair products

- Beer
- Alcohol prep pads
- Smoke

- Movement
  - Poor balance, can't catch herself fast enough; this is possibly due to muscle atrophy in legs
  - Nausea from spinning rides
  - Car sick
  - As a child in gymnastics, no headstands or backbends, but could do back handsprings
  - In the dark, feels "lost in space"
  - TV "moves too much" for her to watch for more than short periods of time

Adaptations Sydney Had Made for Herself Before Learning About SMC

Sydney needs a daily nap due to her physical issues. She uses the couch because she finds that she has fewer nightmares there than in her bed. The couch is in a corner of the living room, placed there for the least exposure to open space (the classic veteran's "back to the wall" vigilant stance). She wakes from her nap feeling very "scared" and very sensory sensitive. She says that all sensations "hit at once" when she opens her eyes, resulting in visual and auditory overload. She can't breathe, feels "overwhelmed," and makes her family turn off the TV and not talk. She can't even tolerate her dog's presence in those moments, as "his body feels prickly."

Sydney, in order to be able to sleep at night, has come up with many ways to decrease her pain and (unknowingly) modulate sensory input. She has a very large 5-pound rice pack which she heats in the microwave and uses to cover her legs. She uses a heated foot warmer and many heavy blankets, and a fan for background noise to cancel out other sounds. Even with all of these measures, she sleeps very little.

Awareness About Sensory Modulation Challenges

After participating in the previously mentioned research study about sensory processing in veterans, Sydney elected to have her results interpreted for her and to engage in a discussion about sensory issues in veterans with PTSD. This *awareness* is the first step in wellness self-treatment for sensory modulation challenges. Sydney stated that she found it "empowering" to know that her issues had a name that was not "just" a mental health label, and to understand why she did the things she did to protect herself from sensations that were too upsetting or bothersome. (She'd never even specifically identified these experiences *as* sensations or sensory input before—just as a list of specific trouble spots.) She said that knowing about sensory modulation challenges "opened up a dialogue on PTSD that we [her family] never had before… about how it affects me and them…we can manage it now!"

After she explained sensory modulation challenges to her family, Sydney reported numerous changes in the ways they responded to her. Her family started recognizing her sensory overload and worked to help decrease it. One good example occurred when her adult daughter, who had not yet been told about sensory modulation challenges, visited unexpectedly. Sydney came home from work to an overwhelming sensory experience: her daughter's talking non-stop as Sydney came in the door, and her dog's barking and jumping on her as someone had forgotten to put him out in the yard. Sydney's adult son, who lived at home, recognized the overload, put the dog outside, told Sydney that she could "go to your room and do your thing" (the sensory break they'd incorporated into her coming home routine), and while Sydney did her chosen modulating activities, he took the time to explain sensory modulation challenges to his sister.

Developing a Sensory Diet

Once Sydney became aware of sensory modulation challenges, she wanted to develop a wellness self-treatment plan in the form of a sensory diet. We began with one of the issues that was troubling her the most: waking from her nap. As stated above, she had always awakened in a very fearful state, and had to (sometimes more abruptly than she intended) ask her family to decrease any stimuli in the living room. So we worked together to develop a sensory-based nap routine to help her modulate her *own* nervous system, rather than only making changes to the sights and sounds around her. We decided that Sydney would keep her eyes closed when she woke up, and while she slowly sat up. We needed to add some heavy joint and muscle work to help her self-modulate, but she didn't have enough strength to do chair push-ups. So, before taking her nap, she started filling two milk jugs partially with water (to her personal weight tolerance) and leaving them beside the couch. When she woke, she did 15 repetitions of bicep curls with each arm while in a seated position before opening her eyes. This produced a successful wake-up transition. Sydney was very pleased, reporting, "The milk jugs work!"

Sydney also developed sensory diet games with her dog Samson. She says that Samson loves to play, and invented the games that Sydney now realizes have a strong sensory diet component. Samson crawls under the covers on the bed, and while Sydney lies on top of the covers, he tries to push her out of bed as she resists (providing both strong vestibular and proprioceptive sensory input). In another game, Samson rolls across the bed to Sydney and expects her to roll with him back and forth across the bed (again, giving an excellent combination of vestibular and proprioceptive input). Sydney has added more sensory "snacks" (lighter, shorter activities) to her day by having Samson use a tugging toy (pulling against Sydney's resistance, giving modulating proprioceptive input to both of them) to ask for a dog treat. And Samson likes to "play soccer" with her, even holding the ball in his paws.

Other sensory diet activities that Sydney felt were within her pain and strength tolerance included the use of exercise tubing (resistance stretching), yoga using restricted positions, and wall push-ups (as initially she did not enough strength for chair push-ups).

Wilbarger Therapressure Protocol™ (WTP)
(Wilbarger & Wilbarger, 2001)

After several weeks of successfully using sensory diet activities, Sydney elected to try the Wilbarger Therapressure Protocol™. She was very interested in the program, as she had previously discovered that rubbing her own skin with heavy pressure or with a bath brush decreased her pain and muscle spasms. She was fascinated to learn that there was an actual research-based procedure that could be used to incorporate this type of sensory input throughout her day. The Therapressure Protocol was added to her existing sensory diet for 4 weeks. (See Appendix IV for a further explanation of the Protocol, which involves a daily schedule of pressure-brushing certain parts of the body using a *special brush* which provides no tickle, scratch, or itch sensations, followed by a specific pattern of firm joint compression.) It is very important that the Protocol be followed exactly, with the correct approved brush, and the correct level of pressure with the brush and during joint compression, or the person can become less regulated (more hyper-aroused). The Protocol must be taught by a specially trained occupational therapist to the person and demonstrated on them, and the person must then show that they can carry it out correctly with the right brush and joint pressure by demonstrating it *on* the therapist and themselves.

The first time the Protocol was demonstrated on Sydney, her pain level dropped from 85 percent in her knees and 70 percent overall, to 45–50 percent in her knees and 45 percent overall, and she found it "energizing!"

Changes

Sydney reported many changes from the combination of her sensory diet and the 4-week Wilbarger Therapressure Protocol™ (WTP). After 2 weeks of the WTP, Sydney reported that her sleep increased from 3 hours per night to 5 hours per night. Previously, she only could sleep when exhausted. Now she gets "sleepy" and falls asleep easily, sleeps "soundly and naturally," and wakes "refreshed." Stress has always increased Sydney's pain levels. After 2 weeks, the WTP was lowering her pain levels for 45 minutes after each session. She reported that others commented on how good she looked, saying that her "eyes and face glowed," and she "looked refreshed." After 4 weeks of the WTP, she reported that she could "safely" watch "assaults" in TV programs, whereas if she'd watched them before, it would take several hours to a day for her to "come down," and "it was the elephant in the room" as the TV had to be turned off. "Now I can watch the rest of the show and enjoy it." She did find that she was more relaxed if she added sensory diet "automatically" by doing some heavy lifting and petting the dog during the TV show.

The WTP was done regularly for 4 weeks and then was only used occasionally as part of Sydney's overall sensory diet. Sydney reported that 4 months after completing the WTP, she took a cruise to the Caribbean and had a great time (her issues had previously made it hard for her to travel). And after that, she successfully handled a very stressful family emergency requiring long drives and staying with family members whose household was not at all sensitive to her sensory or allergy issues. Her relatives smoked, were loud, left the TV and lights on all night, had loud air conditioning units, and ceiling fans with mirrors above them. Sydney's adult son insisted that they reduce sensory input levels, saying, "My mom needs this!" And Sydney kept herself modulated by adding as many sensory diet activities as she could during the stay.

Changes Noted by Sydney Over the Several Months Since She Started "Self-treating" Her Sensory Challenges

Sydney's pain decreased after each session of the WTP. Initially, the decrease lasted 45 minutes; later, it lasted for as long as 4 hours between sessions, with no pain medication needed. (See Appendix IV for research about the Wilbarger Therapressure Protocol™.) By doing her sensory diet work, Sydney gradually became strong enough to incorporate chair push-ups. She invented her own "yoga" poses requiring less strength – for example, on her back with her feet in the air. She can now tolerate new smells, such as candles, cleaning products, and her son's body wash. She is able to handle lighter touch from her husband, but has also asked her husband to use more body weight and heavier pressure during hugs and intimacy (see Chapter 6). Sydney additionally reported that she has had "no nightmares for months!" She enjoys getting up in the morning, and her need for naps has been reduced to 3 per week, although she still has some visual triggers for seizures.

On a visit 7 months after we initially discussed sensory diet, we compared Sydney's scores by having her fill out the Sensory Responsiveness checklists (Miller & Schoen, 2008) a second time. Her scores were dramatically different. Sydney's Sensory Over-Responsivity Scale (SensOR) went from 37 (or a standard score based on preliminary standardization data of +5.15, which is very high) to a score of 20 (standard score of +1.65), a significant reduction. And her Sensory Under-Responsivity Scale (SensUR) and Sensory Seeking Scale both improved.

Final Statements

Seven months after the start of her sensory self-treatment, when asked about her PTSD, Sydney stated: "I don't remember the last time I thought about it. I can't think of when I was startled last; when I was not able to say, 'I'm fine'! This is life-changing! I am taking it for granted and going on with my life!"

CHAPTER 13:

How Wellness Interventions for Sensory Modulation Challenges Fit with Existing Treatments for PTS and PTSD for Post-Traumatic Growth

The "N" in DIAL IT DOWN: "New" Solutions

Throughout this book, we've discussed ways for you to "dial down" the hyperarousal that is often seen in veterans, first responders, and frontline medical workers, especially those who are experiencing post-traumatic stress and PTSD. We've discussed the "staying alive" fight-or-flight response, and why people may respond differently to their daily life environments after having served in sustained-threat situations. We've shown how behaviors caused by your nervous system's interpretation that you need to react at the "staying alive" level can lead to problems in your intimate relationships. And we've shown you how to create your own wellness program, a sensory diet, to keep these "staying alive" responses from being triggered. Your sensory diet will help you to stay modulated so that your behaviors are more "even" and you're more empowered to handle new stressors in your life. You'll be less likely to overreact to sensations from your environment, more able to understand the arousal level at which your nervous system is functioning at any given time, and more able to communicate with others about your sensory responses and your sensory needs. *But* there is more to the PTS and PTSD story. *Your sensory diet will not address the emotions surrounding your initial trauma and sustained-threat stressors.*

These emotions will need to be addressed by other means, such as the programs discussed below. When you combine these methods *with* the Dial It Down program of sensory diet, your nervous system will be modulated and *you will be in a stronger position to "take in" the new information and perspectives they offer, allowing them to have a much greater positive effect on your life.*

Many programs have been developed to help people with PTS, PTSD, and related diagnoses to understand and manage their emotions. Current research studies on the effectiveness of these interventions with veterans, first responders, and frontline medical personnel have shown varying results. This may be because few people know how to "Dial It Down," and these programs are being applied to nervous systems that are easily hyperaroused with the expectation that people with PTS or PTSD will be able to change their hyperarousal patterns by using these mostly *cognitive*, "thinking-related" strategies. But as we've discussed throughout this book, *the nervous system hyperarousal pattern is not under conscious control.* It *is*, however, greatly influenced by sensory input like vestibular (movement of the head through space), proprioceptive (heavy work with joints and muscles), and firm touch activities which have been shown to dial down the fight-or-flight response. *And once the nervous system* is *"dialed down" through sensory diet input,* these other interventions have a much greater chance of getting through and being effective in helping you deal with the emotional components of PTS and PTSD.

This chapter will give you an overview of many of the current interventions for dealing with PTS and PTSD. Notice that some of them do have a heavy muscle work, breathing, or other modulating nervous system component. If you are dealing with any emotions since your active duty or frontline work that are unresolved or concerning to you, it's important that you seek out a professional with a background in one or more of these interventions. Post-traumatic healing and growth have been experienced by countless people, and are available to and possible for you!

Current PTS and PTSD Interventions

The following is a partial list of current interventions used in the treatment of PTS and PTSD. Each will be explained in more detail below.

- Cognitive Behavioral Therapy (CBT)

- Cognitive Processing Therapy (CPT)

- Various Exposure Therapies

  - Prolonged Exposure Therapy (PE)

  - Virtual Reality Exposure Therapy (VRE)

- Mindfulness and Guided Imagery

- Eye Movement Desensitization and Reprocessing (EMDR)

- Psychodynamic Therapies

  - Psychotherapy: Individual

  - Psychotherapy: Group (includes Couples Therapy, Family Therapy, and Peer Groups)

- Movement/Body Related Programs

  - Cranial Sacral Therapy (or CranioSacral Therapy)

    - SomatoEmotional Release

  - Physical Releases (Myofascial release)

  - Yoga

  - Meditation

  - Progressive Muscle Relaxation and Biofeedback

- Therapies using art, poetry, journaling, music, etc.

- Animal-Assisted Therapies, most commonly using horses or dogs

- Psychoeducational Programs

Cognitive Based Therapies

COGNITIVE BEHAVIORAL THERAPY (CBT)

Cognitive Behavioral Therapy (CBT) is a type of psychotherapy based on theories of behavior, conditioning, and learning. It is used to help the person explore how unhealthy thought patterns can result in dysfunctional behaviors and emotions. "From a cognitive psychological perspective, trauma exposure is thought to evoke erroneous automatic thoughts about the environment (as dangerous and threatening) and about oneself (as helpless and incompetent). CBT directly confronts such PTSD-related distortions in thinking" (Friedman, 2006, p. 36). CBT focuses on examining inaccurate automatic negative thoughts and feelings, in order to help the person change their responses to challenging situations. Problematic thoughts and emotions related to the trauma are identified and discussed so that the person can recognize when they're causing difficulties with daily life and functioning. Ways to interrupt the "inaccurate thoughts" and replace them with "reality" are discussed and practiced (Friedman, 2006; Schupp, 2004; NAMI website).

COGNITIVE PROCESSING THERAPY (CPT)

Cognitive Processing Therapy (CPT) is a type of Cognitive Behavioral Therapy that focuses specifically on faulty thoughts or feelings related to trauma that have resulted in changes in the person's overall view of the world or of their self-worth and capabilities. "Many people have problems understanding how to live in the world after trauma. Your beliefs about safety, trust, control, self-esteem, other people, and relationships can change after trauma" (PTSD: National Center for PTSD). Using a written narrative, CPT helps the person examine those thoughts and feelings related to the trauma to identify if they are accurate (based in reality) or inaccurate ("stuck" due to a change in the person's belief system). CPT is conducted in individual or group sessions for approximately 12 weeks, with a 1-month follow-up after completion. Clients are guided by a psychologist through three phases of treatment following a specific protocol.

- Phase One: Analyze, Gather Information, Identify Feelings
- Phase Two: Challenge
- Phase Three: Change

The expected outcome of CPT is for people to be able to challenge and process any distorted feelings and thoughts connected to the trauma (like guilt and shame), modify those beliefs, and arrive at a conclusion that is more accurate and balanced (accommodation), thus allowing them to experience the emotions (often including fear and sadness) which were blocked by distorted beliefs about the trauma (Friedman, 2006; Moore & Penk, 2011). The Veterans Administration has stated that "CPT has been shown to be one of the most effective treatments for PTSD" (PTSD: National Center for PTSD).

PROLONGED EXPOSURE THERAPY

Prolonged Exposure Therapy is a type of Cognitive Behavioral Therapy that uses desensitization by having clients exposed in a structured way to objects or events that were part of the traumatic experience. Thoughts, feelings, places, and even physical sensations in the body related to the trauma may be highly avoided by the person with PTS or PTSD because they can elicit a fear response (the "fight-or-flight" response we've previously discussed). From a cognitive behavioral standpoint, this means that the person overreacts or "overgeneralizes" from one specific trauma to many situations which are not in themselves dangerous. To cognitively challenge and reduce these fear responses, Prolonged Exposure Therapy incorporates the structured use of the following:

1. The person repeatedly retells their personal story of the traumatic event (called imaginal exposure);

2. The person identifies and ranks avoided situations or places, and then, with the help of a therapist, confronts the situations or places in hierarchical order, starting with the least feared, for increasing lengths of time (called *in vivo* exposure);

3. Education is provided on typical responses to trauma and how treatment helps;

4. Breathing techniques are taught to assist with calming (remember that breathing is a technique we have discussed for use in your sensory diet).

Prolonged Exposure sessions are typically 90 minutes long, are conducted once or twice a week for a total of 8 to 15 sessions, and are guided by a psychologist following a precise protocol. Prolonged Exposure Therapy has the expected outcome of lessening a client's anxiety and distress over the habituated fear. The VA reports that this is another of the most effective treatments for PTSD. (Moore & Penk, 2011; PTSD: National Center for PTSD; Schupp, 2004)

VIRTUAL REALITY EXPOSURE THERAPY

This therapy uses the same premise as Prolonged Exposure Therapy, but incorporates a visually interactive computer simulation to retell the client's story. Some research suggests that it may be more effective than traditional exposure therapy in emotionally engaging military personnel.

MINDFULNESS AND GUIDED IMAGERY

Mindfulness is gaining support among psychotherapists and other health professionals as a method to help reduce stress and anxiety. Mindfulness encourages people to keep their thoughts in the present, avoiding past or future concerns. The person observes and is aware of all thoughts and feelings as they occur, but just accepts them and views them as thoughts running through the brain, not reacting to them or allowing the brain to attach *to* any particular thought and "run with it" into automatic processing. This state is most often accomplished by the person's keeping their primary focus on *breathing*, allowing other thoughts and feelings to move through consciousness without responding to them and thus reducing their hold. Mindfulness, in addition to its application in treating persons with PTS and PTSD, has been used by therapists to help decrease cravings in addicts.

Guided Imagery is a method in which a trained professional "guides" you through a relaxation process by keeping you focused on *mental images* that you intentionally visualize in response to a word picture they describe.

Each person will visualize different specifics (a particular stretch of seashore, for instance), but the process of creating and sustaining your own mental image helps to keep the brain focused on the present moment, utilizing many senses (sight, sound, smell, touch, taste, even movement) to elaborate the scene you're experiencing. The purpose of Guided Imagery is to keep you in the present and mentally "in your body." Some people who have difficulty focusing on their breathing may find guided imagery to be the best method for helping them to stay "mindful."

EYE MOVEMENT DESENSITIZATION
AND REPROCESSING (EMDR)

Eye Movement Desensitization and Reprocessing (EMDR) is a psychological method that focuses the person's attention on consciously recalling traumatic memories while at the same time visually tracking specific (fast-moving) stimuli. The theory of EMDR is that sometimes, a traumatic memory may have been stored in the brain in a maladaptive fashion, and that by targeting the distressing memory while focusing on an *external* stimulus, the brain is better able to process that memory more fully, therefore becoming "unstuck" (and hence desensitized to the memory). The external stimuli provided by the therapist are usually bilateral, consisting of rapid hand movements which patients must follow with their eyes, but stimuli can also include finger tapping and/or sound. EMDR is typically performed during 1 to 12 sessions with a therapist trained in this technique. During treatment, the person identifies the target negative image, thought, or feeling from the trauma. Desensitization occurs as the person recalls various parts of the memory while the clinician who is providing the bilateral stimulation stops at certain intervals to check in with them to ensure that processing is occurring.

EMDR seems to facilitate the processing of the negative emotion associated with the trauma by maintaining the patient's conscious attention on *both* the *inner* thoughts and feelings, and the *external* movements simultaneously. Moore and Penk (2011) report that its use is supported by considerable research, but responses may vary widely: some people experience no change, while others have found it extremely helpful (Curran, 2010; Friedman, 2006; Schupp, 2004).

Psychodynamic Therapies

PSYCHOTHERAPY: INDIVIDUAL

Psychotherapy is traditionally known as "talk therapy." There are many types, but all involve discussing your emotional issues with another person who is trained and licensed to guide you in examining problem areas including past memories and current relationships. Many veterans, first responders, and frontline medical personnel feel that they benefit from the combined flexibility and strict confidentiality of this type of therapy. Look for board-certified psychologists, psychiatrists, or social workers, and be sure that you find the right "fit" for you (the personal recommendation of a doctor, VA healthcare worker, or peer whom you trust can be very helpful in this process).

PSYCHOTHERAPY: GROUPS

Psychotherapy can also be provided in the form of couples therapy, family therapy, or peer group therapy. Each type has its benefits, and often a person will engage in more than one type as needed. Several methods of structured group therapeutic interventions have been shown to be particularly helpful for the treatment of PTS and PTSD: Trauma-Focused Group Therapy, Present-Centered Group Therapy, and the Spirituality and Trauma Group Module.

Movement/Body Related Programs

CRANIAL SACRAL THERAPY (CST)

Cranial Sacral Therapy (CST) is a form of physical and emotional therapy based on work done by DOs (Doctors of Osteopathy), who have the same training as MDs but also receive specialized training in wellness approaches to medicine. Practitioners of CST believe that balance in the body leads to a healthier person, and so many of them include physical manipulation (through fast or slow movement of the joints and muscles) in their treatment options. Osteopaths practice in all fields of medicine, and some specialize in manipulation for physical issues, in particular pain management. One osteopath, John Upledger, developed additional techniques to deal with the *emotional* components of physical problems. He felt that injuries to the body resulted not only in physical damage but also in an "internalization" of the emotion that was present at the time of the injury and the incorporation of that emotion into the injury area. He believed that the injury might not heal fully until the emotional component was also healed. To facilitate healing the emotional component, he developed a technique called "SomatoEmotional Release." First, the physical injury (strains, pain, etc.) is worked on through slow releases of restriction in muscle and fascial tissue, and then the emotional component is addressed through additional hands-on work while discussing with the client the feelings that are associated with the painful, tight or "stuck" area. Dr. Upledger found that when the emotion was released, both the physical and emotional pain associated with the injury or trauma usually improved. Unpublished data and a video of an Upledger Institute/VA project in 1999 showed significant improvement in PTSD in Vietnam veterans who had 2 weeks of daily craniosacral therapy after they had exhausted all other treatment options with minimal results (The Upledger Foundation, 2000). Several studies are currently being conducted with veterans receiving craniosacral therapy, one in Florida and one on the West Coast which combines craniosacral therapy with hippotherapy. Results are not yet available.

In addition to DOs, specially trained occupational and physical therapists, chiropractors, nurses, and some massage therapists can also administer CST. Check for proper training with your provider, especially if you want SomatoEmotional Release (SER), as this requires specific certification.

YOGA

Yoga has long been used as a way to "de-stress," and current research confirms that it can help people experiencing PTS and PTSD. The Army conducted a randomized control trial research study using sensory enhanced yoga, which combined yoga with activities known to help with sensory modulation challenges (see Chapter 10). This study showed substantial benefits (Stroller et al., 2012).

MEDITATION

In 1975, Dr. Herbert Benson's book *The Relaxation Response* introduced the use of meditation as a way to manage fight-or-flight reactions. Dr. Benson made meditation understandable with easy-to-follow directions, and a considerable body of research has shown the efficacy of meditation in reducing stress and improving wellness. Today, there are many meditation programs available online and through apps for your phone or tablet.

EXAMPLES OF ONLINE PROGRAMS

- Calm.com (app for phone and tablet): numerous mediation practices and sleep stories
- Head Space.com (app for phone and tablet)
- Insight Timer.com (app for phone and tablet)
- Peloton: guided meditation classes
- Apple Watch can be set to remind you to breathe deeply

PROGRESSIVE MUSCLE RELAXATION AND BIOFEEDBACK

These techniques were developed because muscle tension is often a part of stress responses. They involve systematically *tensing* a given muscle group, and then concentrating on *relaxing* it. Progressive muscle relaxation can be done in the form of a guided individual session; by listening to a prepared audio session; during a live group session; or on your own. Biofeedback (through small monitors attached to a portable device) can be temporarily used to train you to better detect your muscle tension and relaxation by allowing you to view tension levels on a visual screen. These *physical* techniques have a *cognitive* component as well, because you have to concentrate on how tensed the muscle feels, detect the differences when relaxed, and know when and how to use your chosen relaxation approach.

THERAPIES USING ART, POETRY, JOURNALING, AND MUSIC

Veterans, first responders, and frontline medical personnel can find help in addressing their trauma through a wide variety of art therapy programs available throughout the country in clinics, crisis centers, hospitals, and community centers (Ramirez, 2016). The following website lists many types of programs and their individual addresses: https://veteransfamiliesunited. org/art-therapy-visual-performing-written/.

The types of art programs offered include visual arts, performing arts, and written arts. For one specific example, see Chapter 10, Artists for Peace and Freedom.

Music therapy has long been used as a means to prompt and support emotional discussions, and there are now several "Listening Therapy" programs which have shown promise in changing the way the brain processes stimuli and emotion. These have mostly been tested in children with sensory modulation challenges. All involve listening through headphones to music that has been modified to increase its intensity in certain ranges. Different ranges have been shown to result in different positive changes in functioning. A research study on a program called Berard Auditory Integration Training has shown improvement in sensory modulation as well as emotional regulation in children with sensory modulation challenges (Brockett, Lawton-Shirley & Kimball, 2014). Other auditory programs include Samonas, Therapeutic Listening, The Listening Program, and Integrated Listening Systems. All have websites and are backed by research with children and a few with adults as well (Carley, 2013; Hall & Case-Smith, 2007; Frick, 2000; Moore & Henry, 2002). Personal communications with Ingo Steinbach, the developer of Samonas, reveal that he feels his program would be helpful for veterans and others with PTSD (July 2, 2015).

ANIMAL-ASSISTED THERAPIES, MOST COMMONLY USING HORSES OR DOGS

As we discussed in Chapter 11, dogs and horses can offer therapeutic benefits through their potential to provide you with strong sensory diet activities, as well as positive feedback and support. Dogs will get you out walking or running several times a day and provide you with unconditional love. Horses provide the perfect combination of vestibular and proprioceptive movement to modulate your nervous system, as well as the heavy muscle work involved in grooming them and cleaning their stalls. Learning to handle a horse can contribute to building your confidence.

PSYCHOEDUCATIONAL PROGRAMS

Many programs and books are available to teach you about the symptoms of PTS and PTSD. However, if you are looking for additional help, veterans should contact their local Veterans Centers to guide them toward effective programs in their areas; first responders should contact their unions; and frontline medical personnel should be sure to access any programs available through their employers or local hospitals (many hospital systems in cities hard-hit by COVID-19 are now offering a range of group therapy, peer support groups, and individual therapy sessions to help healthcare workers manage PTS). Your colleagues who are experiencing similar issues may also have found resources and activities to help, which underscores the benefits of *talking about it* with family and close friends – and remembering that while the symptoms you're experiencing can feel isolating, *you are not alone* in dealing with sensory challenges and PTS or PTSD.

CHAPTER 14:

What Health Professionals Should Know About Sensory Modulation Challenges

The "N" in DIAL IT DOWN: "New" Solutions

You may (optionally) choose to share this chapter with your health care providers and therapists to let them know about new research and practices regarding sensory modulation challenges, and how these might apply to you.

Review

Many of the symptoms of post-traumatic stress (PTS) and PTSD (PTS that meets specific *DSM-5* criteria) result from the central nervous system's trying to protect a person from dangerous situations by guarding and remaining on alert against any potential repeat of past trauma. Danger activates the brain's prime directive to "first stay alive," the fight-or-flight response. This protective response *is* in fact a lifesaver for veterans, first responders, and frontline medical personnel who have endured sustained-threat situations like war, active shootings, and the risks of overcrowded COVID-19 wards; yet it becomes maladaptive in the civilian world when it cannot be "dialed down." This book introduces a new way to understand some of the behaviors seen in these personnel after they have experienced traumatic events – most notably, their tendency to remain hyper-aroused (hyper-vigilant) or to have unpredictably fluctuating levels of fight-or-flight arousal depending on the level of sensory stimuli from the surrounding environment. Sometimes what looks like severe under-arousal, but is actually "shutting down," can occur when the nervous system has sustained too high a level of arousal for too long and can't process any additional sensory input.

Heightened nervous system responses can result in behaviors like constantly feeling "on edge"; responding angrily to what was once experienced as normal household noise and clutter; and feeling a new aversion to light touch (which, in a heightened nervous system, can provoke a startle/defensive response: one veteran, for instance, reported that he could no longer tolerate light kisses on the cheek from his daughter). These *changes* in feelings and behavior from the person's "normal" range before their trauma or sustained-threat exposure can cause much friction in interpersonal relationships, as everyone wants the returning soldier, first responder, or healthcare worker to "be the same person" they "used to be" before their traumatic experience.

Many such personnel are diagnosed with PTSD, a mental health diagnosis. This book makes the case that both *within* that diagnosis, and within the more general range of PTS (post-traumatic stress that causes notable changes in feelings and behavior but does not fully meet all *DSM-5* PTSD criteria), *some of the most commonly experienced symptoms can be viewed as sensory modulation challenges (SMC), a difference in how the brain interprets and responds to sensations from the environment.* Sensory modulation challenges both affect and are affected by other aspects of PTS and PTSD, and should be treated alongside treatments for the emotional and psychological components of trauma. But the SMC component is primarily *physical* or *sensory* rather than psychological; it is a *heightened nervous system response* of a type that has long been documented in children born with these challenges, but has only begun to be studied in children and adults who acquire these challenges through trauma. There is research evidence (summarized by Weiss, 2007) that trauma stress influences the structure and function of the brain and that these neurobiological changes are related to the symptoms experienced after trauma, most notably hyperarousal, hypervigilance, increased startle, irritability, impulsivity, and angry outbursts. These are major symptoms we identify in SMC.

Sensory modulation challenges can be self-treated using a wellness approach (a "sensory diet") that anyone can access, and this approach—by building and sustaining a more regulated sensory baseline—will help to make *all other* essential PTS and PTSD interventions more effective. Just having *knowledge* about sensory modulation challenges can help veterans, first responders, frontline medical workers, and their families to understand many of the differences in their behaviors following their service, thus empowering them to make changes, reducing blame and self-blame, and helping to preserve key relationships and emotional support systems.

A further benefit may be seen in pain reduction for personnel who've suffered physical injuries: the SMC wellness approach that's outlined in this book (which may be adapted to accommodate any physical disability) will help to modulate and positively influence all sensory systems, including the tactile and proprioceptive systems involved in the processing and perception of pain. Both the "sensory diet" activities and other activities outlined in this book such as the Wilbarger Therapressure Protocol™ (Wilbarger & Cook, 2011; Bar-Shalita et al., 2014) have shown early promise in reducing pain levels (see Chapter 12 and Appendix IV).

Please note that whether or not they have been formally diagnosed with PTS or PTSD, all veterans, first responders, and medical personnel who've experienced sustained-threat situations can benefit from understanding the definition of and wellness treatments for sensory modulation challenges.

Key Points

1. Understanding the contributions of sensory modulation challenges to behaviors following sustained-threat exposure can help in these ways:

   a. Veterans, first responders, and frontline medical workers can recognize and better understand their changed reactions to life "at home."

   b. They can learn that the heightened intensity of their responses is linked to the brain's prime directive to keep them alive: the fight-or-flight response, which their brains used very appropriately to keep them (and the members of their squad, unit, or team) alive and safe during their service;

c. that sustaining the hypervigilance of the fight-or-flight response for extended periods was *specifically "trained in"* during their military, first responder, or medical training to keep them and others alive and safe while managing direct life-or-death threats;

d. and that during sustained-threat situations, the brain can undergo actual *neurochemical changes* that make subsequent over-arousal more likely (see Weiss, 2007, Appendix I).

e. They can also learn that many of the heightened sensory responses that saved their lives during their service can become problematic when they return home;

f. that they and their families are likely to notice at least some (and often *many*) differences in how they react to everyday life events, particularly *stronger* (hyper-aroused) reactions to sounds, sights, smells, and touch (reactions that, again, may have saved their lives while on duty when visual clutter could indicate threats like an IED in the road or a breach of hospital safety protocol).

g. They can learn that, while military, first responder, and medical personnel are trained in how to "dial up" their fight-or-flight arousal responses, they *have not* been trained in how to "dial down" these responses once they are in a safe environment;

h. and they and their families can learn that it *is* possible to "dial down" these responses—through mapping out their own specific sensory-based environmental triggers and through incorporating "sensory diet" and other activities to modulate their nervous systems.

2. Sensory modulation challenges can affect all areas of a person's life, but tend to follow certain patterns:

a. The sensory systems that are most frequently affected in veterans, first responders, and frontline medical workers are auditory, visual, olfactory (smell), and tactile;

b. but within each sensory category, each individual will have highly *specific* environmental triggers for hyperarousal. For instance, in the category of "sight," one person may react extremely negatively to the movement of large outdoor crowds but be fine with household clutter; pre-COVID 19, another might have been fine with stadium and mall crowds but reacted negatively to the closed-in crowds at restaurants; others might be fine with any type of crowd but find themselves yelling at the kids for clutter that never bothered them before. The following sensory questionnaires can help to clarify these individual triggers: The Adolescent/Adult Sensory Profile (Brown & Dunn, 2002), available through occupational therapists; and the Sensory Over Responsivity Scale (SensOR) and the Sensory Under Responsivity Scale (SensUR) (Miller & Schoen, 2008), available by special permission in Chapter 7.

c. Sensory modulation challenges have been shown to be related to increased pain perception; therefore, keeping the nervous system modulated can help personnel who've sustained chronic injuries to manage their pain.

3. Understanding the specific practices that helped to prime the nervous system for peak performance during active- or on-duty work can help veterans, first responders, medical workers, and their families to realize how some of these same practices can be incorporated to "Dial It Down" back home:

a. Most military personnel have never been taught that the physical training they did daily (75-plus minutes per day in the Army, for instance) not only kept them *physically* strong, but also served to keep their nervous systems modulated and calmly alert so that they could make the best choices possible to stay alive and to carry out their missions;

b. and very few military reintegration programs acknowledge that there often isn't time, space, motivation, physical ability, or family support for this type of extensive physical training back home. *But*

c. the good news for "dialing it down" is that high-intensity physical training is *not necessary*. Shorter durations of specific types of activities, called *"sensory diets,"* have been proven to be extremely effective.

d. Most first responders and frontline medical workers have never specifically been taught that their rotating on- and off-duty schedules, before COVID-19, served to "protect" their *sensory systems* by giving them time to rest and recover; and that the increased intensity and duration of their work during this pandemic (tending to many more very sick patients over extended shifts) can disrupt that balance and lead to sensory challenges. *But*

e. as with military personnel, the good news for "dialing it down" is that short durations of specific sensory diet activities can be incorporated into their lives back home (and even, as needed, through smaller "sensory snacks" while on duty) to greatly improve modulation.

4. Adding **sensory diets** can "dial down" some of the most common symptoms of PTS and PTSD:

a. A sensory diet is a wellness approach, controlled by the individual person;

b. sensory diet activities modulate *all* sensory systems (decreasing hyperarousal and increasing hypoarousal), and therefore empower the veteran, first responder, or frontline medical worker to participate more fully in *all* of their occupations (work, play, sleep, self-care, recreation, family life, etc.);

c. sensory diets don't disrupt daily life at home, but instead support and can be easily integrated into existing daily routines.

Sensory diets work well in small doses throughout the day, as little as 5-10 minutes every few hours. Some veterans and others tend to like longer, high-intensity workouts, and these do work well – but *adding* short bursts of physical activity at regular intervals *throughout* the day (in addition to that one long workout) can help to keep them better modulated.

5. Sensory diets are a simple self-treatment wellness approach involving activities using specific types of strong sensory input:

    a. vestibular or rhythmic movement of the head through space (running, jumping jacks, jumping on a rebounder);

    b. proprioception or heavy work with muscles and joints (any pushing and pulling against resistance [like exercise tubing], or carrying weight like a backpack);

    c. and tactile or firm pressure on the skin (like a weighted blanket or massage).

6. Increased sensory modulation means that *other treatments for PTS and PTSD (like individual or group therapy) will work better*, because the person's more modulated nervous system will support them in more fully attending to and taking in information – physically, cognitively, and emotionally.

7. If an active-duty member has sustained a mild traumatic brain injury (mTBI) or concussive syndrome, this can result in decreased ability of the cortex to do its usual job of *inhibiting* stimuli, contributing to a heightened risk for sensory modulation challenges and exacerbating any already-existing SMC. Sensory diet can be a key component of helping to increase inhibition for these individuals.

What Can You Do?

As a health professional working with individuals with PTS, PTSD, or mTBI, being aware of the possibility that sensory modulation challenges may play a role in your patients' behaviors, and supporting your patients in incorporating SMC wellness techniques as part of their treatment, can be a crucial intervention. In addition to the *direct* health and emotional benefits of sensory diet activities, you can contribute to key *indirect* benefits by providing education and encouraging communication. One of the most devastating aspects of SMC issues is their effect on *interpersonal relationships.* In educating veterans, first responders, frontline medical workers, and their families about the effects of SMC and encouraging them to discuss these effects, you will be helping to bridge a huge divide of miscommunication, misunderstanding, and missed opportunities for emotional support. The effects of sensory modulation challenges can be discussed in many ways. (See Chapter 11 for examples and strategies for communication between people with SMC and their family members.)

Combining work on sensory modulation challenges with any of the current therapeutic programs for PTS and PTSD should help to make these programs even more effective. For example, a cognitive behavioral approach will work much more efficiently in a person whose nervous system is modulated so that they can attend to the program in a calm state rather than in fight-or-flight mode.

If additional professional help is desired in developing, implementing, and monitoring a sensory diet program, occupational therapists have extensive training in best practices for sensory diets, as well as in the physical and wellness aspects of client issues that may prevent them from participating fully in all the "occupations" of their lives. Occupational therapists can help with any *functional* problems that arise from physical or mental health issues, for example, providing specific training for amputees, people with spinal cord injuries, brain injuries, and chronic pain. This includes personal care and other activities of daily living such as sexual health and functioning, a very difficult yet little-discussed area for many people experiencing sensory modulation challenges (see Chapter 6).

CHAPTER 15:

DIAL IT DOWN Revisited

The "N" in DIAL IT DOWN:
"New" Solutions and Strategies

The "N" in Dial It Down is ultimately about seeing yourself differently, in a *new* way. It's about taking back control of your body so that you can take back control of your life. It's about putting yourself in a better position to access other positive programs for growth by modulating your nervous system – through combining activities you already like with new ideas and opportunities.

Congratulations! You have discovered and initiated a personal wellness approach to understanding, managing, and improving your sensory modulation challenges. You now know how to Dial It Down!

Summary: What You Have Learned

1. The Dial It Down approach described in this book can help anyone with PTS, PTSD, or mTBI – but you don't need a medical diagnosis to benefit from this program.

2. People with hyperarousal, anxiety, and/or depression can also often benefit from understanding sensory modulation challenges and accessing the wellness strategies outlined here.

3. Sensory modulation challenges can account for many of the behavioral changes that veterans, first responders, and frontline medical

workers may experience following their exposure to sustained-threat situations and/or due to trauma.

4. Sensory modulation challenges represent a difference in the way the brain processes *everyday sensory input* from the environment.

5. Although the behaviors resulting from sensory modulation challenges can sometimes *look like* mental health problems, and may occur alongside or as one component of diagnosed mental health issues (as research suggests in PTSD), SMC is a *physical* rather than mental health issue – it's a measurable *neurophysiological difference in how the brain processes sensory information.*

6. Sensory modulation challenges usually lead to some form of hyperarousal, the "overdoing" of the fight-or-flight response that's a result of the brain's prime directive to "first keep you alive." If you are a veteran, first responder, or frontline medical worker, staying at a heightened level of arousal for long periods while you were on duty kept you and others alive and safe – but sensory modulation *challenges* can occur when you have difficulty "dialing it down" back home. (Sometimes under-arousal, or "shutting down," can occur when the nervous system has sustained too high a level of arousal for too long and can't process any additional input.)

7. Sensory modulation challenges can influence your behavior in many areas of your life including:

   a. Sleep

   b. Touch/Intimacy

   c. Reactions to noise

   d. Reactions to things you see

   e. Reactions to smells

   f. Ability to attend crowded events

   g. Driving

   h. Concentration

8. You can address challenges in these and other areas by "dialing it down" using sensory strategies.

9. Sensory strategies include four steps:

   a. increasing your awareness of sensory modulation challenges in general, and of your own specific sensory issues;

   b. changing your environment to avoid things that can raise your sensory arousal ("fight-or-flight") level;

   c. designing and carrying out your own "sensory diet" using wellness activities consisting of rhythmic movement of your head through space (vestibular), heavy joint and muscle work (proprioceptive), and heavy touch pressure on the skin (tactile);

   d. and finally, you may choose to incorporate a program called the Wilbarger Therapressure Protocol™, which requires training and guidance from a licensed occupational therapist.

10. Of the steps above, the major method you learned to use to "dial down" your SMC is a *sensory diet.* The key points about sensory diets are:

   a. that you have very likely *already used* some sensory diet strategies in the military, during first responder training, or through regular exercise without realizing it;

   b. that in designing your sensory diet, *you* have the freedom to choose the activities you like and that work well for you;

   c. that you can add sensory *power* to many of these activities in easy ways (like wearing a weighted vest, using a weighted blanket, increasing your workout time or changing the type, sitting on a yoga ball while playing video games or using your computer, or using exercise bands);

   d. that, as with a food "diet," you should spread sensory diet activities throughout your day;

e. that you can plan to use specific sensory diet strategies before stressful events you know about in advance, and can also make "backup plans" for unexpected stress triggers;

f. and that you can monitor and adjust the effectiveness of your own sensory diet as needed.

11. Talking about your sensory modulation challenges with family and close friends can help both you and them to:

a. avoid sensory-based misunderstandings;

b. improve your shared intimacy;

c. build key support networks;

d. create the opportunity for new joint physical activities that can benefit everyone's health and wellbeing.

12. A sensory diet (particularly when used along with the Wilbarger Protocol) can help in managing chronic pain.

13. Since a sensory diet involves regular physical activity, a great secondary effect is better physical conditioning and overall health.

14. Dialing down your nervous system's sensory responses will empower *you* to feel more in control, and to participate more fully in every aspect of your life.

APPENDIX I:

The Science of How Modulation Works in the Nervous System: Additional Information

A Short History of Sensory Modulation Challenges

Sensory modulation challenges fall under the umbrella term of "Sensory Integration." A. Jean Ayres, PhD, OTR, first developed the theory of Sensory Integration through her work with children who had coordination issues. As an occupational therapist, Dr. Ayres (1972a, 1972b, 1979) looked at the neurological underpinnings of developmentally based coordination problems (dyspraxia/motor planning) in children, and hypothesized that the nervous systems of some children were not fully taking in and processing the sensory information they were presented with, and that this poor "sensory integration" then made it difficult for them to draw from past sensory experiences in order to accomplish new, non-habitual motor tasks. (For instance, after the vestibular, proprioceptive, tactile, and visual experience of climbing one ladder at a playground, a child with these issues might struggle much more than expected to climb a second, only slightly different ladder at that playground). Ayres hypothesized that sensory integration could be improved by providing additional specific types of sensory input to help the children increase their low muscle tone (background tension and responsiveness in the muscles); improve balance; improve their use of joints and muscles; and improve tactile, auditory, and visual perceptual abilities. The children she treated showed improvements not just in these areas, but also often in their academic performance (Ayres, 1972a, 1972b).

During this time, Ayres also began describing sensory *reactions* she observed in the children, which she labeled "tactile defensiveness." *These reactions were not related to tactile perceptual abilities* (which is being able to discriminate shapes, forms, and textures by touch), but *instead were an observed aversive response to light touch.* These adverse reactions were out of proportion to the actual intensity of the input, as measured against how most children would react to that input level, and *they appeared to result in increased arousal of the sympathetic portion of the autonomic nervous system, triggering the fight-or-flight response.* Dr. Ayres found that the tactile defensiveness became less severe when she used some of the treatments she had developed for dyspraxia. Particularly helpful in reducing tactile defensiveness were "heavy work" activities with the muscles and joints; heavy touch pressure on the skin; and rhythmic movements of the head through space (vestibular input) such as swinging and jumping.

As other occupational therapists, including this author, started to investigate tactile defensiveness, they noted that not just the tactile system but also *every other sensory system* could be defensive. Rather than labeling each system separately, the name of this type of response was changed from "*tactile*" to the more general "*sensory* defensiveness." Occupational therapist Patricia Wilbarger was the first to describe an over-responsive/sensory defensive nervous system as displaying "a constellation of symptoms related to aversive or defensive reactions to non-noxious stimuli across one or more sensory systems." This represents "an over-reaction of our normal protective senses." We may see "patterns of avoidance, sensory seeking, fear, anxiety or even aggression" which "fluctuate widely and can be misidentified as emotionally based." (Wilbarger & Wilbarger, 2001, p. 2)

Patricia Wilbarger (1991), who worked with Ayres, realized that using specific sensory inputs—especially those mentioned above (heavy touch pressure, rhythmic movement of the head through space, and heavy work with joints and muscles)—*on a specific schedule* was the most helpful in decreasing sensory defensiveness. She, along with her daughter Julia Wilbarger, PhD, also an occupational therapist, developed daily routines of sensory input which they called "sensory diets," as they felt that the nervous system needed a regular diet of the "just right" amount of sensation to keep it healthy (meaning "modulated") just as people need food at regular intervals throughout the day to remain healthy. The Wilbargers developed a wide range of sensory diets based on what different individuals liked to do, so that these sensory diets would fit easily into people's busy lives and people would be motivated to continue them.

Around this time, occupational therapists also began to note that while some people were over-aroused or sensory defensive, others were *under-aroused*. This led to a change in the terminology to include both over- and under-arousal: from Sensory Defensiveness to Sensory Modulation Challenges (SMC).

Research on the evaluation of sensory modulation issues led Winnie Dunn (1999) to develop a method for evaluating and describing sensory preferences. She defined and measured two types of sensory modulation issues: "Sensory Sensitivity" (which is the same as sensory defensiveness), and "Low Registration." And she described two types of behavioral reactions to these issues, "Sensation Seeking" and "Sensation Avoiding." Dunn and her colleagues developed three age-related sensory profiles to assess individual sensory processing preferences. These involve self-reporting for adults, and parent reporting for children and infants, asking about the person's reactions to different sensory events. They are the *Adolescent/Adult Sensory Profile* (Brown & Dunn, 2002), the *Sensory Profile for Children* (Dunn, 1999), and the *Infant/Toddler Sensory Profile* (Dunn, 2002). (Dunn's sensory profiles for infants, toddlers, and children were later expanded and incorporated into the *Sensory Profile 2* [2014].) Lucy Jane Miller and her colleagues have since developed the *Sensory Processing Inventory* (Schoen et al., 2008), another evaluation of how a person experiences sensory input, for use with children. They are now in the process of standardizing an examiner-administered scale (in conjunction with Western Psychological Services) for children and adults called the Sensory Processing 3 Dimensions Measure (SP3D) (Miller et al., 2018). They have graciously given this author permission to use two unpublished sensory inventories for adults in my research and for readers of this book: the Sensory Over-Responsivity Inventory for Adults (SensOR) and the Sensory Under-Responsivity Inventory for Adults (SensUR) (Miller & Schoen, 2008).

In an attempt to consolidate all the different terms used for sensory issues and to make them more readily understandable, a group of occupational therapists and physicians developed a taxonomy that described sensory processing issues more completely and specifically. This group produced a model which appears in the *Diagnostic Manual of the Interdisciplinary Council on Development and Learning Disorders (ICDL)* (Greenspan, 2005). It uses "Regulatory-Sensory Processing Disorder" as the overarching term. There are three major subtypes:

1. ***Sensory Modulation Challenges*** (the focus of this book) incorporate sensory over- and under-arousal based on the nervous system's evaluation of danger.

2. ***Sensory Discrimination Challenges*** incorporate problems in discriminating what the sensory input actually is (for example, feeling the difference between a nickel and dime in your pocket; or hearing the difference between similar words like "cat" and "hat"; or perceiving the difference between sloped and even terrain).

3. ***Sensory Based Motor Challenges*** are the developmental coordination problems in children which accompany certain types of sensory processing issues based on poor *discrimination* of sensory input, and result in difficulty in easily learning new motor skills.

Sensory Discrimination Challenges and Sensory Based Motor Challenges are developmental in nature and are seen in children who show difficulties in developing good fine- and gross-motor coordination and perceptual abilities. These are *not* related to the sensory modulation challenges/sensory defensiveness issues that are the focus of this book.

Some of the Science Behind Sensory Modulation Challenges

Why do we need sensory modulation, and how does it work? The central nervous system regulates and organizes the body's reactions to all sensory input. As Miller et al. write (1999, p. 6), the central nervous system does this "in a graded and adaptive manner which involves changes in the responsivity of neurons and allows the nervous system to adapt its output in the face of a continually changing environment." To change and balance our responses, the central nervous system uses the processes of sensitization and habituation. *Sensitization* is the central nervous system process of recognizing that a stimulus is *important* or may represent *potential harm*, thus requiring a *heightened or more focused* response. *Habituation* is the central nervous system process of recognizing a stimulus as familiar or non-threatening and thus decreasing responsiveness to it (Dunn & Westman, 1997). Habituation and sensitization cannot occur in isolation: the central nervous system needs to utilize *both* simultaneously to be able to make *instantaneous survival decisions* in reaction to potentially harmful stimuli, and to ignore other, non-threatening stimuli in the environment at any given time.

Every individual has a different range of sensory thresholds. If a person is to remain in their *individual range of optimal performance*, or to remain "modulated," a balance between habituation and sensitization is necessary. Increases in anxiety and stress can cause people to react as if they have *increased sensitization* – to react more strongly than they otherwise would to stimuli, which can in turn impact their ability to fully and comfortably participate in their lives.

Earlier theory held that when the sympathetic portion of the autonomic nervous system (ANS) becomes "over-aroused," the protective pathway dominates, causing the typical sympathetic fight-or-flight behaviors (Fisher & Dunn, 1983). The intensity of these behaviors was thought to be determined by **the level of the perceived threat.** However, we now know that this intensity can *also* be influenced by **the current level of arousal of the individual's nervous system.** The purpose of fight-or-flight is the safety and survival of the organism: therefore, *if the nervous system is **already** at a high level of sympathetic arousal (as in sensory defensiveness) when the individual perceives a new input (one that would commonly be understood as nonthreatening), **a strong survival response may be evoked** which is **out of line** with the intensity of the new stimulus alone.* In such a case, the survival response would *not* seem out of line **if the previous high arousal state** of the nervous system were recognized (Kimball, 1993, 1999a, 1999b, 2000, 2002).

Research

LeDoux (2002) was responsible for refining the concept of the sympathetic (fight-or-flight) "protective" component of the autonomic nervous system (ANS). He called it the *"evaluative"* rather than *"protective"* system because, in addition to acting to *protect* the organism, it primarily performs a more general *alerting/arousal* function in the nervous system. This includes "preparing for action, processing of low-level affective or highly learned information . . . and [assigning] value and relevance to stimuli" (Wilbarger & Wilbarger, 2001, p. 12). For example, if a car is coming when you start to cross the street, you not only *alert* to its presence, but you also *evaluate* how fast it is coming so that you can make the decision of whether to proceed at a normal pace, stop abruptly, or run quickly to get out of the way.

Stephen Porges' "polyvagal theory" describes the dual nature of the parasympathetic part of the ANS, usually thought of as our calming "rest and digest" system. He reminds us that the parasympathetic part of the ANS is made up of the *two* major pathways of the vagal nerve. "The ventral vagal responds to cues of safety and supports a sense of centeredness and readiness for social engagement. By contrast, the dorsal vagal pathway responds to cues of life-threat, causing us to shut down, become numb, and disconnect from others" (Dana, 2019, p. 20). (Remember our previous discussion of "shut down" from too much sensory input.)

Bessel van der Kolk (2014) further examines Porges' Polyvagal Theory, which explains that when threatened, our ANS responds in one of three ways depending on the severity of the threat. The *first* level of response is a social or relationship one, in which we look around or call out for help or support using our social engagement (ventral vagal). If there is no aid available and/or we are in more serious real (or perceived) danger, the sympathetic part of our autonomic nervous system activates our fight-or-flight response (*second* level). This helps us to escape by putting the hormone epinephrine (adrenalin) into our systems to increase heart rate and blood pressure and shunt blood to the extremities and brain to facilitate fighting or fleeing. If the level of danger escalates even more and we can't escape, our nervous system tries to preserve itself (*third* level) by "shutting down" into freeze mode, expending as little energy as possible (van der Kolk, 2014). This "shut down" is not a sympathetic reaction, but the parasympathetic system's dorsal vagal response. A social worker who worked with Porges states, "from a polyvagal perspective, a key goal of therapy is to help the client find ways to move out of a dysregulated state – either a numbed-out 'dorsal vagal' state or a hyper-aroused 'sympathetic' one – and return to 'ventral vagal', the biological seat of safety and connectedness" (Dana, 2019, p. 21). Remember that *these reactions are not under conscious control*, and that sensory diet can help us move out of fight-or-flight or shut down into feelings of safety, social engagement, and connectedness.

As noted previously in this book, sensory processing can change substantially from this "norm" if someone has a trauma history. *If there is a trauma history, sensory responses may be triggered by specific, individual sensory events associated with past trauma or abuse.* The trauma survivor will react to *specific* sensory experiences, like a specific smell (gunpowder, smoke, disinfectant, aftershave), but not all smells, or some sounds (fireworks, beeping alarms) but not all sounds. However, if a person *is born with sensory modulation challenges or acquires them in childhood, the person is more likely to react to whole categories of sensation,* for example, many types of tactile sensation or many textures of food in their mouths (Koomar, 2009).

While researchers first investigated the theoretical explanations for sensory modulation challenges in children, it now appears that these same issues are present in individuals who acquire SMC *as* adults. Miller and her team (McIntosh et al., 1999; Miller, 2003; Miller et al., 1999) showed that the sympathetic part of the ANS does play a role in sensory modulation challenges. Schaaf et al. (2003) studied the role of the parasympathetic part of the ANS and found that vagal tone (a heartrate-generated measurement of parasympathetic nervous system functioning) was significantly higher in typical children than in children with sensory processing challenges. Remember, the parasympathetic part of the nervous system provides homeostasis or our feeling of a calm and organized state, and is often what we strive for in our hectic lives, the opposite of the sympathetic system. If the parasympathetic nervous system is functioning at a lower level than "normal," we are more likely to stay stressed and over-aroused. Decreased parasympathetic activity is associated with emotional and behavioral over-reactivity, vulnerability to stress, and a narrow range of behavioral adaptation, which is what we see in persons with sensory modulation challenges (Schaaf et al., 2003).

To more fully study sensory defensiveness, a Sensory Challenge Protocol was developed to evaluate sensory challenges in five systems: olfactory, auditory, visual, tactile, and vestibular. The challenges delivered to participants consisted of a smell, a sound, a picture, an air puff to the neck, and the fast movement of tipping a chair backward. Using electro-dermal (skin) responses, this study revealed that the pattern of responses in *one* sensory system predicts the response in *all the others*. Therefore, defensiveness in sensory responses occurs across the five sensory modalities after input to only one (Miller et al., 1999, 2003): in other words, a person with sensory modulation challenges who is triggered by a specific smell will experience increased arousal (and a potential fight-or-flight response) in all these other systems as measured by increased electrodermal (skin reaction) responses, which indicate sympathetic over-activity. Electrodermal responses are correlated with scores on the Short Sensory Profile (a shorter version of the Sensory Profile often used in research) (McIntosh et al., 1999).

Research is beginning to narrow down the areas of the brain involved in Sensory Processing Disorder (SPD), the larger category that encompasses SMC. Diffusion tensor imaging, an advanced form of MRI, was used in one study to compare the integration of white matter in the brains of sixteen boys between ages 8-11 who had sensory processing disorder (including sensory modulation challenges) with white matter integration in the brains of 24 neurotypical boys. The brain's white matter is responsible for perceiving, thinking, and learning (Owen et al., 2013). Results showed differences in the posterior corpus collosum, which is the structure connecting the two hemispheres of the brain. Whether this is an issue in adults with acquired sensory modulation challenges has not yet been studied.

To summarize the research presented above: sensory modulation challenges in children are related to sympathetic over-reactivity; decreased habituation to sensory stimuli; decreased parasympathetic functioning; decreased self-regulation; and emotional and behavioral over-reactivity.

Measuring Sensory Modulation Challenges (SMC) in Adults

The Adolescent/Adult Sensory Profile (AASP) (Brown & Dunn, 2002) is the most consistently used measure of sensory processing with adults. To see how the AASP relates to other measures, this author (Kimball et al., 2012) compared the sensory profile (AASP) with the Basic Personality Inventory (BPI) in 50 typical women between ages 19-59 (see Figure 3). The BPI is not a diagnostic measure but is a standardized measure of personality tendencies. As can be seen in the chart below, Sensation Seeking was not a significant sensory strategy used by the women, while Sensation Avoiding *was* used and correlated with several personality attributes. Of major interest are the two categories involved in sensory modulation challenges, Low Registration and Sensory Sensitivity. Persons with Low Registration showed many correlated (related) personality attributes, as did those with Sensory Sensitivity. Of particular note is that *sensory sensitivity correlated with anxiety, depression, and hypochondriasis, which we commonly see in people with sensory modulation challenges/sensory defensiveness;* while *low registration correlated with many traits we see in persons with low arousal to sensation.* One asterisk in the following chart shows statistical significance, while two asterisks show stronger statistical significance:

Figure 3:

AASP and BPI Correlations (50 Typical Women)

BPI \ AASP	Sensation Avoiding	Low Registration	Sensory Sensitivity	Sensation Seeking
Hypochondriasis	0.322*	0.388**	0.574**	
Depression	0.325*	0.310**	0.298*	
Alienation		0.384**		
Thinking Disorder		0.384**		
Self-Depreciation		0.407**		
Deviation		0.393**		
Anxiety			0.367**	
Social Introversion	0.358**			
**p ≤ 0.01	*p ≤ 0.05			

Neuroscience Research on PTSD

Recent research is showing that the hypervigilance which has long been documented in PTSD has a clear neurological basis. Clancy et al. (2017) compared participants with PTSD, anxiety disorders, and healthy controls using psychological scales, the PTSD checklist, and electroencephalogram (EEG). EEG studies were done during passive viewing of scenes, "5 min. 921 pictures, neutral, positive, and negative randomly intermixed," in order to measure "adaptive responses in the context rich, unceasing sensory input from the environment" (p. 2043). This study found an "exaggerated intrinsic (resting state) sensory activity in patients with PTSD *as if they were constantly bombarded by busy sensory input....*" The study further notes that those with PTSD failed to show adaptation as visual input increased, "*highlighting a rigid, set mode of sensory hypervigilance in PTSD.* This lack of sensory adaptation can cause not only frequent complaints of sensory hypersensitivity and distress...but also in the long run, blunt sensory registration, resulting in paradoxical problems in sensory numbing in PTSD" (p. 2047). The authors additionally state that *with the overload of sensation, the cortex is not able to use its executive functioning abilities:* "PTSD is associated with dysregulation of the hypothalamic-pituitary-adrenal and noradrenergic systems...these neurochemical imbalances, especially dysregulated dopamine-adrenergic systems, can directly influence sensory gating and processing" (p. 2048). These finding were *not* seen in participants with anxiety disorders or healthy controls, which supports the previously discussed research on SMC.

Weiss (2007) presented a thorough analysis of how traumatic stress influences brain structure and function, and how these neurobiological changes are related to the symptoms experienced after trauma. A summary of her work is displayed in following chart. Note that the symptoms she highlights are related to SMC.

Brain Area, Issue	Result
Decreased ability of the prefrontal cortex to inhibit	Hypervigilance, startle, misinterpreting innocuous stimuli as potential threats (p. 115)
Relay from thalamus to cortex under high arousal	If person pays high attention to trauma information, this can contribute to hyperarousal. If they pay low attention, this can contribute to dissociation (p.116)
Hippocampus, decreased cell volume	Avoidance, numbing
Amygdala hyperresponsivity	Hyperarousal, startle, irritability, angry outbursts, hypervigilance (p. 117)
HPA Axis: hypothalamus, controls endocrine function, with stress secretes CRH which stimulates ACTH from pituitary	ACTH stimulates adrenals to produce cortisol, the stress hormone (p.117)
Cortisol increases sensitivity of thalamus to threatening stimuli	Lower-level threats can cause alarm (p. 118)
Glutamate also from adrenals creates prolonged excitation of cell firing patterns	Creates strong, vivid memories, intrusive thoughts. Excess causes excitotoxicity (cell death) leading to numbing, avoidance, dissociation (p. 118)
Increased adrenal activation results in increased sympathetic nervous system activation and to increased cortisol and increased epinephrine	Increased heart rate, respiration, metabolism, attention, startle, "overgeneralization of trauma-related arousal to other situations and events" (p. 120)

Norepinephrine sharpens focus during fight-or-flight with chronic stress, loses inhibitory ability	Increased norepinephrine contributes to anxiety, sleep problems, nightmares, hypervigilance, startle, irritability, and consolidation of long-term trauma memories leading to reexperiencing, flashbacks, intrusive memories (p.120)
Serotonin calms and decreases anxiety; chronic activation due to reexperiencing leads to depletion	Depletion contributes to hyperarousal, impulsivity, and irritability (p.121)
Dopamine is increased by stress	Increased levels "contribute to feelings of depersonalization" (p.121)

Judah et al. (2018) tested 104 veterans with PTSD. Their findings "suggested that hyperarousal, but not other PTSD symptoms, explained the relationship between neurobehavioral symptoms and cognitive functioning" (p. E10). Their results were "consistent with evidence in the PTSD literature which shows that hyperarousal is associated with attention and working memory dysfunction. Features of hyperarousal, such as hypervigilance, may interfere with the efficiency of working memory through preoccupation of cognitive resources" (p. E14). The authors suggest that "beyond PTSD our findings highlight a need for research to investigate hyperarousal as a transdiagnostic source of attention and working memory impairment" (p. E14).

Research on Sensory Modulation

Research on sensory modulation challenges in adults is fairly new. The Adolescent/Adult Sensory Profile (AASP) has been used in several studies. As is further discussed in Appendix IV, I was the primary author of a treatment study of four women with PTSD from trauma they experienced as adults (Kimball et al., 2017). The women used the Wilbarger Therapressure Protocol™ (see Appendix IV) as a sensory self-treatment and were assessed with the AASP as well as two unpublished sensory profiles, the Sensory Over Responsivity Inventory (SensOR) and the Sensory Under Responsivity

Inventory (SensUR) (Miller & Schoen, 2008), which readers of this book will recognize from Chapters 7 and 9. After following this sensory modulation self-treatment (the Wilbarger Therapressure Protocol™) for 2 weeks, results showed positive changes in *modulating* cortisol levels, which resulted in normalizing arousal. This was reflected in decreased stress, increased concentration, increased participation in life activities, improvement in some personality measures, and improved sensory scores on the SensOR. In fact, the SensOR, which registers hyperarousal, appeared to be the most sensitive to change of any of the sensory assessments. Cortisol was measured because it is indicative of arousal levels, and hyperarousal is one of the major symptoms of PTSD. The modulation of cortisol levels after self-treatment with the Wilbarger Therapressure Protocol™ is particularly noteworthy, as previous research had shown that 8 weeks of treatment for PTSD using psychotherapy or pharmacotherapy (Sertraline) did *not* result in changes in total cortisol output even when the treatment was successful enough to allow removal of the PTSD label (Pacella et al., 2014).

Two studies I conducted (Kimball, 2021; Kimball, 2021a) revealed that veterans with a medical diagnosis of PTSD had significantly more issues with SMC when compared to veterans who thought they might have PTSD but lacked a medical PTSD diagnosis (2021). Using the AASP (Brown & Dunn, 2002), this author (Kimball, 2021) determined that veterans with a medical diagnosis of PTSD showed significantly increased Sensory Sensitivity, Low Registration, and Sensation Avoiding (types of sensory modulation challenges). On the unpublished SensOR (Miller & Schoen, 2008), the PTSD group also showed significantly higher scores. Of interest are the correlations among the Basic Personality Inventory (BPI) and the AASP (see Figure 4). The BPI factors are grouped in ways that make behavioral sense with what we know about AASP factors, lending further validity to using both inventories when working with those with PTSD.

Figure 4:

Veterans with PTSD, Correlations Among BPI and AASP Factors

BPI \ AASP	Sensory Sensitivity	Low Registration	Sensation Avoiding	Sensation Seeking
Hypochondriasis	.659**		.519**	-.442**
Depression	.516**		.584**	-.418*
Denial				
Interpersonal Problems	.467**		.403*	
Alienation			.340*	-.408*
Persecutory Ideas	.424*	.370*	.427*	
Anxiety	.648**	.389*	.561**	-.379*
Thinking Disorder	.411*	.430*	.398*	
Impulse Expression	.519**	.536**	.447**	
Social Introversion	.603**	.350*	.663**	-.371*
Self-Depreciation	.376*		.382*	-.384*
Deviation	.583**	.442**	.515**	-.364*
**p≤ .01 *p≤ .05				

Additionally this author (Kimball, 2021a) used the unpublished SensOR as well as the unpublished SensUR (Miller & Schoen, 2008) to compare the responses of six groups. Eighty-six people self-selected one of six categories and filled out the SensOR and SensUR. As there are no published norms for these inventories, the mean (average) scores were compared. Both scales showed the same order in their average scores from highest to lowest, with higher scores indicating more sensory modulation issues. The order was 1. Veterans with PTSD; 2. Non-veterans with a trauma history; 3. Non-veterans with PTSD; 4. "Regular" people (not a veteran and no history of a traumatic event); 5. Veterans without PTSD who were deployed to a combat area; 6. Veterans without PTSD who were not deployed to a combat area. It is interesting that groups 5 and 6 had lower SensOR and SensUR scores than "regular" people. It is possible that these veterans had comparatively lower scores because they didn't experience trauma and that they had participated in strong daily sensory diets while in the military, which kept their nervous systems in well-modulated states so they could handle higher stress if it occurred, or that there is much more stress in our "regular" environments than we like to admit. (Note: This study was conducted pre-COVID-19.)

The AASP has been used as a metric in several yoga studies, one conducted by the Army on reducing combat stress in deployed soldiers (Stoller et al., 2012). In this study, the AASP did not show the changes after the yoga program that *were* picked up by other sensory measures, perhaps indicating that the AASP may be a good diagnostic tool but may not be as sensitive in showing functional *change* after treatment. (I found the same pattern in my Wilbarger Therapressure Protocol™ study [Kimball et al., 2017], in which the AASP did not show change but the SensOR did.) However, yoga practice contains the basic sensory diet components of deep breathing and heavy work, and Stoller et al. (2012) stated that "results support using sensory enhanced hatha yoga for proactive combat stress management" (p. 59).

Yoga is recommended as a possible treatment for PTSD by numerous authors. Most of these authors use psychological measures and do not measure sensory modulation; however, they interpret the improvements in PTSD symptoms as likely being due to the breathing and mindfulness portions of yoga (Reinhardt et al., 2018; Cushing et al., 2018), which we know can be part of a sensory diet to reduce SMC.

Sensory Modulation and Pain

Researchers have begun to examine the relationships between sensory modulation and pain perception, and the ability to cope with pain. One study conducted with samples of "healthy adults" looked at what is referred to as "pain catastrophizing," which is defined by Engel-Yeger and Dunn (2011) as "an exaggerated negative cognitive response to actual or anticipated pain... associated with enhanced pain experience and pain related outcomes" (p. e1). The researchers considered this to be a coping strategy and found that it was positively correlated with AASP Sensory Sensitivity, as well as with Sensation Avoiding and Low Registration (remember that these are all terms for sensory modulation challenges and related behaviors). Meredith et al. (2015) found that AASP Sensory Sensitivity and Sensation Avoiding are directly related to higher levels of pain catastrophizing. This may be interpreted to mean that some people with sensory hyperarousal may have a more difficult time taking an active role in coping and dealing with pain.

In a study of women with fibromyalgia, Wilbarger and Cook (2011) found that the women self-reported more sensory hypersensitivity to sensations found in daily life in the areas of smell, audition, taste, and touch when compared with a group of women who do not experience chronic pain and a group with rheumatoid arthritis.

Neurotransmitter Research: An Interesting Question

As we have discussed previously, traumatic events or prolonged exposure to highly stressful situations result in a sympathetic nervous system response which can lead to hyperarousal and even "shut down." We discussed that hyperarousal is *not* primarily a mental health issue, but a difference in how the brain is interpreting sensory input from the environment resulting in more frequent sympathetic activation. The "staying alive" fight-or-flight response originates in the amygdala which along with the hippocampus makes up the limbic system which governs emotion. During fight-or-flight, the amygdala activates the sympathetic nervous system to "produce high levels of neurotransmitters (i.e., epinephrine, norepinephrine, and dopamine). These neurotransmitters are charged with activating certain physical reactions, such as, constricting blood vessels, increasing heart rate, and dilating pupils" which are necessary to fight or flee successfully. The amygdala also communicates with the hippocampus which forms memories of the trauma (Ramirez, 2016, p. 40). As we have discussed, sensory modulation challenges are the result of the nervous system's staying in a state of hyperarousal and continuing to react to sensations from the environment with a fight-or-flight response.

Future research may help us to better understand the relationship between sensory modulation challenges, neurotransmitter changes, and mental health. Compulsive behaviors are often seen in persons with sensory modulation challenges, as they use compulsions to try to feel safer in a world that their nervous systems frequently interpret as "unsafe." In the late 1980s, research started to be reported that showed changes in the neurotransmitter glutamate, including some cell death caused by excess glutamate under extremely stressful conditions. This led me to question whether this cell death could lead to SMC in the case of trauma in adults. Up to that time, we had been focused primarily on SMC in children who were born with it. The research indicated to me that "sensory defensiveness can be 'acquired' ...and that the mechanism is not psychological but physiological. Cell death leads to lessening the ability of the cortex to inhibit incoming sensory stimulation. Research has shown that rats lose cortical sensing cells in their hippocampus under abusive conditions and that abused women who experience increased anxiety, depression, and trouble with stress show hippocampal differences" (Kimball, 1999, p. 131).

Glutamate tends to stimulate neurons in many regions of the brain, including areas found to be active in obsessive compulsive disorder (OCD). Glutamate fuels neuronal circuits involved in decisions leading to rewarding outcomes, especially *when the choices require sifting through data and experience* (using a part of the brain called the cortical-basal ganglia circuit). Mutations in the glutamate transporter gene might impair the ability to regulate activity in this circuit, leading to decisions and behavior that do not objectively make sense. This appears to alter a person's ability to sift through data and make decisions based on experience, "leading them to see danger when none is present and obsess over it" (Moyer, 2011, p. 39). This study provides more evidence regarding the question of whether the neurotransmitter glutamate may be related to some of the symptoms seen in sensory modulation challenges.

Berger et al. (2019) have found another surprising piece of the puzzle. The release of adrenalin is not the exclusive stimulating component many believed it to be that causes the fight-or-flight response in our nervous systems after a high-stress threat. Instead, it appears that acute stress also causes the release of *osteocalcin* from *bones* within minutes. Osteocalcin inhibits the parasympathetic tone from mediating the sympathetic (fight-or-flight) stress response. And the neurotransmitter glutamate "is required for osteocalcin release during an acute stress response."

Holmes et al. (2017) studied possible dysfunction in the glutamate system in persons with PTSD versus healthy controls. They stated that "glutamate is thought to play a key role in the pathogenesis of PTSD for several reasons: glutamate underlies synaptic plasticity and memory formation, stress significantly impacts glutamate transmission, and the glutamate receptor antagonist ketamine may have efficacy in treating PTSD" (p. 8390). Many people consider ketamine to be a wonder drug (Lyford, 2019) as it "targets the glutamate system thought to restore neural connections that regulate mood and the ability to feel pleasure" (p. 11). "Esketamine, a variation of the ketamine molecule, was granted FDA approval for depression treatment" (Lyford, 2019, p. 12) – though it bears noting here that ketamine also has the potential for addiction and abuse, and its use must be closely monitored by a prescribing physician.

What Does This Research Mean?

Most practitioners are trained in, or aware of, the medical and psychological applications of research and treatment for people who are "stressed out" on a regular basis to the point where their stress level negatively impacts their physical health and daily functioning. If we do not know about or consider sensory modulation challenges, we may miss an important contributing cause of this high stress. This is especially true of the specific ways in which sensory modulation challenges can contribute to behaviors that are often seen as mental health issues like PTS, PTSD, and mTBI. Our understanding needs to change so that a fuller range of treatment and self-treatment choices may be made available to the many veterans, first responders, and frontline medical workers who have developed sensory modulation challenges.

APPENDIX II:

More About Interpersonal Relationships

The Second "I" in DIAL IT DOWN:
"Interpersonal Relationships and Intimacy"

How Do Sensory Modulation Challenges Affect How We
Demonstrate and Participate in Our Relationships?

As discussed throughout this book, sensory modulation challenges can affect many different aspects of our most intimate relationships, as well as our casual interactions with others. This appendix includes a list of some common types of social interactions that may be *difficult for* and evoke a *different response in* people with SMC – differences that could potentially lead to misunderstandings and unintended consequences. It also suggests ways to *modify your environment* in these interactions so that your reactions will be less bothersome to you and others. Remember that *modifying your environment is one of the key ways of dealing with sensory modulation challenges*. Note that the social interactions below are sorted by category. (Please also note that while some of these interactions, such as greeting others with handshakes or hugs and dealing with crowded spaces, have been curtailed or altered for safety reasons during COVID-19, traditional [pre-COVID-19] customs are discussed here, as looking back at past interactions will help you to better understand yourself and your social relationships, and normality will return.) As with all issues related to SMC, please remember that *it's individual*, and while some of the information below may be highly relevant to your daily life and functioning, other information may not be: choose what works for *you*.

GREETING OTHER PEOPLE

ACTIVITY: HANDSHAKE WITH A FIRM GRIP

How It's Usually Done: Standard way, your right hand to other's right hand.

Sensory Safety Level: Handshakes generally feel very sensory safe for people with SMC as long as the other person does not try to touch you with their other hand (for instance, a *light* touch on your shoulder with their left hand while shaking your right), or if they have a very light grip.

Why: Standard handshakes usually feel okay because heavy firm touch is modulating.

Alternatives to Make It Feel Safer for Your Sensory System: In appropriate contexts, you can prevent the other person from touching you with their other hand by putting your left hand on their shoulder to (subtly) keep them at arm's length. If you know you'll be going to a meeting or large social gathering where you'll be shaking hands with strangers, be sure to include sensory diet activities *beforehand*; and if you're meeting a new "boss" or someone you feel it's important to impress, you can *visually* check in on their handshake style before they reach you by observing how they shake hands with others. This cognitive awareness and readiness will help you to anticipate and modulate your own responses to things like a light shoulder touch (if you *know* it's coming, there's much less of a chance that your sensory system will react with surprise).

ACTIVITY: HUGGING

How It's Usually Done: Many types, including bear hugs, light hugs, hugs with back rubbing or patting.

Sensory Safety Level: How "sensory safe" a hug feels to someone with SMC depends very much on the type of hug. Hugging firmly with a back rub or pat is usually the most modulating. The lighter the hug, the more it arouses the sensory system.

Why: Heavy touch pressure is modulating.

Alternatives to Make It Feel Safer for Your Sensory System: If you don't want a hug, reach out for a handshake. If you want to hug someone with SMC, ask first if it's okay to hug them and let them know that the hug will be firm. If you have SMC, communicate your hug preferences to your friends and family members (even fairly young children will appreciate and incorporate things like, "Mom likes BIG hugs best!"). For people with sensory modulation challenges, *bear hugs rule!*

ACTIVITY: GREETING KISS ON THE CHEEK

Sensory Safety Level: If done firmly with dry lips to a cheek, this can be tolerated by someone with SMC; if lips are wet, it can feel a little like "spitting," which is very alerting. Also alerting (and confusing, if you're not dating!) can be the "friend" who likes to hello-kiss you on the lips.

Why: Light touch and wetness can both be over-alerting. The entire face is a highly sensory-sensitive area as it connects to multiple senses (eyes, ears, nose, and mouth) that are crucial to survival.

Alternatives to Make It Feel Safer for Your Sensory System: Initiate a hug instead. If the person is someone you see regularly and they are a "kisser," you can teach them about sensory-safe ways to show you affection. Again, *bear hugs rule!*

ACTIVITY: GREETING IF YOU DON'T WANT TO BE TOUCHED

How It's Done: Wave, smile, and say "Hi."

Sensory Safety Level: Very safe.

Why: You have avoided touch.

Alternatives to Make It Feel Safer for Your Sensory System: In our culture, it's not always possible to avoid social touch entirely without appearing rude – which may be challenging in the workplace and at work-related gatherings (where you can use the sensory techniques outlined above in dealing with handshakes and cheek kisses). But you *can* speak openly to family, friends, and even casual acquaintances (if you feel at ease with the latter) about the fact that social touch isn't always comfortable for you, with a simple statement like, "That's just the way I'm made," or with a fuller description *if you want. Your comfort level* in both touch and conversation matters!

REST AND SLEEP

ACTIVITY: HOW TO HAVE SOMEONE WAKE YOU UP SAFELY

How It's Done: People with SMC often startle or have a big reaction to being awakened suddenly (and may unintentionally move their arms or legs with force to avoid perceived danger). Ask the person who will be waking you up to make noise while they're still some distance away from you. Discuss in advance your preference for the type of noise and how far away from you they should be. If you are a veteran, ask them to use a sound that would not commonly be interpreted as a threat during active duty – for example, singing a favorite children's song, or striking a mellow-sounding ringing bowl.

Sensory Safety Level: Low – wake-ups can be challenging.

Why: Sleep can be very difficult for people with SMC; you may sleep very lightly to stay "on guard," or "conk out" when exhausted into a very deep sleep.

Alternatives to Make It Feel Safer for Your Sensory System: Have the person who's waking you make noises that are "as safe as possible" for you. This will help to you realize who they are and where they are so that you don't unintentionally strike out at them. Though many veterans choose to sleep with guns beside them, *this is not a safe practice in a home setting.* Take the weapon out from under your pillow and unload it! (Remember the veteran in Chapter 2 who almost accidentally shot his wife.) On the off chance that a real threat does enter your house, you will, with your training, almost certainly have time to quickly retrieve and load your weapon – and "guarding" against an unlikely threat is *simply not worth the very present danger* of accidentally harming your spouse or kids. You can also install an alarm system in your home, preferably one with a panel that you can visually reference in the night (from bed) for reassurance if you wake suddenly.

ACTIVITY: ABILITY TO FALL ASLEEP

How It's Usually Done: While people without SMC can generally fall asleep with no specific preparation at the end of the day, people *with* SMC often find it very difficult to get to sleep no matter how tired they are.

Sensory Safety Level: Low – sleep often doesn't feel "safe."

Why: The sensory systems of veterans, first responders, and frontline medical workers are often "on guard," hyper-aroused to threats.

Alternatives to Make It Feel Safer for Your Sensory System: Use preparation activities for sleep. Lower your arousal level before sleep. Use slow push-ups, slow movements with hand or ankle weighs, a rocking chair (for calming vestibular input), or a warm bath. Some people use "white noise" machines. Others don't, for fear that this would mask sounds they might consider dangerous. Assess the level of actual threat and, as stated before, consider installing an alarm system to give you visual reassurance.

ACTIVITY: FATIGUE

Sensory Safety Level: Low; poor sleep is particularly problematic for people with SMC.

Why: When a person with SMC is fatigued, their sensory sensitivity actually *increases*. They have much less tolerance for sensory input from the environment, even those things that don't *usually* bother them.

Alternatives to Make It Feel Safer for Your Sensory System: Be aware of times when you're fatigued, and try to engage in extra sensory diet activities and/or to decrease sensory input. When you're extremely fatigued, ten minutes of jumping on a mini trampoline might do you a great deal more good than would lying down for a nap (if you *can* sleep, great, but fatigue often has the counter-intuitive effect of *heightening* arousal levels in people with SMC and making sleep more difficult). Lower your arousal level through calming sensory diet activities before any attempt at sleep.

ACTIVITY: HOW TO STAY ASLEEP

How It's Done: Improved sleep has been reported by service members sleeping under a special heavy weighted blanket (up to 30 lbs.). Research shows that these blankets are safe and effective in reducing anxiety (Mullen et al., 2013).

Sensory Safety Level: Highly safe and calming.

Why: Weighted blankets provide heavy touch pressure, which is modulating.

TOUCH

ACTIVITY: SOMEONE TOUCHING YOUR HAIR

How It's Done: This is often done to children to demonstrate affection, in the form of a quick head/hair rub.

Sensory Safety Level: Low – this can feel very uncomfortable for people with SMC.

Why: Hair is protective to the head, and light touch in this area will be very alerting.

Alternatives to Make It Feel Safer for Your Sensory System: Fortunately, this kind of touch is most often done by family members, to whom you can talk about your own or your child's SMC. If you are particularly sensitive in this area, you can also consider using a hat to prevent anything/anyone from unexpectedly touching your or your child's head.

ACTIVITY: SOMEONE BRUSHES AGAINST YOU

How It's Done: This often happens in crowded areas, as a light accidental touch – which, for someone with SMC, is actually more bothersome than a heavy bump.

Sensory Safety Level: Low – this is uncomfortable.

Why: Light touch alerts you to danger, while heavy touch is modulating.

Alternatives to Make It Feel Safer for Your Sensory System: Before you go to a crowded area like a mall, a supermarket during peak hours, or a concert, be sure that you've done your sensory diet work, and carry portable sensory diet items with you (for example, an exercise stretch tube or band to use for a few quick arm exercises).

ACTIVITY: ELEVATORS

Sometimes you must take an elevator even if you don't want to. Stairs are always a better option for people with SMC because they provide heavy work, and function as a sensory diet activity. Stairs also give you more space and movement options, which is key for veterans and first responders who've been trained to "always look for an exit."

Sensory Safety Level: Low – elevators can be very uncomfortable for some people with SMC.

Why: Elevators have "no exit," can be very crowded, and put you in close proximity with many smells (perfumes, cologne, body odors).

Alternatives to Make It Feel Safer for Your Sensory System: Try to stand with your back to a wall (the classic protective/defensive stance for active-duty personnel in close quarters). Some people prefer the back wall, while others prefer the areas of the side walls that are as close to the elevator doors as possible. Before you get in, take a few deep breaths or do hand pushes.

ACTIVITY: UNPLEASANT SUBSTANCES ON HANDS

How It's Done: Putting your hands in sticky or unpleasant substances or into any area you can't see: people with SMC who have children find themselves facing this type of "mess" much more frequently than those who don't!

Sensory Safety Level: Low – this can be very uncomfortable for people with SMC.

Why: Unpleasant substances or even just the thought of "what's in there?!" can activate tactile defensiveness.

Alternatives to Make It Feel Safer for Your Sensory System: If you need to deal with unpleasant substances, wear vinyl gloves (always keep a box of these around if you have kids or pets), and use a flashlight when reaching into dark places (or explain your sensory sensitivity in this area to your spouse or partner and use an "I" statement to ask them to help by reaching in for you).

CONVERSATIONS/SOUNDS

ACTIVITY: LISTENING TO OTHERS WHEN IN A SENSORY STIMULATING ENVIRONMENT

How It's Done: Difficulty with *hearing* what others are saying can be a problem for people with SMC due to their difficulty in *screening out* background noise.

Sensory Safety Level: Low – this can be very uncomfortable.

Why: When you are hyper-aroused by the environment, your nervous system is focused on "finding danger and reacting," not on listening to the content and emotion of the person who's talking to you. This is an *involuntary* sensory response – you are not deliberately ignoring them.

Alternatives to Make It Feel Safer for Your Sensory System: Using sensory diet strategies before going into a sensory stimulating environment will lower the set-point of your nervous system so that you can tolerate the environment for a longer period of time. And *talking about* your SMC issues with friends and family members can help to keep "blame" out of these types of situations: for instance, you can say to your brother-in-law before going to a pro basketball game with him, "My issues sometimes make it hard for me to tune into conversations when there's lots of stuff going on around me; let's grab a beer afterwards (or beforehand) to catch up." Similarly, if you're going Christmas shopping at the mall with friends or family, you can mention your issues and pick a quiet spot where you can more easily listen and talk for lunch. You can also try to plan ahead and pick venues for get-togethers that will be more comfortable and less sensory-stimulating for you – and while this isn't always possible in social relations, you may find that if you explain your challenges using some of the conversational strategies we've discussed, many friends and family members will be open to adapting. And, of course, always plan to do sensory diet activities before you go out to any sensory stimulating place.

ACTIVITY: LISTENING TO OTHERS WHEN ON HYPERAROUSAL

How It's Done: Even in a quiet environment, if you're on "high arousal," you won't really be able to "listen" well to what the other person is saying.

Sensory Safety Level: Low – this is very uncomfortable for people with SMC.

Why: Same as above. When your sensory system is alerted and "looking out" for danger, it's hard to focus on any type of conversation – and this can become particularly fraught and problematic with emotionally charged material or something the other person feels it's really important for you to hear and react to.

Alternatives to Make It Feel Safer for Your Sensory System: Use your sensory diet strategies, and find a time of day for important conversations when your nervous system is less likely to be over-aroused. Be honest and open with family members about your sensory issues and how they can affect your ability to listen. Consider developing a code word or signal to use with your spouse or partner if emotionally charged issues come up when you're not in a modulated sensory place to address them as fully as you'd like to. This can help to reduce the kinds of blaming and "You're not listening to me!" spirals that can make the issues that are bound to come up in *any* intimate relationship even *more* charged and difficult for people with SMC. Keep your signal simple, and make it something that's impersonal so that blame is not attached; something like, "I want to listen to you, but my body's not in a good place for that right now." One veteran who had a very understanding spouse kept a "rain check" chip in the form of a clock-face magnet on the refrigerator to hold up when he needed space before engaging in emotionally charged conversations with his partner or kids: everyone in the family understood that this meant he needed a few minutes of sensory diet time before being able to listen fully.

ACTIVITY: SINGING

Sensory Safety Level: High – singing alone or as part of a choral group can be modulating for people with SMC.

Why: Deep breathing is modulating; and the high-frequency sounds and overtones in live singing are modulating. The sounds you're making also cover bothersome environmental sounds.

Alternatives to Make It Feel Safer for Your Sensory System: If you're considering participating in a chorus, make sure that the practice times and spaces feel "sensory safe" to you (and/or that you can incorporate sensory diet work beforehand). Some contemporary songs involve short, "choppy" vocal riffs, and this is less modulating (and can even be overly stimulating); the best types of music for SMC are choral music, classical music, or music accompanied by a distinct beat (drumming).

ACTIVITY: LISTENING TO CLASSICAL MUSIC OR MUSIC WITH A STRONG BEAT

How It's Done: Live or via recordings.

Sensory Safety Level: High – this can help people with SMC.

Why: Classical music has high-frequency sounds and overtones which are very modulating to the nervous system. Music with a steady beat (rhythmic drumming) is also modulating. Remember that live music is particularly good for SMC because all sounds are present; none have been removed to make the music fit an electronic format.

Alternatives to Make It Feel Safer for Your Sensory System: If you're planning to go to a concert, think about the concert venue (crowds, incidental noises, and smells) beforehand. Use your sensory diet strategies before you go, and keep an emergency sensory diet "kit" on hand for the concert (elastic stretching band, or a plan for wall pushups in a bathroom stall, etc.) in case you start to feel your sensory arousal level rising. If you have a choice of seating, consider an aisle seat (with a ready "exit") or a seat with wall space around you so that you don't have to feel 360-degrees "on guard."

VISUAL ISSUES

ACTIVITY: THINGS OUT OF PLACE

How It's Done: Anything out of place can trigger a survival response in people with SMC who are visually sensitive.

Sensory Safety Level: Very low – this can be profoundly uncomfortable.

Why: Military, first-responder, or medical training and experience have shown you that anything out of place could pose a life-or-death threat.

Alternatives to Make It Feel Safer for Your Sensory System: Use sensory diet activities throughout the day to keep your nervous system in that "just right place" so that you can make informed decisions about the actual danger of a given situation. If your nervous system starts out in a modulated place, the survival trigger will not have as much of a chance to "take over."

ACTIVITY: CLUTTER

How It's Done: Every household has some degree of clutter – and kids in particular are clutter-making machines!

Sensory Safety Level: Low – clutter can be very uncomfortable for people with visual SMC.

Why: Anything out of place increases your arousal level, as you never know what may be concealed under the clutter. Again, your first responder, military, or medical training taught you to constantly scan the environment for anything "unusual" or "out of place".

Alternatives to Make It Feel Safer for Your Sensory System: A steady sensory diet will help to keep your nervous system in a modulated range so that the "danger arousal" of seeing things out of place won't take over. If this is a big issue for you, then *talking* to your family is crucial; many veterans have voiced the frustration and remorse they feel about their at-times-reflexive tendency to "yell at the kids" about clutter. Explain to your kids, if they're old enough, that clutter just doesn't feel "safe" to you. If particular times of day are frequent triggers—for instance, the clutter you trip over when you come home in the evening—then you can work together to make a "family plan" to manage this. You can even make a "game" out of it, cupping your hands around your eyes like exaggerated "blinders" when you first come in the door, and having a clutter-cleanup playlist with the kids laughing and competing to clean everything up by the time a fun song is done. Organize your environment so that clean-up is easy (plastic storage bins and drawers that toys or crayons can quickly be tossed into can be placed in kids' rooms and also in the kitchen or any room where kid clutter accumulates).

ACTIVITY: EYE GAZE

How It's Done: Some people with SMC find direct eye gaze to be threatening to their sensory systems.

Sensory Safety Level: This varies by person; some people aren't bothered at all and even welcome direct eye gaze, while others experience uncomfortable sensory-defensive reactions and/or quickly look away.

Why: The tendency to find direct eye gaze threatening is probably a hold-over from our "reptile" brains, a time way back in evolution when direct eye contact meant a physical challenge. If your sensory system is on high-alert, these "survival brain" holdovers will have more force.

Alternatives to Make It Feel Safer for Your Sensory System: Sensory diet throughout the day will modulate sensory responses including response to eye gaze. If you've developed an eye gaze aversion that's affecting your work, consider seeking out an occupational therapist for specific training in this area. One commonly used strategy is to train yourself to look at the other person's eyebrows, not their eyes (this is close enough that most people won't notice the difference). If you work in a military context and your eye gaze aversion developed as part of SMC resulting from active duty, consider explaining this to your commanding officer. And as always, if it's affecting your personal life, it's important that you *talk about* and explain this specific challenge to your family and friends.

ACTIVITY: FAST MOVEMENTS

How It's Done: Fast-moving cars, some carnival rides.

Sensory Safety Level: Varies: some people with SMC find fast movements very threatening, while others don't.

Why: Fast movements can *alert* some people to danger, but others find this type of movement modulating, especially if *they have control* over the speed and sensory input, like driving a fast car or motorcycle (motorcycles also add proprioceptive and vestibular input – though, wear a helmet), or if the movement is predictable and repetitive like it is in some carnival rides (though not in others).

Alternatives to Make It Feel Safer for Your Sensory System: Keep your nervous system in the "just right place" through sensory diet so that you have the ability to react from a modulated rather than a heightened sensory starting point. This will allow you to make a cognitive decision about the fast-moving sensory input, not just a survival one. If unpredictable fast movements bother you, avoid settings like a fast-moving hockey game, or a gymnastics competition with many different events going on at once (always explain specific issues that affect your kids—like missing a gymnastics or track meet—to them in an age-appropriate way, and follow up by having a spouse or friend take a video of your child's event and watching it with them afterward to show them you *do* care; even if kids *say* they "don't mind," they usually do!). If you *like* to drive fast, explain this to your spouse or partner and realize that fast driving may scare others, even though it might modulate you: go for drives on your own (*follow the law, and wear a helmet on a motorcycle or ATV*), and always respond to your passenger's concerns just as you'd like them to respond to yours.

SMELLS

ACTIVITY: ALL SMELLS

Sensory Safety Level: Varies widely based on a person with SMC's specific issues.

Why: Smells primarily go straight to the emotional (limbic) centers of the brain, so your response will have a survival (fight-or-flight) quality. Certain smells will initiate past memories, and if these are related to past trauma, they can act as triggers. Things like diesel fuel, gasoline, burning rubber, and smoke may have an increased effect on veterans; hospital-related smells like alcohol swabs and disinfectant may have an increased effect on frontline medical workers when they're experienced outside of a hospital setting (for instance, when your spouse cleans up a child's wound or when you're cleaning the bathroom at home).

Alternatives to Make It Feel Safer for Your Sensory System: It your nervous system is modulated through a regular sensory diet, then your sensory *reactions* will be more modulated – and you'll also have the chance for a mental "pause" to think about what the smell is and what it means rather than responding automatically. If you know that certain smells tend to be triggers, you can avoid them when possible (you can for instance avoid fireworks, and speak openly to your spouse about the smell of gasoline and make a plan for them to be the one who usually fills up the car). You can keep sensory "tools" handy – for instance, keep a stretch band in the car for a quick sensory diet activity before you get out to fill it up.

PLACES/EVENTS

ACTIVITY: SHOPPING (CROWDED MALL, LIKE AT CHRISTMAS)

How It's Done: Stores can have what may feel like "too many" sounds, visual contrasts, strong smells, people touching you, etc.

Sensory Safety Level: Low – this can be a very uncomfortable setting for people with SMC.

Why: Sensory overload – there's too much stimuli for your high-alert system to process.

Alternatives to Make It Feel Safer for Your Sensory System: If you have to go to a space like this, use sensory diet activities before going and keep your time there short. Make a shopping list in the order of how things are arranged in the store so that you don't have to backtrack. Plan to shop at "down times" like late at night or early in the morning when there will be fewer people present. Plan to go on days when there are likely to be the least number of shoppers – for example, a weekday instead of a weekend.

ACTIVITY: SPORTS EVENTS

Sensory Safety Level: Low – these events can be very uncomfortable for people with SMC.

Why: Crowds, noises, and smells mean sensory overload, which activates sensory defensiveness; also, the constant background clamor and noise mean that you "can't hear danger" and you'll be (unconsciously) straining to listen for it.

Alternatives to Make It Feel Safer for Your Sensory System: Sit high in the stands so that you can scan the environment around you, preferably against a wall so that nobody can "sneak up" behind you. Add sensory diet before you go, and while you're there incorporate sensory "snacks" like jumping (heavy work), cheering (deep breathing), and singing team songs. Think of quiet places like restrooms (*not* at halftime) where you can take a longer sensory break if you need to. While having a few drinks is fine (check in with your doctor about any potential medication interactions), try to avoid drinking to the point of self-medicating with alcohol; one of alcohol's first effects is to disinhibit – including disinhibiting your sensory system's ability to screen out stimuli, which may make you *more* rather than less alerted; and drinking heavily can come at the cost of a jittery rebound with your senses in overdrive, the exact opposite of what you need.

ACTIVITY: CHURCH

Sensory Safety Level: Moderate to high. Church and other places of worship or religious practice usually feel "safe" for people with SMC.

Why: Prayer, singing (deep breathing), and meditation decrease blood pressure and overall sensory arousal levels. The high-frequency sounds and overtones you're likely to hear in church music are modulating. Music with a distinct beat also works.

Alternatives to Make It Feel Safer for Your Sensory System: As with other venues, you can plan ahead to pick a seating spot that will work best for you. If you're sensitive to light touch, you can make a plan to leave either before or *after* the milling-around "touchy" time that tends to occur immediately following a standard church service (you can remain in the pews for ten minutes of quiet, for instance). Use hand pushes or leg presses if you need a "sensory snack" during the service or just before leaving.

ACTIVITY: MOVIE THEATER

Sensory Safety Level: Varies. Some people with SMC love going to the movies, while others experience heightened sensory-defensive reactions and anxiety.

Why: The movies involve not just sitting and watching, but also the expectation that you must remember many things all at once: which movie, what time, how many tickets of each type, what each person wants to eat. You're likely to experience people standing too close in line and might feel hemmed in by seating. This can result in sensory overload for you – which will in turn *decrease your ability to attend to details and remember them* (leading, for instance, to crabby kids – "Mom always gets the wrong popcorn!" "Dad can never remember that I want Twizzlers!" and additional upset).

Alternatives to Make It Feel Safer for Your Sensory System: Do sensory diet activities before leaving for the movies. Write down details about tickets and food orders, or designate someone else to get the food. Buy your tickets online if that's an option, and plan to get there a little early so you can pick the seat where you feel safest: last row, aisle, etc. Remember "sensory snack" tips like hand presses and leg pushes while seated. Communicate your sensory needs to your friends and family: you may choose to find a quiet spot to go to (a corner of the hallway, restroom, etc.) while the ads for upcoming movies are playing, as these are sometimes deliberately played at a higher volume by the theater, and ask your friend or partner to text you when the credits start to roll, or wear earplugs. Many movie theaters now run "sensory friendly" movies with the theater lights left on low and the volume also set lower. Ask the theater manager if you can take a peek at one of these before you commit to going, as there may be many children with sensory challenges attending, which may add too much distraction for you.

ACTIVITY: FAMILY EVENTS

How It's Done: These events contain many opportunities for sensory and emotional overload.

Sensory Safety Level: How these events feel to people with SMC varies widely based on the type of event and the people attending.

Why: Lots of unexpected sensory input is possible: physical crowding, loud voices, loud music, different foods and smells, unexpected light touch (like hugs, light touches on the shoulder, kisses on the cheek), and possibly alcoholic beverages, which can lower your sensory system's ability to inhibit.

Alternatives to Make It Feel Safer for Your Sensory System: Do your sensory diet before you go. Take portable sensory diet activities like exercise tubes with you. Do not drink excessively. Communicate your sensory issues to your family, and take a break or leave if you need to. Wear a thick shirt or layers to lessen light touch sensation, and wear a hat or sweatshirt with the hood up if needed. Explain your seating needs to the hosts if possible (back against the wall, near an exit, etc.). When seated, do chair push-ups, or if you don't want anyone to know what you are doing, do chair pull-ups. Chair push-ups: push your body off the chair by placing your hands on the seat at the sides of your legs. Chair pull-ups: put your hands under the seat of your chair and pull your buttocks firmly into the seat (this won't work on a chair with solid arms).

ACTIVITY: BIRTHDAY CELEBRATIONS

How It's Done: The stand-out challenge of kids' birthday parties for veterans and first responders with SMC is the sound of popping balloons and noises made by children popping large air-filled packing "pillows" or small packing plastic (bubble wrap).

Sensory Safety Level: Low.

Why: Popping balloons and packing "pillows" may sound like gunshots.

Alternatives to Make It Feel Safer for Your Sensory System: Mylar balloons are very hard to pop, so choose these if you're the host – or get your kids involved in choosing alternate fun decorations. Tell kids they can't pop balloons and packing plastic at the party and, if it's age-appropriate, tell them why. Check in with the hosts ahead of time if your child is going to a party and you're planning on staying; tell them about your SMC if you feel comfortable doing this, and/or plan to take a sensory break when you need one. Always do sensory diet activities *before* a party or any other social gathering so that you're starting out from a modulated place.

ACTIVITY: VACATIONS

How It's Done: Plane flights, driving in traffic, staying with relatives or in hotels can all bring different challenges.

Sensory Safety Level: Low to moderate, depending on your familiarity and comfort level with the place and routines.

Why: New places mean new sights, smells, sounds, and activities. Typical daily routines are modulating (this is why some people with anxiety develop compulsive behaviors to calm down). If you're staying with relatives, emotional issues may be added to the mix. If you'll be staying in a big city and aren't accustomed to this, all sensory input will be increased. The discomfort of sleeping on a pull-out couch or in a shared room when you're not used to doing so may increase your fatigue level and "amp up" any pre-existing SMC issues.

Alternatives to Make It Feel Safer for Your Sensory System: When possible, plan trips to less congested areas, or areas where you can be outside in a natural environment. Participate in outdoor heavy sensory diet activities such as bike riding, running, swimming, etc. Use one particular hotel chain (preferably one that has a "gym" or exercise equipment) so that you know the general room and hotel layout, and can pick a room that has the sensory qualities you need. Ask for a room in a corner, away from the elevator and not over a restaurant or meeting room to reduce background noise. Consider traveling with a white noise machine. Keep up your sensory diet as much as possible, and plan "sensory snack" activities for long waits in airports – like walking carrying a heavy bag, hand presses, etc.

ACTIVITY: DISNEY PARKS (OR OTHER AMUSEMENT PARKS)

How It's Done: A day spent with family: long lines, noise, crowds, new and moving sights, different foods, etc.

Sensory Safety Level: Low – this experience can be extremely uncomfortable for people with SMC.

Why: The dream "Disney" vacation is *not* a dream for everyone due to the potential for extreme sensory overload.

Alternatives to Make It Feel Safer for Your Sensory System: Use the Disney (or other amusement park) app to get FastPasses before you go to avoid having to stand in long lines. Do a few "fast rides" first to get your nervous system modulated (unless you have a movement sensitivity); these rides can give strong sensory input to modulate you quickly. Plan to go on a day that's less crowded. Rent a hotel room nearby so that you can retreat to it if needed. The Disney parks all have customer service representatives who can help you with tips and information to decrease unwanted sensory overload. Many of their ideas are found in materials designed for those with autism spectrum disorders because sensory processing disorder (SMC) is not yet widely understood as a standalone issue, and individuals with diagnosed autism all experience some sensory issues (in other words, even though you do not have any of the other issues seen in autism, you have a similar issue with SMC which Disney is beginning to address). One important consideration is that Disney has ways to help you manage your sensory issues including ways to exempt you from having to stand in long lines and information on what types of sensations each ride contains. There are also several unofficial guide books for Disney that include information for people with sensory issues (look for the term "sensory-friendly environments"). With any amusement park, be sure to do sensory diet activities before going, and plan for portable "sensory snacks."

ACTIVITY: BARS AND OTHER PLACES WHERE ALCOHOLIC BEVERAGES ARE CONSUMED

Sensory Safety Level: Low – these environments can be noisy and crowded, and "peer pressure" to over-consume may pose additional challenges.

Why: Although many people "self-medicate" with alcohol, the initial effect of alcohol is to decrease your ability to *inhibit*, which means that sensory input may affect you more strongly. You may also experience a jittery rebound as the effects of alcohol wear off.

Alternatives to Make It Feel Safer for Your Sensory System: Consider reducing your consumption of alcohol. Many bars now carry non-alcoholic beers if you don't want to stand out. If a bar you went to before developing SMC now makes you feel "on edge," look for another one to try instead. Small differences in lighting, seating, and background noise can have a big impact in reducing sensory input. Do a sensory diet activity before going out. And plan to take sensory breaks as needed.

ACTIVITY: NATURAL ENVIRONMENTS

How It's Done: Being in nature.

Sensory Safety Level: High – this can feel very safe and even restorative for people with SMC.

Why: The sights and sounds of the natural environment are basically modulating.

Alternatives to Make It Feel Safer for Your Sensory System: Go to places you're familiar with, and if possible, go at times when there are likely to be fewer people around. You can just sit and enjoy the calm environment, or engage in a strong sensory diet activity such as hiking, bike riding, walking, skiing, canoeing, surfing, running, etc.

YOUR TURN

Fill in an activity that currently "bothers" you, assess its sensory safety level, and think about alternatives to make it feel safer before you go:

ACTIVITY:

How It's Done:

Sensory Safety Level:

Why:

Alternatives to Make It Feel Safer for Your Sensory System:

ACTIVITY:

How It's Done:

Sensory Safety Level:

Why:

Alternatives to Make It Feel Safer for Your Sensory System:

ACTIVITY:

How It's Done:

Sensory Safety Level:

Why:

Alternatives to Make It Feel Safer for Your Sensory System:

ACTIVITY:

How It's Done:

Sensory Safety Level:

Why:

Alternatives to Make It Feel Safer for Your Sensory System:

APPENDIX III:

Sensory Modulation Challenges at Different Ages

The "L" in DIAL IT DOWN: "Likes/Dislikes"

Check-In #15: Is it Possible That You Were Born With Some Sensory Modulation Challenges or Acquired Them in Childhood?

In this book, you have already charted what sensory modulation challenges may look like in you as an adult. Is there a possibility that you were *born with* some sensory modulation challenges or that you could have acquired them in childhood, either from a traumatic event or from repeated concussions through sports participation? If you think you may have been showing signs of sensory modulation challenges as a child, this appendix will help you to understand how childhood SMC may have affected you both back then and now. If you acquired sensory modulation challenges only as an adult, you can skip this section for yourself (*but* if you have a child who might have sensory modulation challenges, read on and fill in the questionnaire below about them). If you do not remember how you reacted to sensations as a child, you can review the later sections in this appendix to jog your memory, and/or ask your parents or siblings.

1. Given what you now know about SMC, is it possible that you were born with some sensory modulation challenges or that you acquired some in childhood?

   a. Yes: _____Continue

   b. Maybe: _____Continue

    c.   Definite No: _____Skip this Check-In.

2.   As a child, do you remember having a sensory experience that you did not like?

    a.   Yes_____

    b.   No _____

    c.   If yes, what was the experience?

    _____

    d.   At what age did it occur?

    _____

3.   Do you remember someone telling you that you should not be reacting to a sensory experience in the way you were reacting to it?

    a.   Yes_____

    b.   No _____

    c.   How old were you? _____

    d.   What was the experience?

    _____

4.   Do you remember organizing some aspect of your life around your expectations (either negative *or* positive anticipation) of the *sensory qualities* of an event?

    a.   Yes _____

    b.   No _____

    c.   Was it a positive sensory experience? _____

    d.   Was it a negative sensory experience? _____

    e.   How old were you? _____

    f.   What was the event?

    _____

5. Did you ever avoid an event due to its sensory qualities?

   a. Yes _____

   b. No _____

   c. What was the event?

   _____

6. How did you prepare yourself for a negative sensory event that you could not avoid, and/or modify your participation in that event?

   _____

Examples by Ages

The following sections give a few examples of how SMC looks at varying ages. Adults may also find some parts of the "Teen" section to be relevant to them. Remember that, as with the adult checklists earlier in the book, children with SMC may experience some of these issues but not others.

WHAT SMC LOOKS LIKE IN BABIES (THIS VARIES AMONG CHILDREN)

- Colic: While colic is generally considered to be a digestive problem, many instances of so-called "colic" actually represent an immaturity of the nervous system which leads to irritability, difficulty with modulation of sensory input, and decreased ability of the baby to "self-soothe." (Given that babies can't "speak for themselves," these types of issues are often diagnosed by well-meaning pediatricians under the general rubric of "colic," without an understanding of potential contributing sensory factors.)

- Sleep problems: For example, a baby might not fall asleep easily, might need to be held and rocked to sleep, might not stay asleep, and may be bothered by any noises, any differences in light in the room, or being set down in the crib when already asleep.

- May sleep best when bundled: Bundling provides deep touch pressure and "neutral warmth," both of which are modulating. Be careful that the blanket used for bundling is firmly fastened so as not to come undone during sleep. (Note: "Neutral warmth" works for all ages. I like to describe neutral warmth as that perfect temperature that your bed gets to just before the alarm goes off in the morning.)

- May sleep well when carried by mother in "snuggly": same as above (neutral warmth and deep pressure).

- Baby is difficult for parent to calm, needing constant holding, rocking, pacifier.

- Baby has poor *self*-calming abilities: The baby cries more than other babies, does not do well spending time alone, and may not even reach for easily accessible pacifier when upset.

- May dislike lying on stomach. "Tummy Time" is very upsetting to some children but is essential for many aspects of their development. Remember that the stomach is an area of the body that has many touch receptors and is an area easily alerted by touch. The ventral surface (front of the body) is one that all animals protect due to the presence of vital organs, so a baby with SMC may react against this added stimulation.

- May dislike being placed on their back for diaper changes: "Gravitational insecurity" makes moving through space toward the back feel frightening. To reduce this "scary" sensation, try holding the baby tightly against your chest while leaning all the way down to the changing table. Do not release your hold or the baby's contact with your chest until the baby is firmly on the changing area.

- May dislike diaper/clothes changing: Movements of the clothes on and off the body and the change in temperature may activate tactile defensiveness.

- Poor nursing/bottling: Child may not like things in their mouth. They may be slow to "latch on" to the breast, or have difficulty accepting a nipple for bottling. If bottling, try to find the nipple with the "just right" fit for the mouth and the "just right" texture and flexibility (the breast conforms to the baby's mouth). Sucking on the breast requires more force than a bottle, and the heavy pro-prioceptive work of nursing on a breast is modulating, but many babies have trouble latching on to the breast or resist the extra work once they have experienced success with the bottle. Reach out for guidance from your pediatrician and/or a trained nurse or occupational therapist if this is an issue.

- Difficulty transitioning to solid food: A child may dislike many textures of foods, making it difficult to find things they will eat. They may only want the bottle or breast longer than most babies.

- May dislike bath time: Many aspects of baths can activate tactile defensiveness, like the splashing of water, the temperature of the water, being undressed then redressed, the coarse feeling of a washcloth, or the slippery feeling of shampoo or soap.

- May fall asleep quickly if in a very noisy or chaotic situation and stay deeply asleep until taken to a quiet environment. This could be a result of the nervous system's being very over-stimulated and "shutting off" any more stimulation by sleeping in an attempt to protect itself.

WHAT SMC LOOKS LIKE IN YOUNG CHILDREN

Some earlier behaviors may persist. Varies from child to child.

- Hates socks: use the "socks secret" of putting them on *inside out* so that the texture of the seam is not felt.

- Only likes certain clothes: usually cotton, well-washed, with no fuzzy pile, sometimes only in limited colors.

- Dislikes new clothes: new clothes feel stiff; new clothes also smell different due to the "sizing" in the material.

- Difficulty regulating body temperature: over- or under-dresses for the weather. For example, wears shorts and no socks even in winter, or wears long-sleeved shirts in the summer. This is due to either not liking the feeling of the clothes or not liking the feeling of a breeze on the skin.

- May want to keep many stuffed animals in the crib or bed; likes to burrow into them. The heavy touch pressure of these objects is modulating.

- Picky eater: Does not like many textures of foods. Food has to be at a certain temperature. Will not eat certain foods just because they "look funny."

- Feels small bumps/touches as very painful.

- Does not seem to feel more serious bumps/accidents as painful.

- May hate baths (still).

- May hate showers due to water in the face or the "prickling" of the water.

- Does not adapt to changes in routine. Routines are reassuring as you know in advance what the sensory experiences will be. Changes mean you don't know what's coming, which raises your arousal level.

- Trains parents to do things the child's way. As the child needs routine to feel safe from unexpected sensory experiences, they will insist that parents do things a certain way by crying, having tantrums, and later by telling them in words. The *feeling of safety* provided by *routine* may lead to behaviors that look like obsessive compulsive disorder.

- Transitions are difficult: Once the child is engaged in something, it is hard for them to change gears, especially if transitioning means going somewhere with potential sensory threats.

- Dislikes noisy or busy places due to too many sensory threats and too many opportunities to be surprised by sensory input.

SMC IN SCHOOL-AGED CHILDREN

Varies from child to child.

- Younger behaviors may continue.

- Trouble getting up in the morning: The "neutral warmth" of the bed feels too good to leave. And the child is now old enough to consciously anticipate (and dread) sensory-intensive morning activities like needing to change into clothes from pajamas, and needing to ride to school on a noisy, bumpy, smelly bus with many kids who could accidentally touch them.

- May have trouble getting dressed in a timely manner. Changing clothes activates many sensory experiences. And verbal arguments may ensue if the child always wants to wear the same well-washed, comfortable clothes and a parent wants them to wear something nice that may be new, smell funny, be stiff, be the wrong material, or have "poky" tags.

- Only wears "favorite" clothes, usually well-washed sweats or T-shirts. The ones that "feel right" are the ones they will choose.

- Only wants to wear cotton or linen. These natural fabrics always feel good and get softer the more often they're washed. Synthetic fabrics have fibers that break off after use, and these little broken fibers can "pick" at the skin, feeling irritating to people with sensory modulation challenges.

- New clothes may need to be washed many times before the child will wear them. Washing many times makes the cloth softer and eliminates any smell of the sizing that comes in new fabric.

- Dislikes stores: odors, crowds that can bump into them, noise, and visual clutter all contribute to sensory discomfort.

- To deal with their sensory modulation challenges, the child may either seek sensation or avoid sensation, and will do activities which reflect that preference, such as constantly being on the move, or only wanting to sit in front of a computer.

- May not understand safety, and may try high-risk behaviors. May not understand how high something is that they want to jump off of. They want the thrill of the movement but don't consider the consequences.

- Conversely, they may know what they *can't* sense (inability to accurately estimate heights, proprioceptive and/or vestibular challenges), and may as a result be overly cautious.

- Trouble "sitting still" in school.

- Dislikes sitting close to other kids, as this may lead to accidental light touch.

- Complains that other kids hit or bump them when this is not apparent to adults (due to their heightened sensitivity to light, incidental touch).

- "Over-reacts" to slight injuries (like scratches).

- "Under-reacts" to larger bumps, injuries.

- Dislikes cafeteria and art class. Those environments are messy, noisy, full of smells and visual clutter, and hard to move around in easily, especially if the person is carrying something like a tray of food.

- May dislike gym class due to the echoing sounds in the gym and too many people moving all at once.

SMC IN TEENS

Varies from child to child.

- Difficulty with developing intimacy (see Chapter 6, and Appendix II). As touch is such a large part of intimacy, it can be difficult for teens with SMC to develop romantic relationships, and sometimes even close friendships. Light touch, which is used by most people in a loving way, may activate sensory modulation challenges and feel uncomfortable. Heavy touch, which can be positive when used correctly, may be used to excess *by* the person with SMC, who may not accurately assess the force they exert in a hug, for instance, and may therefore cause others to feel uncomfortable. There is a fine line between using heavy pressure to decrease your own tactile defensiveness and using it a bit too hard with someone else because that is how you need and like it. The person with sensory modulation challenges needs to know that others might find heavy pressure uncomfortable.

- May masturbate to self-calm. Masturbation, as part of the normal human sexual response, brings the nervous system into a parasympathetic mode, or modulation; and as it's typically done alone (and in a quiet space), there is no possibility of others setting off any tactile defensive responses. You do not set off your own tactile defensiveness as you know and control the feeling of your touch on yourself. A majority of teens experiment with masturbation, but for a teen with SMC, masturbation may become a self-calming habit. This is not in and of itself a problem; as a parent, try to avoid attaching shame to any discussions of this, and try to "let it go" as long as it's done appropriately (in private, in the home) and doesn't interfere with other life activities. Discuss with a healthcare provider if you are uncomfortable with or have questions about this.

- Clothes may continue to be a problem, one that's now additionally complicated by the teenager's difficult search to balance *style* with comfort. Wearing pants loose and low on the hips avoids the stomach, which is one of the areas that is most sensitive to touch. Sweatshirts and sweatpants provide sensory comfort but are not appropriate socially in some situations.

- Teens with SMC may experiment with high-risk behaviors like fast driving or racing, jumping or diving off of high spaces, binge drinking, and drugs. These high-risk behaviors are a way for those who modulate their arousal levels by "sensation seeking" to get large amounts of sensory input in a short amount of time. If your child is involved in any of these activities, consult with a healthcare provider for guidance, and try to find alternate ways of incorporating more appropriate "sensation seeking" activities – like rock-climbing, skiing, rafting, skateboarding, surfing, etc.

- Anxiety around social events may lead to "self-medicating" in an attempt to decrease uncomfortable feelings. A teen with SMC may self-medicate with drinking, street drugs, or "borrowing" others' prescription medications. Some teens say they like the feeling that drinking and some drugs provide as they appear to "take the edge off" and make them feel less anxious. Again, as a parent, you should consult with a healthcare provider if you have any concerns, and also discuss ways to use sensory diet to safely modulate anxiety around social events.

- May want to wear coat and hat in school. Some schools equate jacket and especially hat-wearing with gang behavior and have banned it. But some teens wear these to control sensory input. A jacket can keep others from touching you and provide "neutral warmth," while a hat can provide heavy touch pressure to the head, an especially sensitive area. Consider alternatives like a hooded sweatshirt with the hood up (check in with your child's school to see if this will be tolerated).

- May have difficulty with (and anxiety about) transitioning between classes in middle and high school. This occurs because the noise, incidental touching, visual stimulation, and fast-moving crowds in the halls can activate sensory defensiveness. If this is a big problem and your child doesn't mind your involvement, consider seeking an accommodation from the school for a dismissal from class that's several minutes early so that your child can transition through an empty hallway (an occupational therapist can help to provide the documentation of sensory challenges that you may need in order to add this to an Individualized Education Plan [IEP] or 504 Plan). Always try to involve your teen in making decisions like this about their life, in order to avoid compounding any anxiety. An occupational therapist can be a valuable resource in helping you understand and talk to your teen about SMC.

- Some students may find that they have less difficulty in middle and high school because carrying their heavy backpacks provides a built-in sensory diet.

Summary

This has been a short introduction to some behaviors seen across ages that may indicate someone is dealing with sensory modulation challenges. Remember that each person is different, but these examples can give you a starting point in developing an understanding of how the symptoms of SMC can cross the lifespan. This can be especially important to you if you were born with some sensory modulation challenges or acquired them in childhood, or if you know a child with these issues and are in a position to seek evaluation and treatment for them.

APPENDIX IV:

Professional Treatment for SMC:
The Wilbarger Therapressure Protocol™

Throughout this book, I have discussed the use of a self-administered sensory diet to modulate hyperarousal and hypoarousal. The Wilbarger Therapressure Protocol™ (WTP) is a specific treatment technique used to decrease sensory defensiveness symptoms (hyperarousal), a type of sensory modulation challenge. As with sensory diet, the WTP works by modulating the nervous system (Miller et al., 2007; Wilbarger & Wilbarger, 2011). But in contrast to many of the sensory diet options discussed throughout this book, the WTP is a technique that you *cannot teach yourself.* In fact, if you do it incorrectly, you may actually *increase* your sensory defensiveness. You must be taught the technique and monitored by a specially trained occupational therapist. Before occupational therapists receive official certification to prescribe and supervise the WTP for clients, they must take a 3-day course about current research on and treatments for sensory defensiveness and must be evaluated on their application of the WTP technique using the special Therapressure™ brush (Wilbarger & Wilbarger, 2011). Once you as a client have been taught the technique and have been monitored for a short time by a trained occupational therapist, you may then self-administer it. In order for it to work effectively, you must commit to doing the whole program and doing it exactly as it was taught to you.

The WTP is one part of a professionally guided treatment approach to sensory modulation challenges/sensory defensiveness that was developed by occupational therapists Patricia and Julia Wilbarger (Wilbarger & Wilbarger,

1991, 1995, 2001, 2007). The WTP, which should always be used in conjunction with a sensory diet, is designed to move the nervous system toward decreased defensiveness by providing "spatial and temporal summation of modulating input." In other words, it is done in a short amount of time and covers many sensory receptors, specifically the tactile receptors in the skin and the proprioceptors in the joints. It utilizes very deep touch pressure on the skin, and proprioception through firm joint compression. "The skin pressure is given using a special Therapressure™ brush with 224 bristles, which when used with the appropriate deep pressure, delivers non-noxious input with no tickle, scratch, or itch. The WTP is done in a prescribed manner with a specific pressure, order and duration" (Kimball et al., 2018, p. 91).

The Therapressure™ brush is used first to apply several long swipes of *very specific firm pressure brushing* to the arms, back, legs, hands, and feet. The head, neck, chest, and stomach are *never* brushed, as these are areas with numerous sensory receptors resulting in increased sensation (receptors that evolved to *alert* rather than decrease your fight-or-flight response). The Therapressure™ brushing is followed immediately by specific firm joint compression ten times each to most joints of the body. The WTP should be done approximately every 90-120 waking minutes (8-10 times per day) for a minimum of 2-3 weeks (usually more) to be effective in reducing or even eliminating some sensory defensiveness symptoms. If it is done for fewer days or fewer times per day, especially when it is first prescribed, it will be far less effective in reducing symptoms.

The Science Underlying the WTP

There are only a few published studies on the WTP, most of them conducted with children. None of these studies involved veterans, first responders, or frontline medical personnel. Moore and Henry (2001) studied the use of the WTP in three women with histories of sensory defensiveness and self-injurious behaviors. Their symptoms, patterns of engagement in their life roles, and incidents of self-injury were compared. The WTP was done in the prescribed manner for one month along with prescribed sensory diet activities. At 9 months post treatment, all three subjects were "re-engaged in valued roles with no incidents of self-injury" (p. 43). The WTP "appeared to have positive influence on Sensory Defensive symptoms" (p. 43).

Bhopti and Brown (2013) used the WTP along with sensory diet activities with five children aged 3 to 8. Parents of four of the five children reported "significant changes to their everyday routines due to marked reductions in sensory defensive behaviors" (p.128).

Kimball et al. (2007) used a modified procedure based on the WTP with four children, 3 to 5 years of age, with sensory defensiveness. It was called the "Wilbarger Protocol-based procedure" because the whole protocol was not used: rather than applying the protocol numerous times daily for several weeks as it was originally designed, the brushing/proprioception procedure was used only once a week for 4 weeks during a controlled occupational therapy session. The purpose was to investigate if the modified Wilbarger Protocol-based procedure was effective in influencing sympathetic arousal. To do this, saliva for cortisol measurement was collected before and after each application of the procedure. Cortisol findings are significant as cortisol is directly related to stress levels (high cortisol equals high stress). Results showed that each of the four times the Wilbarger procedure was administered to each child, it moved their cortisol in the direction of modulation. When these children came to the therapy setting with elevated cortisol levels, the Wilbarger Protocol-based procedure measurably reduced cortisol, and when they came in with cortisol levels that were too low (indicating hypoarousal), the procedure raised it. In other words, the procedure modulated the cortisol levels to the moderate range each time.

This is not the way the WTP was designed to be implemented; this study was intended solely to measure its direct impact on the stress hormone cortisol. Extrapolating from this study, if the WTP is used every 2 waking hours daily for several weeks in combination with a sensory diet, it has the potential to significantly reduce stress-related sensory defensiveness symptoms.

Kimball et al. (2018) conducted a pilot study to determine the efficacy of the WTP in modulating arousal in four women, non-veterans, who had developed PTSD as a result of trauma as adults. The protocol was done for

2 weeks. Daily testing was conducted on cortisol levels as well as stress and concentration levels. Pre/post assessments included the Adolescent/Adult Sensory Profile (Brown & Dunn, 2002), a preliminary research edition of the Sensory Over Responsivity Scale (SensOR) and the Sensory Under Responsivity Scale (SensUR) (Miller & Schoen, 2008), the Basic Personality Inventory (Jackson, 1996), and ability to engage in life activities. Results showed positive changes in modulating cortisol levels, which resulted in decreased hyperarousal. This was reflected in decreased stress, increased concentration, improved sensory scores on the three sensory profiles listed above, increased participation in life activities, and improvement in some personality measures. Results also showed a dosage relationship when using the WTP: one participant who only did the protocol 2-3 times per day showed limited improvement when compared to those who did it as prescribed, 8-10 times per day.

Although more research is needed, it appears that the WTP holds promise as a means of helping veterans, first responders, and frontline medical personnel to deal with the sensory modulation challenges associated with PTS and PTSD. As mentioned earlier (see Appendix I), the modulation of cortisol levels after using the Wilbarger Therapressure Protocol is notable as previous studies of other treatment modalities for PTSD did not demonstrate changes in cortisol output (Pacella et al., 2014).

Remember, the protocol must be taught to you by a therapist *who has taken the Wilbarger training course* to ensure that they know the correct pressure of brushing (which is very firm), and to ensure that the correct brush is used. *Too little pressure, or the incorrect brush, would be likely to produce scratch, tickle, or itch responses that could make your sensory symptoms worse instead of better.* The WTP should always be tried first in conjunction with a sensory diet.

If you cannot commit to doing the whole WTP in conjunction with a sensory diet, you can still try a sensory diet alone at any time. Many veterans, first responders, and frontline medical workers find the knowledge that they can positively influence their own nervous systems through sensory diet to be life-changing information.

NOTE: For best results with the WTP, find an occupational therapist who has taken the Wilbarger training course. If a therapist claims to know how to do the technique, but has not taken the course, please find another therapist who has completed the appropriate training.

Jim's Experience With the WTP

Jim is a Vietnam-era veteran. At the time this experience occurred, he was a high-level professional engineer and department head in a large military-related company. He knew me personally but knew little about my job. He heard of my interest in working with veterans, and as we began talking, he stated that he was experiencing some anxiety at work. I told him about sensory diet, and he said that he was very involved in sports on weekends and vacations (winter: aggressive fast skiing over bumps and snowshoeing; summer: wind surfing, sailing, kayaking, and cross-country biking including hard courses in Europe), but had little time during the week except to go for an occasional bike ride or run. I pointed out to him that his weekend sports and running were part of a sensory diet and that running or biking every day, even for a short time, would help him. I then told him about the WTP, which he thought sounded "weird," but he agreed to let me demonstrate it on him. He said that he felt better afterward and was surprised that it took so little time each day. I reminded him that he had to do it 8-9 times a day for 3-4 weeks, and that he should keep up or expand his sports, running, and biking during the week, and he agreed to try. I trained him and gave him the special brush. I checked with him a few days later and he said he was following all the directions. Several weeks later, he called and reported that it worked very well for him. He had stuck with and completed the protocol with good results, and had shifted (as we'd discussed) to only using the brush as part of his sensory diet especially before stressful situations. He said, "I will never be anxious before a big meeting again!"

Several months later, he called to report that a major problem had occurred with his house, and he'd known exactly how to handle it. He'd had significant ice damming on his roof, and one evening, as he walked into his kitchen after work, the whole ceiling caved in, the cold water and wall board just missing him. He was calling to tell me that the WTP was his most valuable "tool" in handling this because he immediately got out his brush from his briefcase, used it, and was able to quickly calm down and handle the situation effectively and without anxiety.

REFERENCES

Allen, C. K., Austin, S. L., David, S. K., Earhart, C. A., McCraith, D. B., & Riska-Williams, L. (2007). *Manual for the Allen cognitive level screen-5 (ACLS-5) and Large Allen cognitive level screen-5 (LACLS-5)*. ACLS and LACLS Committee.

American Psychiatric Association. (2013). *Diagnostic and statistical manual of mental disorders* (5th ed.). https://doi.org/10.1176/appi. books.9780890425596

Archer, J., & Lloyd, B. (2002). *Sex and gender*. Cambridge University Press.

Ayres, A. J. (1972a). Improving academic scores through sensory integration. *Journal of Learning Disabilities, 5*, 338-343.

Ayres, A. J. (1972b). *Sensory integration and learning disorders*. Western Psychological Services.

Ayres, A. J. (1979). *Sensory integration and the child*. Los Angeles: Western Psychological Services.

Benson, H. B. (1975). *The relaxation response*. Avon Books.

Berger, J.M., Singh, P., Khrimian, L., Morgan, D. A., Chowdhury, S., Arteaga-Solis, E., Horvath, T. L., Domingos, A.I., Marsland, A. L., Yadav, V. K., Rahmouni, K., Gao, X., & Karsenty, G. (2019). Mediation of the acute stress response by the skeleton. *Cell Metabolism*. https://doi. org/10.1016/j.cmet.2019.08.012

Bhopti, A., & Brown, T. (2013). Examining the Wilbarger deep pressure and proprioceptive techniques for treating children with sensory defensive-ness using a multiple-single-case study approach. *Journal of Occupational*

Therapy, Schools, & Early Interventions, 6(2), 108-130. https://doi.org/1 0.1080/19411243.2013.810944

Brockett, S. S., Lawton-Shirley, N. K., & Kimball, J. G. (2014). Berard Auditory Integration Training: Behavior changes related to sensory modulation. *Autism Insights, 6,* 1-10. https://doi.org/4137/AUI. S13574 (open access)

Brown, C. E., & Dunn, W. (2002). *Adolescent/Adult Sensory Profile Manual.* The Psychological Corporation.

Carley, K. (2013). Sound therapy: A complementary intervention for individuals with sensory integration and processing disorders, part 1. *Special Interest Section Quarterly: Sensory Integration, 36*(1), 1-4.

Clancy, K., Ding, M., Bernat, E., Schmidt, N. B., & Li, W. (2017). Restless "rest": Intrinsic sensory hyperactivity and disinhibition in post-traumatic stress disorder. *Brain: A Journal of Neurology, 140,* 2041-2050. https:// doi.org/10.1093/brain/awx116

Curran, L. A. (2010). *Trauma Competency: A Clinician's Guide.* PESI Publishing.

Dana, D. (2019). The touch taboo. *Psychotherapy Networker, 23*(2), 18-25.

D'Apice, M., & Foley, R. (2017). A different journey full circle. https://vimeo. com/92670725

D'Apice, M., & Foley, R. (2018). Artists for peace and freedom. https://vimeo. com/257540407

Dunn, W. (1999). *Sensory Profile: User's Manual.* The Psychological Corporation.

Dunn, W., & Westman, K. (1997). The sensory profile: The performance of a national sample of children with disabilities. *American Journal of Occupational Therapy, 54,* 25-34.

Engel-Yeger, B., & Dunn, W. (2011). Relationship between pain catastrophizing level and sensory processing patterns in typical adults. *American Journal of Occupational Therapy, 65,* e1-e10.

Frick, S. M. (2002, Spring/Summer). An overview of auditory interventions. *Sensory Integration Quarterly,* 1-3.

Friedman, M. (2006). *Post-traumatic and acute stress disorders.* Compact Clinicals.

Geissler, J., Romanos, M., Hegerl, U., & Hensch, T. (2014). Hyperactivity and sensation seeking as autoregulatory attempts to stabilize brain arousal. *ADHD Atten Def Hyp Disord, 6,* 159-173.

Goldin, P. R., & Gross, J.J. (2010). Effects of mindfulness-based stress reduction (MBSR) on emotional regulation in social anxiety disorder. *Emotion, 10,* 83-91.

Greenspan, S. (2005). *Diagnostic manual for infancy and early childhood: mental health, developmental, regulatory-sensory processing, language and learning disorders.* Interdisciplinary Council on Developmental and Learning Disorders (ICDL).

Hall, L., & Case-Smith, J. (2007). The effect of sound-based intervention on children with sensory processing disorders and visual-motor delays. *The American Journal of Occupational Therapy, 61,* 209-215.

Hession, J. (2003). *Love is an Intention: An Interview with Jerry Jud about the Principles and Skills of Loving.* Friends of Shalom Mountain.

Holmes, S. E., Girgenti, M.J., Davis, M. T., Pietrzak, R. H., DellaGioia, N., Nabulsi, N., Matuskey, D., Southwick, S., Duman, R. S., Carson R. E., Krystal, J. H., Esterlis, I., and The Traumatic Stress Brain Study Group. (2017, August 1). Altered metabotropic glutamate receptor 5 markers in PTSD: In vivo and postmortem evidence. *PNAS, 114*(31), 8390-8395.

ILS Integrated Listening Systems. https://www.integratedlistening.com

Jackson, D. N. (1986). *Basic personality inventory manual.* SIGMA Assessment Systems, Inc.

Jackson, H. (1978). *The human side of human beings: The theory of re-evaluation counseling.* Rational Island Publisher.

Judah, M. R., Renfroe, J. B., Wangelin, B. C., Turner, T. H., & Tuerk, P. W. (2018). Hyperarousal symptoms explain the relationship between cognitive complaints and working memory performance in veterans seeking PTSD treatment. *J Head Trauma Rehabil, 33*(4), E10-E16.

Junger, S. (2016). *TRIBE on homecoming and belonging*. Hachette Book Group.

Kimball, J. G. (1976, July). Vestibular stimulation and seizure activity. *Center for the Study of Sensory Integrative Dysfunction Newsletter (Sensory Integration International)*.

Kimball, J. G. (1977). Case history follow-up report. *Center for the Study of Sensory Integrative Dysfunction Newsletter (Sensory Integration International)*.

Kimball, J. G. (1993). Sensory integrative frame of reference. In P. Kramer & J. Hinojosa (Eds.), *Frames of reference for pediatric occupational therapy* (pp. 87-195). Williams & Wilkins.

Kimball, J.G. (1999a). Sensory integrative frame of reference: Theoretical base, function/dysfunction continua, and guide to evaluation. In P. Kramer & J. Hinojosa (Eds.), *Frames of reference for pediatric occupational therapy* (2nd ed., pp. 119-168). Williams & Wilkins.

Kimball, J.G. (1999b). Sensory integrative frame of reference: Postulates regarding change and application to practice. In P. Kramer & J. Hinojosa (Eds.), *Frames of reference for pediatric occupational therapy* (2nd ed., pp. 169-204). Williams & Wilkins.

Kimball J. G. (2000). When individuals with high IQ experience sensory integration or sensory modulation problems. In K. Kay (Ed.), *Uniquely gifted: Identifying and meeting the needs of the twice-exceptional student* (pp. 227-243). Avocus Publishing, Inc.

Kimball, J. G. (2002). Developmental coordination disorder from a sensory integration perspective. In S. A. Cermak, & L. Larkin (Eds.), *Developmental coordination disorder* (pp. 210-220). Delmar.

Kimball, J. G. (2021). Sensory Modulation Challenges: The missing piece in the diagnosis and treatment of PTSD. In Preparation.

Kimball, J. G. (2021a). Differences in measurements of sensory modulation challenges among six groups including veterans with trauma, veterans without trauma, nonveterans with trauma and nonveterans without trauma. In Preparation.

Kimball, J. G., Lynch, K. M., Steward, K. C., Williams, N. E., Thomas, M. A., & Atwood, K. D. (2007). Using salivary cortisol to measure the effects of the Wilbarger Protocol-based procedure on sympathetic arousal: A pilot study. *American Journal of Occupational Therapy, 61*, 406-413.

Kimball, J. G., Birstler, C.T., Frank, E.M., Nelson, L.M., & Woods, M.R. (2012). The relationship among body mass index, temperament, and sensory processing: A pilot study. *Journal of Occupational Therapy in Mental Health, 28*(1), 72-87.

Kimball, J. G., Cao, L., & Draleau, K. S. (2017, October). Efficacy of the Wilbarger Therapressure Program™ to modulate arousal in women with Post-Traumatic Stress Disorder: A pilot study using salivary cortisol and behavioral measures. *Occupational Therapy in Mental Health, 34*(4). Advance online publication. https://doi.org/10.1080/01 64212X.2017.1376243 (Print version: [2018]. *Occupational Therapy in Mental Health, 34*(4), 86-101.)

Koomar, J. (2009). Trauma-and attachment-informed sensory integration assessment and intervention. *Sensory Integration Special Interest Quarterly, 32*(4), 1-4.

LaMotte, A. D., Taft, C. T., Reardon, A. F., & Miller, M. W. (2015). Veteran's PTSD symptoms and their partners' desired changes in key relationship domains. *Psychological trauma: Theory, research, practice, and policy, 7*(5), 479-484.

Land Combat Study. Castro, C.A., & Hoge, C.W. (2005, August 18-21). Psychological impact of modern warfare: The WRAIR Land Combat Study (symposium). American Psychological Association Annual Convention. Washington, D.C.

Lanius, R. A., Vermetten, E., Loewenstein, R. J., Brand, B., Schmahl, C., Bremner, J. D., & Spiegel, D. (2010). Emotion modulation in PTSD: Clinical and neurobiological evidence for a dissociative subtype. *Am J Psychiatry, 167*, 640-647.

Lawlis, F. (2010). *The PTSD breakthrough.* Sourcebooks, Inc.

LeDoux, J. (2002). *Synaptic self.* Penguin Books.

Lyford, C. (2019, May/June). Ketamine: The latest wonder drug? *Psychotherapy Networker,* 11-13.

Masters, W. H., & Johnson, V. E. (1966, 1981). *Human Sexual Response.* Bantam.

McIntosh, D.N., Miller, L.J., Shyu, V., & Hagerman, R.J. (1999). Sensory modulation disruption, electrodermal responses, and functional behaviors. *Developmental Medicine and Child Neurology, 41,* 608-615.

Meredith, P. J., Rappel, G., Strong, J., & Bailey, K. J. (2015). Sensory sensitivity and strategies for coping with pain. *American Journal of Occupational Therapy, 69,* e1-e10.

Miller, L.J., McIntosh, D.N., McGrath, J., Shyu, V., Lampe, M., Taylor, A.K., Tassone, F., Neitzel, K., Stackhouse, T., & Hagerman, R.J. (1999). Electrodermal responses to sensory stimuli in individuals with fragile X syndrome. *American Journal of Medical Genetics, 83,* 268-279.

Miller, L.J. (2003, February). Empirical evidence related to therapies for sensory processing impairments. *NASP Communiqué, 31*(5).

Miller, L. J. STAR Institute. https://sensoryhealth.org

Miller, L.J., & Schoen, S.A. (2008). The Sensory Over-Responsivity Inventory for Adults. Unpublished manuscript.

Miller, L.J., & Schoen, S.A. (2008). The Sensory Under-Responsivity Inventory for Adults. Unpublished manuscript.

Moore, K. M., & Henry, A. D. (2002). Treatment of adult psychiatric patients using the Wilbarger Protocol. *Occupational Therapy in Mental Health, 18*(1), 43-63.

Moore, B. A., & Penk, W. E. (2011). *Treating PTSD in military personnel.* The Guilford Press.

Mozart for Modulation; More Mozart for Modulation; Baroque for Modulation, modulated recordings available at: https://tempospaceproductions. bandcamp.com

Mullen, B., Champagne, T., Krishnamurty, S., Dickson, D., & Gao, R. X. (2013). Exploring the safety and therapeutic effect of deep pressure stimulation using a weighted blanket. *Occupational Therapy in Mental Health, 24*(1), 65-89. https://doi.org/10.1300/J004v24n01_05

NAMI website. (n.d.). *Psychotherapy.* https://www.nami.org/About-Mental-Illness/Treatments/Psychotherapy

National Center for PTSD. https://www.ptsd.va.gov/

Pacella, M. L., Feeny, N., Zoellner, L., & Delahanty, D.L. (2014). The impact of PTSD treatment on the cortisol awakening response. *Depression and Anxiety, 31,* 862-869.

Performance Triad P3 Program. *Performance Triad (P3): Optimize health with sleep, activity and nutrition.* https://p3.amedd.army.mil/

Porges, S. W. (2009, April). The polyvagal theory: New insights into adaptive reactions of the autonomic nervous system. *Cleveland Clinic Journal of Medicine, 76*(Suppl 2), S86-S90. https://doi.org/10.3949/ccjm.76.s2.17

PTSD: National Center for PTSD, U.S. Department of Veterans Affairs. (n.d.) *PTSD basics.* https://www.ptsd.va.gov/understand/what/ptsd_basics.asp

PTSD: National Center for PTSD, U.S. Department of Veterans Affairs. (n.d.) *Cognitive processing therapy for PTSD.* https://www.ptsd.va.gov/understand_tx/cognitive_processing.asp

PTSD: National Center for PTSD, U.S. Department of Veterans Affairs. (n.d.) *Prolonged exposure for PTSD.* https://www.ptsd.va.gov/understand_tx/prolonged_exposure.asp

Ramirez, J. (2016). A review of art therapy among military service members and veterans with post-traumatic stress disorder. *Journal of Military and Veteran's Health, 24*(2), 40-51. https://jmvh.org/article/a-review-of-art-therapy-among-military-service-members-and-veterans-with-post-traumatic-stress-disorder/

Rogers, C. M., Mallinson, T., & Peppers, D. (2014). High-intensity sports for posttraumatic stress disorder and depression: Feasibility study of Ocean Therapy with veterans of operation enduring freedom and operation Iraqi freedom. *American Journal of Occupational Therapy, 68*(4), 395-404.

Rosso, I. M., Crowley, D. J., Silveri, M. M., Rauch, S. L., & Jenson, J. E. (2017). *Neuropsychopharmacology, 42,* 1698-1705.

Schaaf, R.C., Miller, L.J., Seawell, D., & O'Keefe, S. (2003). Children with disturbances in sensory processing: A pilot study examining the role of the parasympathetic nervous system. *The American Journal of Occupational Therapy, 57,* 442-449.

Schneider, K. J., Meeuwisse, W.H., Nettel-Aguirre, A., Barlow, K., Boyd, L., Kang, J., & Emery, C. A. (2014, September). Cervicovestibular rehabilitation in sport-related concussion: A randomised controlled trial. *British Journal of Sports Medicine, 48*(17), 1294-1298. https://doi.org/10.1136/bjsports-2013-093267

Schoen, S.A., Miller, L.J., & Green, K,E. (2008). Pilot study of the Sensory Over-Responsivity Scales: Assessment and Inventory. *The American Journal of Occupational Therapy, 62*(4), 393-406.

Schupp, L. J. (2004). *Assessing and treating trauma and PTSD.* PESI Publishing.

Shapiro, F. (1995). *Eye movement desensitization and reprocessing: Basic principles, protocols, and procedures.* The Guilford Press, New Press.

Stoller, C.C., Greuel, J. H., Cimini, L. S., Fowler, M. S., & Koomar, J. A. (2012). Effects of sensory-enhanced yoga on symptoms of combat stress in deployed military personnel. *American Journal of Occupational Therapy, 66,* 59-68. http://dx.doi.org/10.5014/ajot.2012.001230

The Interdisciplinary Council on Development and Learning Disorders. (2012). *Diagnostic manual for infancy and early childhood.* ICDL-DMIC.

The Listening Program. http://advancedbrain.com/the-listening-program.

The Upledger Foundation. (2000). *Post-Traumatic Stress Disorder in Vietnam veterans* [video]. Available from The Upledger Foundation, West Palm Beach, Florida.

Tural, U, Aker, A.T., Onder, E., Sodan, H. T., Unver, H., & Akensel, G. (2018). Neurotropic factors and hippocampal activity in PTSD. In *PLoS ONE, 13*(5), e0197889. https:///doi.org/10.1371/journal.pone.0197889

Van der Kolk, B. (1996). *Traumatic stress: The effect of overwhelming experiences on mind, body and society.* Guilford Press.

Van der Kolk, B. (2014). *The body keeps the score.* Viking.

Wagner, D. (2016, June 27). Polyvagal theory in practice. *Counseling Today, Member Insights: A Publication of the American Counseling Association.*

Walsh, R., & Shapiro, L. (2006). The meeting of meditative disciplines and western psychology: A mutually enriching dialogue. *American Psychologist, 60,* 227-239.

Weiss, S. J. (2007, July). Neurobiological alterations associated with traumatic stress. *Perspectives in Psychiatric Care, 43*(3), 114-122. https://doi.org/10.1111/j.1744-6163.2007.00120.x

Wickelgren, I. (2012, Jan/Feb). Forgetting is key to a healthy mind. *Scientific American Mind, 22*(6), 32-39.

Wilbarger, J. L., & Cook, D. B. (2011, April). Multisensory hypersensitivity in women with Fibromyalgia: Implications for well being and intervention. *Arch Phys Med Rehabil, 92,* 653-656.

Wilbarger, P. & Wilbarger, J. L. (1991). *Sensory defensiveness in children aged 1-12.* Avanti Educational Programs.

Wilbarger, P. (1995). The sensory diet: Activity programs based on sensory processing theory. *Sensory Integration Special Interest Section Newsletter: American Occupational Therapy Association, 18*(2), 1-4.

Wilbarger, P. & Wilbarger, J. (2001). *Sensory defensiveness: A comprehensive treatment approach.* Avanti Educational Programs.

Wilbarger, P. & Wilbarger, J. L. (2007). *Sensory Defensiveness: A Comprehensive Treatment Approach.* Avanti Educational Programs.

ACKNOWLEDGMENTS

Many thanks are necessary as this book has been a long time in development and numerous people helped along the way.

Especially thank you to all the veterans who started me on the path to writing this book. These included my father who was an Air Force officer for 20 years (yes, I am a "brat"), my brother, son-in law, and clients I have seen over the years in my practice as an occupational therapist. Your descriptions of what you were going through after deployment fit with new information that I was learning about sensory modulation from my practice and research working with children and their parents and moved me to working mainly with adults. Thank you to all the veterans who took part in my research and to those of you who were willing to try some of my suggestions to deal with your hyperarousal. You continue to amaze me and teach me every day! You humble me!

My sister Susan Giencke, PhD, a psychologist, was invaluable during the early work on this book. She spent many, many hours discussing with me ideas on how to present the material in an organized and interesting manner and read multiple early drafts of chapters. She and I had taught workshops together on sensory modulation challenges in children, so she had expert knowledge of the topic and a great interest in applying it to adults. She suggested the title of the book, *Dial It Down*. And she suggested my wonderful editor.

My daughter, Amy Kimball Carpenter, an occupational therapist at a VA hospital, presented the earlier versions of this work with me in two professional meetings. The first was a 3-hour juried workshop at the American Occupational Therapy Association Conference in San Diego, CA (2013), and the second, the VA Occupational Therapy Monthly Education Conference Call, a 3-hour online conference that was open to all occupational therapists in the VA system (2014). The wonderful reception we got at both conferences was very motivating and confirmed that we were on the right path.

Many thanks to Sue Wilkinson, an occupational therapist, who after thoughtfully reviewing an early version of the first section of the book, gave it to a retired police chief she knew who told her that the information in the book was exactly what first responders need. Thank you, Mark Kissel, for this comment which was responsible for my expanding the book to include first responders.

And as you read the book, you will note that Patricia and Julia Wilbarger's groundbreaking work on sensory defensiveness with children is the basis of, and inspiration for, this application to adults. I feel privileged to have worked with them on applied projects for 45 years and have applauded as their important work has been expanded by them and others. They have changed the lives of numerous children and their families and have enriched the field of occupational therapy.

Ultimate thanks go to my exceptional editor, Deborah Murphy. Due to life experiences, she understands sensory modulation challenges. But, more importantly, she has the ability to expertly edit without changing meaning and is inspired with her change suggestions, including that I expand the book to include healthcare workers as all of us are living under traumatic stress. She also suggested I put most of the research articles in Appendix I where people who were interested could find them, but they wouldn't interrupt the flow of the book. In addition, she has been an invaluable partner through the book production process.

And many thanks and much love to my husband, Charlie, who put up with my numerous extra hours of teaching, research, and writing over many years. He has been my primary teacher as we learned to love, live, and prosper through his sensory modulation challenges.

ABOUT THE AUTHOR

Photo by Charlie Kimball

Judith Giencke Kimball, PhD, OTR/L, FAOTA, has worked as a clinician and university professor in occupational therapy for over 50 years. She was the Founding Director and is now Professor Emeritus of the Occupational Therapy curriculum at the University of New England in Portland, Maine. She has served as Occupational Therapy Director at a University Hospital, Occupational Student Education Coordinator at a VA Hospital, a consultant to many school-based occupational therapy programs, and has consistently maintained a part-time private practice. She worked extensively with Dr. A. Jean Ayes, the developer of Sensory Integration theory and practice, and Patricia Wilbarger, the originator of clinical treatments for sensory defensiveness. Dr. Kimball speaks widely at professional conferences, and her numerous publications include book chapters and research articles in peer-reviewed journals. Her academic degrees include a BS in Occupational Therapy, an MS in Special Education, a Certificate in Marriage and Family Therapy, and a PhD in Psychology.